TUESDAY. NOVEMBER 20. 1877.

AT JEFFERSONVILLE, INDIANA.

From PADDLE WHEELS to PROPELLERS

The Howard Ship Yards of Jeffersonville

From PADDLE WHEELS *to* PROPELLERS

by
CHARLES
PRESTON
FISHBAUGH

Indiana Historical Society
Indianapolis 1970

in the Story of Steam Navigation on the Western Rivers

PREFACE

DESPITE the many floods on the Ohio since 1834 and the several fires that swept the Yards, four generations of Howards in Jeffersonville succeeded in preserving most of the correspondence, ledgers, and other records of the family enterprise. As a result, the Howard Ship Yards and Dock Company collection in the Lilly Library, Indiana University, Bloomington, now numbers over 265,000 manuscripts. It is rare indeed that so great a collection of private papers about so historic a firm has been saved and made available for research.

Primary credit for preserving the manuscripts rests on all the members of the Howard family. But special notice should be made of the work of James E. and Loretta M. Howard in protecting the collection in the great flood of 1937 and the dislocations caused by the Navy's wartime operation of the plant. It was James E. Howard, grandson of the founder, who commenced organizing the records. He was immensely helpful to the first serious researcher who combed the records, the late Stephen G. Savage.

Profiting from the recollections of James E. Howard and the others who had been intimately connected with both the Ship Yards and the rivers, Stephen G. Savage wrote his master's thesis in history on the founder of the company. It was entitled, "James Howard of Jeffersonville, Indiana, Master Steamboat Builder." It had been his intention to prepare a book on each of the Howard shipbuilders, and he worked diligently to help bring the Howard manuscripts to the protection and safe-keeping of the Lilly Library. But his duties as a faculty member of

Indiana University kept him busy with other things too long, and he died in 1964, before he could carry out his project. Nevertheless, his text on the founder, James Howard, still serves as an excellent introduction to the Howards and their steamboats.

Under the direction of Doris M. Reed and Elfrieda Lang of the Manuscripts Department of the Lilly Library order has been brought to the manuscripts of the Howard collection. Identification and retrieval of items has been facilitated, but the very bulk of the papers renders a careful, comprehensive study almost impossible. Therefore, this present work is concentrated on the story of the Howard Ship Yards as they reflect the economic history of steam navigation of the Western Rivers. An important contribution is as complete a listing of the boats and barges comprising the output of the Yards from 1834 to 1942 as could be made at present. This list, which appears as Appendix A, is based on records kept by the Howards themselves. In compiling it the work of Mr. Savage was very helpful for the output between 1834 and 1876. Future researchers combining the papers will undoubtedly uncover additions and errors.

The research for this study was originally enabled by a grant from the Inter-University Committee on Economic History of Indiana University upon the recommendation of Professors Ross M. Robertson and L. Leslie Waters. Both men helped greatly in directing the research.

For Loretta M. Howard, widow of James E. Howard, is reserved special thanks. Without her gracious help the meaning of many scraps of paper and whole volumes would still remain a puzzle.

The assistance of Mrs. Catherine B. Richardson, custodian of the Clark County Historical Society Howard Steamboat Museum, Jeffersonville, and Ernest M. Ellison, of Louisville, in the selection of the illustrations, is gratefully acknowledged as is the contribution of Gayle Thornbrough in editing the manuscript and seeing it through the press.

I am deeply indebted to Professor Robertson for his patience while checking the manuscript. Professor Joseph A. Batchelor deserves an award for his role in bringing the project to completion.

CHARLES P. FISHBAUGH
Louisiana State University in New Orleans

CONTENTS

LIST OF ILLUSTRATIONS

LIST OF TABLES

LIST OF FIGURES

From PADDLE WHEELS *to* PROPELLERS

James Howard (1814–1876), founder of the Howard Ship Yards

The Launching, 1834

CHAPTER I

The *Hyperion*

JAMES HOWARD walked down a steamboat's gangplank to the Louisville levee one day in May 1834. Shortly afterward he had in his pocket a contract to build his first steamboat hull. He was nineteen years old that spring.

But he did not enter into the steamboat-building industry blindly or without experience. When Jim walked down the gangplank that morning, he resigned a job as a steamboat clerk where he had counted passengers, baggage, and freight, and tallied accounts for four months. He knew from the intimacy of the ledgers the revenues, the expenses, and the profits to be earned in steamboating. He knew even better, apparently, the rewards to be gained by building the boats themselves. Then, too, a few months earlier James Howard had left the Cincinnati yards of the steamboat builder, William Hartshorn, to whom he had been apprenticed. While the apprenticeship contract had over a year to run at the time Jim left, he was by then already well experienced in joining oak and pine into hulls that floated lightly on the Western Rivers.

Where and how James Howard met Captain Leonard of Apalachicola, Florida, is not recorded. Fate, perhaps? But how Jim persuaded him to invest several thousand dollars in the ability of a greenhorn steamboat clerk is a greater mystery. It is, perhaps, a tribute to Jim's sincerity, honesty, and enthusiasm, his character in short, that led Captain Leonard and thousands of others to invest in him. It is also an indication of the times—an era of rampant individualism and enterprise, particularly in the West and especially on the rivers. Whatever the amalgam, James Howard contracted in May 1834 to build a steamboat hull 107 feet long, 18 feet in beam, and 8 feet deep from gunwale to keel for Captain Leonard. It was named the *Hyperion*.

STEAMBOATS COME TO THE OHIO

ONE more boat builder probably did not create much of a stir that year in the yards clustered around the Falls of the Ohio. In the preceding season, some eight steamboats had been constructed in the region, while the year before had seen nine leave the ways.[1] They were sizeable craft, too; averaging some 115 tons in displacement.[2] Innumerable flat-boats, keelboats, and barges also took shape in the area in response to the burgeoning demand for transport. Growth, expansion, increase, and development were synonyms for the West of that day. One more boat-builder seemed but inevitable, if not even foreordained.

This growth in numbers west of the Appalachians was readily apparent to one who had the time to pause and count. Some of the hamlets along the Ohio had already grown into towns and a few had become truly cities. Louisville itself was by the spring of 1834 a fair-sized city with at least 15,000 population. During the decade of the thirties, that city doubled its size, adding in ten years as many citizens as had settled there from its founding to 1830.[3] While the growth of the river towns was, perhaps, the most evident and easily verified criterion of development, a similar increase of settlers was occurring in the forests on either side of the Ohio and along the Mississippi. From the unrecorded handful of settlers in the Territory Northwest of the Ohio and the 73,677 citizens of Kentucky in 1790, the combined population of Kentucky and the states carved from the old Northwest grew by 1830 to 2,157,935.[4]

[1] T. C. Purdy, "Report on Steam Navigation in the United States," U.S. Bureau of the Census, *Tenth Census* (1880), IV, *Transportation*, p. 671.
[2] *Ibid.*
[3] Charles H. Ambler, *A History of Transportation in the Ohio Valley* (Glendale, Calif.: Arthur H. Clark Co., 1932), p. 156.
[4] U.S. Bureau of the Census, *Historical Statistics of the United States Colonial Times to 1957* (Washington, D.C., 1960), p. 13.

Such an influx of settlers augured well for a new boatbuilder. It was not just that the Ohio, alone among important rivers in North America, flowed from east to west, and that the tide of humanity was running westward, for there were other feasible westbound routes. In the north, there were the Mohawk Valley and the Great Lakes. There was the Wilderness Road through the Cumberland Gap, for many years the safest route for settlers.[5] The great National Road, of course, traversed the Appalachian barrier and terminated for a while at the banks of the Ohio, reaching Columbus, Ohio, in 1833.[6] But with the exception of the Mohawk Valley route, traversed by the Erie Canal by 1825, all other routes but the Ohio were land routes. The superior ease of floating goods in a boat compared to hauling them by pack horse, wagon, or on foot must have been a paramount consideration for the weary, footsore immigrants on the National Road by the time they caught a glimpse of the Ohio at Wheeling, and many of them proceeded to float the rest of the way to their new homes.

Contrast these descriptions of land and river travel by a traveler in 1842:[7]

> . . . the road we went over that day was certainly enough to have shaken tempers that were not resolutely at Set Fair, down to some inches below Stormy. At one time we were all flung together in a heap at the bottom of the coach, and at another we were crushing our heads against the roof. Now, one side was down deep in the mire, and we were holding on to the other. Now, the coach was lying on the tails of the two wheelers; and now it was rearing up in the air, in a frantic state, with all four horses standing on the top of an insurmountable eminence, looking coolly back at it, as though they would say, "Unharness us. It can't be done." . . . A great portion of the way was over what is called a corduroy road, which is made by throwing trunks of trees into a marsh, and leaving them to settle there. The very slightest of the jolts with which the pon-

---

[5] Caroline E. MacGill et al., *History of Transportation in the United States before 1860* (Washington, D.C.: The Carnegie Institution of Washington, 1948), pp. 7–10, 94.

[6] George R. Taylor, *The Transportation Revolution, 1815–1860* (*The Economic History of the United States*, New York: Rinehart and Co., 1951), p. 22.

[7] Charles Dickens, *American Notes* (London: Thomas Nelson and Sons, n.d.), pp. 170, 171–72, 205.

derous carriage fell from log to log, was enough, it seemed, to have dislocated all the bones in the human body. . . .

A fine broad river always [the Ohio], but in some parts much wider than in others. And then there is usually a green island, covered with trees, dividing it into two streams. . . . but the banks are for the most part deep solitudes, overgrown with trees, which hereabouts, are already in leaf and very green. For miles, and miles, and miles, these solitudes are unbroken by any sight of human life or trace of human footstep.

All this I see, as I sit in the little stern-gallery. . . . Evening slowly steals upon the landscape and changes it before me, when we stop to set some emigrants ashore.

The greater ease of water transport was translated into costs; that such costs for river traffic were significantly lower than for road or any other mode of transport should not be surprising. As an example, in 1827 a hundredweight shipped overland by wagon from Philadelphia through Pittsburgh to Cincinnati cost over three times as much as a similar hundredweight shipped by water, in spite of the long ocean passage from Philadelphia to New Orleans and the trip up the Mississippi and Ohio to Cincinnati.[8] Accordingly, by 1834 the turnpike boom in the United States was drawing to a close. Hard-surfaced roads alone were not sufficient to allow cheap, long-distance hauling, particularly for bulky commodities. For immigrants or Yankee peddlers with little to carry but themselves, turnpikes were a boon. They also served for the sizable local traffic around Boston, New York, or Philadelphia. But elsewhere the turnpikes were not earning enough to cover maintenance expenses, or, frequently, even the cost of collecting the tolls. By 1835, more than half of the turnpikes built had been abandoned in whole or in part.[9]

The greater ease of water transport and its lower cost did provide in that day what the turnpikes could not—economical long-distance transportation. This fact, dictated by technology, had been translated into a new boom then sweeping the nation. Canals were a-building. They only proved the economic superiority of water transportation. Canals also demonstrated the superiority, the bounty, of a *natural* waterway.

[8] Thomas S. Berry, *Western Prices before 1861: A Study of the Cincinnati Market* (Cambridge, Mass.: Harvard University Press, 1943), p. 81.
[9] Taylor, *The Transportation Revolution*, pp. 27–28.

For along the Ohio, its tributaries and its contributories, in a region short of currency as well as capital, to transport a farm's annual surplus to market and to return with tools, cloth, sugar, and salt, took only a boat. To be sure, a steamboat was highly preferable for the return trip, but for a poor country man the only outlay for a boat in those days was some timber, some tools, some skill, and considerable enterprising ingenuity.

Until the steamboat hove into view on the Western Rivers, the flow of traffic had been mostly in the direction of the current. On the Mississippi it was estimated that the tonnage carried upstream from New Orleans was barely one tenth that of the down-bound commerce.[10] The current, and all the flotsam that it carried with it, virtually precluded up-bound traffic for all but a slender keelboat or an occasional barge with a modeled bow. Even the passage upstream of these famous craft was accomplished only with travail and despair. A keelboat would be alternately sailed, rowed, cordeled, and pushed upstream by a dozen men or more. She might carry as much as fifty tons, but more likely only fifteen. From New Orleans to Louisville would take three months, with luck, and cost $8.00 per hundredweight.[11] Just a few years following Captain Shreve's successful *Washington*, however, steamboats had permanently left their mark upon the river trade. Then, from New Orleans to Louisville took but two weeks and cost only $2.00 a hundredweight.[12]

From 1811, the year of the first western steamboat, the *New Orleans*, to 1834, the Western Rivers had floated over 450 new steamboats. In 1834 alone some sixty-two steamboats took form, most of them built along the banks of the Ohio.[13] The ability and ingenuity displayed in constructing and adapting the steamboat for the Western Rivers sprang from two sources: the western need for transportation and the experience already gained from building other craft.

Boatbuilding around the junction of the Monongahela and Allegheny

[10] MacGill *et al.*, *Transportation in the United States before 1860*, p. 109, and Berry, *Western Prices before 1861*, p. 22.

[11] Leland D. Baldwin, *The Keelboat Age on Western Waters* (Pittsburgh: University of Pittsburgh Press, 1941), pp. 44–46, 192.

[12] *Ibid.*, p. 193; MacGill *et al.*, *Transportation in the United States before 1860*, pp. 86–90.

[13] Purdy, "Report on Steam Navigation in the United States," *Tenth Census* (1880), IV, *Transportation*, p. 671.

rivers must have begun before the French and Indian War, for in the winter of 1762–63 the Army found some old boats at Fort Pitt and constructed twenty more.[14] The traders that followed that war also built boats there, importing the shipwrights as well as the tools, the iron, the sails, and even the rope. The American Revolution accelerated the pace of construction and dispersed it up and down the Ohio. Along the Monongahela upstream as far as Elizabeth and even Brownsville boat yards were scattered, with Brownsville turning out a hundred boats a year for westbound settlers.[15] The yards at Elizabeth in 1793 launched the *Polly*, a schooner built for the high seas.[16] After the turn of the nineteenth century, flatboats were built anywhere and everywhere; but the building of a keelboat or a barge required more skill, and the construction of these craft was more concentrated.

The capabilities of a few yards in particular allowed the construction of oceangoing sailing vessels. Two warships were built in Pittsburgh in 1798 for use against the Spanish in New Orleans and Florida. At least ten or eleven other seagoing vessels were constructed at Elizabeth and Pittsburgh. One, the *Western Trader* built in 1804, measured some 400 tons and was equal in size to some of the later steamboats. Twenty-five sailing craft were built around Marietta and sailed to the Gulf. Other centers were located in Allentown, Freeport, Wheeling, Cincinnati, and Louisville.[17]

The Secretary of the Treasury took note of the industry in a report to the Senate on March 2, 1807.[18] But in 1811, Zadok Cramer, editor and publisher of the *Navigator*, a veritable Baedeker of the Ohio and Mississippi, noted that there was "on foot a new mode of navigating our western waters—boats propelled with the power of steam," and predicted that they would prove an immense advantage.[19] These early ventures into

---

[14] Baldwin, *The Keelboat Age on Western Waters*, p. 50.
[15] *Ibid.*, p. 52.
[16] Richard T. Wiley, "Ship and Brig Building on the Ohio and Its Tributaries," Ohio Archaelogical and Historical *Publications*, XXII (1913), 60–62; Ambler, *Transportation in the Ohio Valley*, p. 84.
[17] Ambler, *Transportation in the Ohio Valley*, p. 84, 89, 97.
[18] *Ibid.*, p. 99.
[19] Zadok Cramer, *The Navigator* . . . (Pittsburgh: Cramer, Spears & Eichbaum, 1811), p. 31.

ship building, as opposed to knocking together haphazardly a floating box or flatboat, were undoubtedly instrumental in causing craftsmen of ship's carpentry, rigging, ropemaking, and machinery to migrate west and settle along the rivers to ply their profitable trade.[20]

So it was in the spring of 1834. Canoes and batteaux, Indians and fur traders and soldiers, all had retreated before the barges and keelboats. And these craft had in turn been left in the wake of the upbound steamboat. Each successive technological evolution admitted more settlers to and through the old Northwest. As the self-sufficient Indian and trapper were superseded by the farmer and miller and tradesman, the need for transport increased. At first in dribbles, the corn as whiskey in jugs or as pork on the hoof, then in a larger and larger stream, the annual output of Kentucky, Ohio, Indiana, and Illinois sought its final consumer, who by the 1840s valued it at over $100,000,000.[21] So the demand for boats appeared insatiable. It was a "solid" demand, based on more than just a passenger's conception of relative ease. It was a demand for a technically superior, and economically superior, mode of transportation; a mode of transportation for use largely on natural waterways, supplemented to be sure by the Ohio, Indiana, and Kentucky canals as well as the rutted roads that led to a stream. In 1834, even the steam-powered toy called a railroad appeared destined for nothing more than the role of carrying goods to the superior steamboat!

This was the industry James Howard entered one May morning. It was ebullient, boiling along like a spring flood in a mountain gorge, carrying one and all with it in a crest of excitement, enterprise, and energy. It seemed that a man could not fail. So it was for many years. In no other part of the world were so many steamboats built and operated.[22]

THE FIRST HOWARD SHIP YARD

IF James Howard had gone ashore at Pittsburgh to find his first contract, perhaps he would have built his first boat on some bank near that city. But he met Captain Leonard in Louisville, and he began his boatbuilding

[20] Ambler, *Transportation in the Ohio Valley*, p. 83.
[21] Berry, *Western Prices before 1861*, p. 22n.
[22] Taylor, *The Transportation Revolution*, p. 63.

career there. He selected a site across the river in Indiana in Port Fulton (now a part of Jeffersonville). With an advance payment from Captain Leonard for his capital, the young boatbuilder rented a river-front lot at the foot of Mechanic Street. He bought timber already floating in the river and hired his crew of sawyers, shipwrights, and caulkers. Then he probably drew in the mud an outline of the hull and set his men to building. So the *Hyperion*, which recalled the Titan who fathered the sun god, took shape as a shallow-draft, side-wheel steamer for the Chattahoochee River.

As the number of yards and their locations attest, there were not compelling reasons for building a boat in one place and one place alone. As transportation improved in the West, the materials and labor for boatbuilding became highly mobile. Pine logs from the upper Allegheny or Clarion rivers could be floated to Louisville as well as to Pittsburgh. White oak timber from the Kanawha Valley was also easily rafted downstream. In 1834 there was timber for boatbuilding virtually anywhere along the banks of the Ohio. In fact, the hills of Clark County, Indiana, only a few miles from Jeffersonville, supplied the timber for many a steamboat. Perhaps this was a factor that helped Jim Howard to locate his yard where he did.

Labor with the needed skills was available from Louisville, New Albany, or Jeffersonville. The area had several boat yards. In 1833, at least eight of the forty-four steamboats built on the Western Rivers had been launched from Louisville.[23] Or else a cash-hungry farmhand from the back country could be hired to saw the planks and timbers under the skilled direction of a master craftsman such as Jim Howard.

The technology of steamboat construction, as well as the prevailing business arrangement, required only that a boatbuilding yard offer sufficiently deep water to float the completed hull. At first, specialized machinery was not used in the actual construction of the hull. And, as was the practice of that day, James Howard contracted to build only a hull for Captain Leonard. The owner then contracted with another specialized firm for the engines and machinery. Perhaps even a third would be

[23] Purdy, "Report on Steam Navigation in the United States," *Tenth Census* (1880), IV, *Transportation*, p. 671.

utilized to construct the boilers and flues. Another contract would have been required to build the cabin and maybe yet another for the painting. Once the hull was afloat, the vessel could readily be towed to the other yards for completion.

By 1818, Louisville claimed at least one establishment—Prentice-Bakewell—that could turn out steam engines.[24] Since 1826 New Albany had boasted a foundry for their repair, which may have shortly thereafter begun the manufacture of new shafts, cranks, anchors, pipes, and fastenings.[25] Thus to either Louisville or New Albany the hull that Jim Howard built could be towed for competent completion. And it was. The *Hyperion* left in September that year for the Chattahoochee River trade.

The Voyage of a Century

WITH the *Hyperion*, young Jim Howard launched his name into the mainstream of American history. For over a century four generations of Howards built steamboats, barges, towboats, and ferryboats for the Western Rivers for Alaska and South America too.[26]

The Howard Ship Yards of Jeffersonville, Indiana, flourished in the days of the packet. It is easy to understand why, for even a novice soon could tell a Howard-built belle by her graceful lines and stately beauty. When the packet's glorious day in the West waned, the Howard Ship Yards turned out equally famous towboats and barges. The Yards successfully survived the lean years when all but a few in the nation forgot the advantages of river transportation. Then with the resurgence of the riverboat after the old channels had been improved, Howard-built towboats and barges again were seen in number on the Western Rivers.

[24] Henry M'Murtrie, *Sketches of Louisville and Its Environs* (Louisville: Printed by S. Penn, 1819), pp. 131–32.
[25] Victor M. Bogle, "A Flourishing Place," in *Indiana Magazine of History*, XLIX (1953), 7.
[26] The four generations are represented by the direct line of James Howard (1814–1876), Edmonds J. Howard (1840–1919), James E. Howard (1876–1956), and Edmonds John Howard (1910–   ). While Edmonds John was too young to play a leading role in the story of the Howard Ship Yards before their demise, he worked there in his youth and was preparing to continue the family enterprise.

This is the chronicle of the Howard Ship Yards of Jeffersonville, Indiana, from their beginning in 1834 until the eve of the Second World War. It is a voyage for a century by steamboat and diesel towboat along the Mississippi and the rivers that flow into it.

Competition and Craftsmanship

CHAPTER II

HARD TIMES

THE HISTORY of an era, and the passing of an age, can be easily traced through the procession of names men have painted on their steamboats. The *New Orleans* heralded her goal despite the scoffs and sneers of the skeptics in Pittsburgh. The third Western steamboat, the *Enterprise*, lived up to her name for she was the first boat to come upstream from New Orleans to Louisville under steam. It took her but twenty-five days in contrast to the keelboat's two or three months.

By the time of the first Howard-built boat, the appellation game was just entering its golden age. It was fitting, and prophetic, that the launching of the *Hyperion* signaled the beginning of a titan's career. There had been little to single Jim Howard out of the crowd of pioneers prior to 1834, nor was there much of extraordinary note for the next decade. But these early years were a time of seasoning, aging in wood, meeting and mastering the competition. It was the time for the making of a master craftsman and an entrepreneur.

The sixth Howard-built hull was launched in 1837. It was aptly named the *Hard Times*. To Jim at the time it perhaps seemed more a summary of his life thus far than an omen for the future.

The first child of John and Martha Howard, James was born in September 1814, in Oldham Parish, Lancashire, England. The father was a weaver there until the spring of 1819 when he took his wife, James, and three-year-old Daniel to the United States. After a six weeks' voyage, the family settled in Brooklyn for a while before they joined a westward-bound wagon train.[1]

By the age of six then, young James knew much of the world and many means of travel. It was not an unusual or hard life for the times, even though Jim had had to walk all the way from New York to Wheeling. So had his mother, for his father fell ill early in the trip and had to ride in the crowded wagon. It was simply one of the myriad experiences that conditioned and selected the hardy. At Wheeling, the Howards boarded a flatboat and floated down to Cincinnati. There John Howard built a small wool-finishing mill with quarters for his family adjoining.

The whole family worked in the mill, father, mother, and all the Howard sons as each grew old enough. Following Jim was Daniel, then John C., and finally Tom. Living and working with water and machinery was good training and experience, but when each son became old enough for an apprenticeship, each one, in his own manner, escaped from the wool mill and took after the steamboats.

Jim worked first for William Gordon, a Cincinnati boatbuilder, as a water boy. But it was not only water that the water boy measured out to the sawyers, carpenters, and caulkers. He also poured out each man's measure of whiskey twice a day. He also worked for Burton Hazen for a time, too, in his Cincinnati shipyards, but he had himself apprenticed finally to William Hartshorn and it was from this man and his crew that James Howard learned his craft. Daniel, too, was later apprenticed to Hartshorn.

The term of apprenticeship had some time yet to run when Jim up and quit the boat yards and disappeared from Cincinnati. He took a job as a clerk on a steamboat in the Cincinnati–St. Louis trade for that winter of 1833 and 1834, and that, too, was good experience and training. It was decisive for the launching of the *Hyperion* the next fall and the beginning of the Howard Ship Yards.

Jim's first partner in the steamboat-building business was David Barmore, who also had been apprenticed in Cincinnati. Together they built

---

[1] Biographical material on James Howard is given in Stephen G. Savage, James Howard of Jeffersonville, Master Builder of Steamboats (Unpublished Master's Thesis, Indiana University, 1962) and Lewis C. Baird, *Baird's History of Clark County Indiana* (Indianapolis: B. F. Bowen & Company, 1909), pp. 431–32.

a ferry, the *Black Locust*, in 1834, but the partnership as businessmen was dissolved after the launching of the *Tecumseh* in 1835. Just why is undetermined, but on October 20, 1836, James Howard was married to Rebecca Barmore, his partner's sister.

Jim with his new wife settled at Madison, Indiana, for the next decade. His second partner was P. Emerson. At Madison, in 1836, the firm of Emerson and Howard launched two packets, the *Irwinton* and the *Livingston*. The next year came the barge *Hard Times*, to be shortly followed by a sister hull, the barge *Natches*. But 1838 saw no launchings from their yards.

Three side-wheeler hulls were floated during 1839, then a small packet hull in 1840. But the next contract for a steamboat did not come until 1843. They were hard times, indeed, and Jim had to run on the river as carpenter and engineer in order to keep his family. Jim's son Edmonds J. Howard was born at Madison in March 1840 .

The Demand for Steamboats

STEAMBOAT launchings waxed and waned with the tides of business in the Western River valleys. A surge of trade one season would call forth an increase in hulls launched the next, and this gain in turn would usually curtail an individual boat's trade and profits the following year. As long as each succeeding crest of trade surmounted the past one and as long as each trough descended to a level not so low as the one preceding it, orders for steamboats were still forthcoming. But there were often several years between peaks of activity in the yards, especially after 1834. The depression in steamboat construction after the Panic of 1837 lasted fully until 1844.

During these depressed years the local papers noted that passage from New Orleans to Pittsburgh was but $15.00, a sum that amounted to carrying passengers for nothing and boarding them for less than a dollar a day.[2] The Cincinnati, Louisville, and St. Louis newspapers all made

[2] Cincinnati *Gazette*, February 14, 1842, quoted in Louis C. Hunter, *Steamboats on the Western Rivers . . .* (Cambridge: Harvard University Press, 1949), p. 385, note 111.

mention of the unprofitable operations on the rivers. Some blamed excess competition; others blamed high wages. There were, of course, a few boats that conspicuously earned a good return—in 1839 the *Ione* in one round trip from St. Louis to Galena was able more than to repay her original cost. Possession of a large new boat with the latest machinery and construction, as in the *Empress* or the *Diana*, allowed an able manager to earn $25,000 a year even during hard times.[3] It was the stories about such successes as these that persuaded Charles Pancost to desert his drugstore in a small Missouri town, or John Jones at the flour mill in Rising Sun, Indiana,[4] to forsake his humdrum life, buy into a steamboat, and escape onto the river. Their demand built steamboats. There were too many such entrepreneurs after 1837, however.

From 1820 to 1841, the freight landed at New Orleans by steamboats increased to 542,500 tons from 106,706—a full fivefold gain. In 1820, the freight arrived at the New Orleans levee in only 198 boat trips, with an average of 539 tons per boat. But in 1841, each of the 1,958 arriving steamboats carried an average of only 277 tons.[5] Such a decline in volume when translated into declining earnings and profits would have adversely affected the construction of new steamboats.

In 1820 the average size of the river steamboat was about 200 measured tons. During the inaugural era of steam, from 1811 to 1820, 41 per cent of the 89 hulls launched measured in excess of 199 tons. Nine per cent were larger than 399 tons. Throughout each successive quinquennium, however, the percentage of boats built larger than 200 tons declined. For the period 1831–1835, only 17 per cent measured over 199 tons, and but 3 per cent were larger than 399 tons. For the decade of the thirties, the average tonnage of the steamboats built was but 147, down from the 200 ton average of the first decade.[6]

The decline in the average size of the Western steamboat between 1820 and 1840 was striking. It had some economic explanation, at least

[3] Hunter, *Steamboats on the Western Rivers*, p. 385.
[4] *Ibid.*, pp. 388–89; Richard E. Banta, *The Ohio* (*Rivers of America*, New York: Rinehart & Co., 1949), pp. 294–96.
[5] Emerson W. Gould, *Fifty Years on the Mississippi* . . . (St. Louis: Nixon-Jones Printing Co., 1889; reprinted Columbus, Ohio: Long's College Book Co., 1951), p. 214.
[6] Hunter, *Steamboats on the Western Rivers*, pp. 106, 647.

in part, given the ease of entry into the steamboat industry and the free enterprise of the era. One such reason might well have been that a 300-ton steamboat only half or three-quarters loaded most certainly would have been less profitable more of the time than a smaller craft carrying the same tonnage but at its optimum efficiency. It would suggest a shortage of capital, curtailing the construction of the larger, more expensive steamer. Again, earnings would have been a factor.

Technical problems could partially explain the trend toward a smaller boat. In the 1820s the steamboat was still an awkward duckling, sired by the ocean ship that had used the wind as its motive power for centuries and had been adapted to such requirements as wind and the wind-swept ocean had dictated for survival. The still pools of the Ohio, where ripples were the only waves, dictated a far different answer, as did the current and debris of the Mississippi or the shallow, muddy bottom of the Missouri. Some early steam-propelled craft in the West carried mast and sails, as the *St. Louis* and the *Western Engineer* of 1819.[7] They doubtlessly were built under the influence of the shipwrights and masters who came over the Alleghenies from the Coast. The invention of the Western Rivers steamboat took a generation to accomplish.

A seagoing ship's hull, regardless of the superstructure's configuration and adornment, would be poorly suited for most of the Western Rivers. The *New Orleans* showed this in 1811, when it was found that her hull depth of twelve feet effectively excluded her from the intended New Orleans-Louisville trade and limited her to the Lower Mississippi.[8] A sailing vessel's hull was of necessity deep, not only to withstand the tremendous seas of the North Atlantic, but to stabilize the masts, rigging, and the power of the sails at the end of their tall levers. Then, too, in beating to windward (that is, going as nearly as possible in the direction from which the wind is blowing) the sailing vessel needed a deep keel to bite into the water and prevent a drift to leeward. The superstructure needed to be low and small to reduce both wind and the occasional wave resistance. The hull had to be compoundly curved and heavily planked in order to gain adequate strength for the seas encountered. The swells

[7] *Ibid.*, p. 65.
[8] *Ibid.*, p. 70.

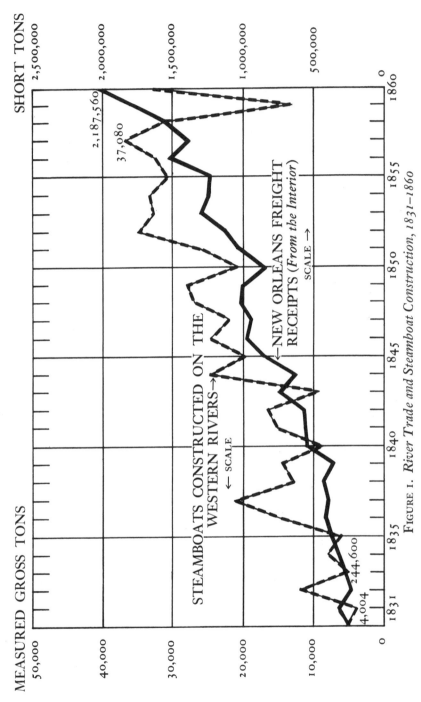

FIGURE 1. *River Trade and Steamboat Construction, 1831–1860*

SOURCE: U.S. Bureau of the Census, *Tenth Census* (1880), IV, *Transportation*, pp. 671–72, and *Report on the Internal Commerce of the United States. Commerce and Navigation*, Pt. II (Washington, D.C., 1888), pp. 199, 221.

also dictated a strong backbone or keel to hold the hull together when the middle was unsupported while the stem and stern were borne up by two wave crests. All that a river steamboat required in common with an ocean-sailing ship, however, was that they both had to float. The river steamboat, though, had to float on the water; the ocean ship could float in it.

At sea, a grounding frequently meant the destruction of the vessel, either from the pounding of the waves against a hull without resilience as a result of being impaled upon the shore, or from the bottom poking holes through the hull and causing it to founder. In the river, a grounding might not automatically cause the destruction of the vessel, though the likelihood of rupturing the hull was always there. A grounding was to be avoided, as was a collision with another craft, a log, or other flotsam. In the rivers where the depth of water was often measured in inches rather than fathoms or feet, groundings were catastrophic enough even if not fatal. For a grounding on a sandbar with the river in a falling stage might well mean a week's delay, or a month's. Thus, the shallow rivers dictated smaller hulls that floated lightly on the water. By the 1840s, then, the external keel and skeg were gone, as was the heavy internal keel. Compound curves were replaced by a flat-planed bottom curved, or modeled as it was described, to turn the water aside and under. The strength needed to carry a profitable tonnage was found now in trusses, keelsons, and longitudinal bulkheads within the hull, as well as a system of beams and chains extending upward through the superstructure—the hog chains. The *Magnet* of 1822 measured 150 tons and when lightly loaded drew 42 inches. The *Old Hickory* in 1845 drew but 40 inches similarly loaded, but she measured 445 tons. Likewise the shoal-draft *Velocipede* in 1820 drew 24 inches and measured 109 tons, while the *General Taylor* in 1846 drew 24 inches but measured 199 tons.[9] But still in any one year, the smaller vessel had less draft. As the frontier moved, so too did the steamboats move farther and farther up the progressively shallower streams.

By the decade of the forties, the frontier began to pass the regions in which the steamboat (however small or light in draft) could profitably operate except for a few months of the year. The Census of 1840 placed the frontier at just above the present Illinois–Wisconsin border, then

---

[9] Hunter, *Steamboats on the Western Rivers*, p. 647.

down fifty to one hundred miles west of the Mississippi to the Iowa-Missouri border, thence west to near Kansas City. From there it extended down to the eastern edge of Texas.[10] By 1850, the progress of the frontier had pushed civilization up to and often beyond the margin of practical navigation. Occasional exploits were recorded, of course, similar in character and bravado to that of bringing a steamboat up the White River to Indianapolis. When it is realized that that feat required the spring flood, rollers, winches, and teams for the last few miles, its commercial value for transportation can be doubted.[11]

Thus, the regions of easy conquest for the steamboat diminished. When faced with a poor season in one trade in the twenties or early thirties, a captain could push off to the newer region where the shortage of boats would insure a profitable trip or two, but in the late thirties and early forties competition appeared everywhere. The ability of the builders to expand the navigable regions by technological innovations and triumphs had also reached a zenith. Accordingly, then, the tonnage afloat, if denied access by low water or excessive draft to new areas for exploitation, could only turn to the deep, natural, and public waterways from Cincinnati to New Orleans, from St. Louis to New Orleans, or any two places in between. Since their alternative was to tie up to the bank somewhere and take a loss, many chose instead to stay in operation even if it meant that they would have to do business a little cheaper than their neighbors.[12]

A steamboat's expenses were largely fixed costs such as depreciation, insurance, interest, painting, and the like. The costs that varied directly with the freight hauled were relatively small—some additional fuel, more roustabouts' wages, increased wharfage fees, and canal tolls. A decline in freight carried of 20 per cent or so, with perhaps an even greater decline in freight revenues, might not have caused a steamboat owner to bank the fires and suspend operations. If he had no other vocation or opportu-

[10] Clifford L. Lord and Elizabeth H. Lord, *Historical Atlas of the United States* (Rev. ed. New York: Henry Holt and Co., 1953), Maps 68 and 69.

[11] Emma Carleton, "First Steamboat on White River," in *Indiana Magazine of History*, II, No. 2 (June, 1906), pp. 95–96; Jacob P. Dunn, *Greater Indianapolis . . .* (2 vols. Chicago: Lewis Publishing Co., 1910), I, 18–19.

[12] Gould, *Fifty Years on the Mississippi*, p. 589.

nity, he might well elect to stay and fight it out. He could cut his rates, ignore the insurance premiums, forego depreciation charges, let the paint peel. As long as he could buy fuel and pay his crew, the boat could steam up and down the rivers searching for cargo. The 50 per cent decline in freight rates from 1841 to 1844 suggests that such cut-throat competition did occur in the lean years.[13]

Price cutting can be expected where excess capacity exists. It could, of course, also come about where costs of operation have declined, but in the river trade of the early 1840s such a decline in costs would not explain adequately the sudden deep drop in freight rates that occurred after 1841. Rates on freight from Cincinnati to New Orleans during September 1841 were exceptionally high for the year, indicating either a brisk trade or a great shortage of water. Thereafter, however, the freight rates declined. In 1842 the average rate for the year was some 35 per cent below the annual average of 1841. In 1843, rates declined by 5 per cent more. Through 1844, freight rates showed a further drop of 12 per cent. But by 1845 a small increase had occurred. Thus, from 1841 to the trough of 1844, Cincinnati–New Orleans freight rates dropped by 51 per cent.[14] Such a decline was more severe than that shown by most other prices during the same period. Prices of northern agricultural products in Cincinnati during the period dropped by but 10 per cent; prices on commodities other than of northern agriculture declined by 18 per cent through 1844 and began to increase thereafter.[15]

The fleet of steamboats on the rivers in 1845 numbered 557, with a measured tonnage of 98,246.[16] The natural life of a Western steamboat was generally estimated to have been but five years. Those operated on some difficult river, such as the Missouri, often would not last over three years.[17] Consequently, at least 110 new steamboats, one fifth the fleet, were needed each year just to replace those worn out or wrecked. If the growth in the need for steamboat transport in the West continued to increase at a rate of about 15 per cent annually, as it had up to this time, the

[13] Berry, *Western Prices before 1861*, p. 557.
[14] *Ibid.*
[15] *Ibid.*, p. 564.
[16] Hunter, *Steamboats on the Western Rivers*, p. 33.
[17] *Ibid.*, pp. 100–101.

increased demand for steamboats added to the expected replacement demand would have required around 199 to 255 new steamboats each year.[18] Yet the greatest number of hulls launched in the antebellum era was but 163 in 1857. Six hundred and thirty-eight new boats were launched in the five years ending in 1850, and the fleet in 1850 numbered 740 steamboats.[19] From 1846 to 1850, then, the fleet of steamers was virtually replaced with new, and on the average slightly larger, craft (176 tons and 193 tons average in 1845 and 1850, respectively). But the annual average production of but 128 boats in those years was in accord only with the expected replacement demand. Expansion in the size of the fleet of steamboats accounted for but 17 vessels each year. Expansion was apparently taken care of by the larger hull's greater carrying capacity or by faster boats making a greater number of trips each season. Thus, it appears that the steamboat had reached an age of maturity and stability.

Many a steamboat man returned to his drugstore or his flour mill poorer in purse but never able to forget the adventure of steamboating on the rivers. These men had played a necessary role in the metamorphosis of the river steamboat. The era of wild, speculative expansion, innovation, and change had ended with the Panic of 1837 and its aftermath. By 1845, when Jim Howard survived with his skills as a master craftsman intact, the steamboat was ready to enter the "palmy days" of its existence, and James Howard, too, was ready.

The Second Start

In 1846 James Howard once more elected to build steamboats. In that spring he settled in Shippingport, near the terminus of the Louisville and Portland Canal. He commenced building the *Courier* and during the year he launched six steamboat hulls while in early 1847 he had two more on the ways and near completion. The spring flood, however, inundated his yard and carried the boats to destruction. Undaunted, he formed a part-

---

[18] Trend computed from the annual steamboat arrivals in New Orleans as quoted in Hunter, *Steamboats on the Western Rivers*, pp. 644–45.

[19] See Appendix B, pp. 231–232, and Hunter, *Steamboats on the Western Rivers*, p. 33.

nership with John Enos at his fourth location, this time in Louisville opposite Towhead Island. This enterprise was barely started when John Enos died. Although work on the seven hulls under contract continued until they were completed in 1850, James chose once more to move his own operations to Jeffersonville, where he settled on a site between Graham and Divisions streets on the river. The work on the Louisville bank was left to his younger brother, Daniel. The brothers formed a partnership, then, D. & J. Howard, and began in earnest to make their mark on the waters on the Western Rivers.[20]

One of the larger hulls that they launched in 1848 from Jeffersonville became the *Louisiana*, their first boat for an enterprising Southerner named John W. Cannon. But she had a short life. In the evening of November 15, 1849, in New Orleans, when, fully laden with cargo and carrying a large number of passengers,

> she disengaged herself from the wharf and began to back out into the river, all the boilers exploded with a concussion which shook all the houses for many squares around to their very foundations. The *Louisiana* was lying between two other steamers—the *Bostona* and *Storm*—the upper works of which were completely wrecked. . . . It is generally admitted that this disaster caused a greater loss of life than ever took place on the Mississippi. . . . the number of killed [was estimated to be] one hundred and fifty; and some estimates extend to two hundred. . . . Capt. Cannon . . . was on the wharf at the time of the explosion. He had stopped for a moment to speak to an acquaintance and this delay probably saved his life.[21]

The accident left Captain Cannon over $20,000 in debt, but he recovered and in 1851 was back in Jeffersonville to arrange for the purchase of the *S. W. Downs*, built the previous year at the Louisville yards, for which he paid $150 down. Presumably, the rest of her $17,000 cost came from the boat's earnings.[22] Captain Cannon was among the first of a long list of

[20] Savage, James Howard of Jeffersonville, pp. 27–32.
[21] Gould, *Fifty Years on the Mississippi*, pp. 469–72.
[22] Correspondence, 1851, in Howard Ship Yards & Dock Co. MSS, Lilly Library, Indiana University, Bloomington (hereinafter cited as Howard MSS).

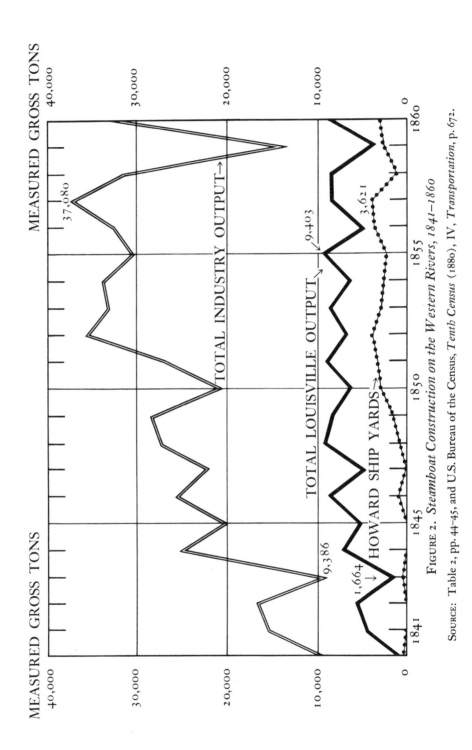

MEASURED GROSS TONS

37,080

TOTAL INDUSTRY OUTPUT→

9,403

TOTAL LOUISVILLE OUTPUT→

3,621

HOWARD SHIP YARDS→

9,386

1,664→

MEASURED GROSS TONS

FIGURE 2. *Steamboat Construction on the Western Rivers, 1841–1860*

SOURCE: Table 2, pp. 44–45, and U.S. Bureau of the Census, *Tenth Census* (1880), IV, *Transportation*, p. 672.

captains, masters, and merchants who contracted with the Howards for their first boat, then a second, and a third. The Howards' customers proved steady.

The *Louisiana* explosion was no fault of the Howards nor, likely, of Captain Cannon, for the steamboat conquered the West only with fearful explosion and a great loss of life. Up to 1848, in fact, 185 reported boiler explosions had occurred and claimed 1,443 lives. Fires ranked second to explosions in dollar value of losses and in loss of life. While steamboats were also easy prey for groundings, snags, and collisions, these accidents and losses were so commonplace that they were more or less accepted as inevitable. They caused little public outrage, but the distrust of steamboats' boilers, which seemed to blow up one or two a week in season, eventually resulted in the Steamboat Inspection Act of 1852 which strengthened an earlier but weaker law.[23]

There was little doubt in the minds of competent observers of the time that the unprofitable operations of the majority of the boats contributed greatly to the frequency not only of explosions but also of collisions, fires, and groundings. The frequent, thrilling, and celebrated races were more than just races, for to the victor often would accrue thereafter a ready freight, a full load, and larger profits.

The excitement of running at night with only pitch pots on the jack staff for illumination was ably portrayed by Samuel Clemens in his *Life on the Mississippi*. Near misses and collisions both with flatboats and barges and unlighted rafts were well-nigh inevitable, according to him. That the river men considered such hazardous navigation a risk worth running, or a mark of virility, is but another commentary on the nature of the times and the conditions that surrounded the antebellum steamboat industry. They ran the risks because they increased their total number of trips thereby. If successful, they expanded their total revenues, the source of all compensation for the risks undertaken. If they were not, another boat could be gotten. Many paid down just a draft drawn on New Orleans, payable when the captain got his new boat and his first freight to that levee.

[23] Hunter, *Steamboats on the Western Rivers*, pp. 272, 287, 537–39; U.S. *Statutes at Large*, X, 61–75.

47962

An eyewitness of the industry, a steamboat pilot and captain, Emerson W. Gould commented on the scene:[24]

> The accidents, which are almost wholly the result of bad management, were set down as among the unavoidable chances of navigation, and instead of adopting measures to prevent them, they were deliberately subtracted from the supposed profits, as matters of course. As the boat was not expected to last more than five or six years . . . within that period, it was considered good economy to reduce the expenditures, and to make money by any means, during the brief existence of the vessel. Boats were hastily and slightly built, furnished with cheap engines, and placed under the charge of wholly incompetent persons; the most inexcusable devices were resorted to, to get freight and passengers, and the most criminal indifference to the safety of the boat and those on board, observable during the trip.

It took force to make the Western Rivers steamboat a safer craft. One hundred and eighty-five separate boiler explosions from 1816 to 1848, with the loss of 1,443 lives, paled in comparison with the 628 lives lost in the twelve months before July 1851. To that carnage in the next eight months were added seven more major steamboat disasters and 600 more lives.[25] In August 1852 both houses of Congress passed the new steamboat bill that required the hydrostatic testing of boilers and fixed the maximum pressure allowable. The manufacture of boiler plate was subjected to inspection. Navigation rules to reduce the chance of accidents were formulated. Fire engines, hoses, and life preservers were made mandatory. Just as important, provisions were made to examine the competence of both engineers and pilots and license those qualified; and adequate inspection and enforcement machinery was spelled out to give teeth to the law. It was effective, for lives lost because of boiler explosions numbered but 224 for the entire United States in the years 1854 to 1858. Before the Act, 1848 to 1852, 1,155 lives had been lost as a result of boiler explosions.[26]

Thus, the industry for which James Howard intended once more

[24] Gould, *Fifty Years on the Mississippi*, p. 122.
[25] Hunter, *Steamboats on the Western Rivers*, pp. 287, 537.
[26] *Ibid.*, pp. 537 ff.

to build steamboats in 1846 was made up of 557 steamboats with an average displacement of 176 tons. The fleet was owned by some two thousand entrepreneurs,[27] perhaps many of whom were in financial straits most of the time, although the shrewder managers obtained handsome returns indeed. It was an industry of free enterprise, small in scale and consequently fiercely competitive. But it served, and well.

COMPETITION

A typical boat yard in the mid-1840s was likewise a small enterprise. At first it required little capital as James Howard well knew. Specialized equipment was not necessary then. It was simply a site along a river where a small band of craftsmen built boats.

Under the plane, saw, and hammer of a thousand such riverfront craftsmen, the Western Rivers steamboat had evolved. By the time Jim Howard located his yard in Jeffersonville for the second time, the steamboat already had been made in its final form and it remained unchanged in general design for half a century or more. To be sure, elegant side-wheelers were displaced by stern-wheelers, but many an old river man never accepted that change as progress. The antebellum side-wheeler— floating palace or plain-faced tramp—was a work of art, built by artists. In a generation, the riverboat had evolved into a reasonably efficient answer for its purposes.

The Howards, James and his brother Daniel, were artists, too, masters of their craft. For in spite of their lack of formal schooling, hard times, and inadequate financial backing after four starts, how else could these young men have built a boat yard that in only the third year of its existence was able to construct 10 per cent of the hulls launched in the West?

Their competition was formidable. By 1850 New Albany had nine established shipyards. Cincinnati had at least five yards: Gordon's, Hartshorn's, Huger's, Leatherwood and Littleberry's, and Week's.[28] Alto-

---

[27] Computed from data in *ibid.*, p. 311.
[28] *Gabriel Collins' Louisville and New Albany Directory, and Annual Advertiser, for 1848* . . . (Louisville: G. H. Monsarrat & Co., n.d.); Ambler, *Transportation in the Ohio Valley*, p. 162.

gether, the Cincinnati yards built seventeen boats in 1850. Marietta, Ohio, and Wheeling, West Virginia, also boasted yards of some importance, and some smaller steamboats as well as keelboats and flatboats were turned out in yards at Madison, Indiana, and Ripley, Ironton, Portsmouth, Galipolis, and Steubenville, Ohio. Along the Ohio and its tributaries from Beaver, Pennsylvania, upstream to Elizabeth were scattered yards, too. The ten in Pittsburgh turned out fifty steamboats in 1850. Down river at St. Louis were one or two yards, and there were perhaps a few more down the Mississippi.[29] But despite the efforts of these more than fifty competitors up and down the Ohio, the Howards built twelve hulls in 1850. The Howard Ship Yard's reputation was established after that.

The advantage of the Jeffersonville location would have redounded to the advantage of all the dozen other builders located around the Falls of the Ohio. The principal advantage of the location was the pool of deep water extending from the Falls all the way to Madison, although the Falls were just as great an obstacle for Jeffersonville-built boats as for Cincinnati or Pittsburgh boats, or even Louisville-built boats in fact, inasmuch as the Falls stretched two miles downstream from Louisville, ending at the eastern edge of New Albany. But a hull started in the autumn or early spring in Jeffersonville would be launched by April or May when the water over the rocks was most likely to be deep enough to afford a safe and free passage. Access could then be had to the engine and boiler builders and the cabin builders and outfitters located in New Albany or Portland. If need be, a boat could be towed all the way to Cairo or St. Louis for its finishing touches.

For the southern market it was no mean advantage to get a new boat to Memphis or Natchez by September. Boats from Cincinnati or Pittsburgh starting out at the time of summer completion would often be stranded at the Falls when the water fell to less than the minimum needed for the boat's passage. A week's delay at the peak of the season could well spell the difference between a profit and a loss to the steamboat owner. Boats from New Albany enjoyed at least five feet and more all the way to New Orleans.

[29] Hunter, *Steamboats on the Western Rivers*, p. 107; Purdy, "Report on Steam Navigation in the United States," *Tenth Census* (1880), IV, *Transportation*, pp. 671–72.

In later years the passage over the Falls assumed an even greater importance than it did at first, for the early boats of the Howards could generally have passed through the 182-foot-long locks of the Louisville and Portland Canal. After about 1855, however, boats with lengths in excess of 200 feet began to leave the Howard ways with greater frequency. Until the locks were enlarged in 1872 and on occasions even until the Falls were dammed in the twentieth century, it was the practice of the Howards to take an incompleted vessel over the Falls for finishing at New Albany or Portland whenever the water level threatened to drop.

In the 1850s there was plenty of wood on the knobs surrounding Jeffersonville, and when that had been consumed, the forests at the head of the local rivers and creeks were utilized. As the years rolled on, lumber for boats and barges was brought from points farther and farther away. In the matter of timber supplies, the location of the yards around Louisville seems not to have been a deterrent to boat construction until the turn of the century and after. James Howard and his local competitors suffered no great disadvantage over the yards of Pittsburgh in the matter of a supply of timber. Neither did they have any real advantage.

The early growth in the number of yards situated around Pittsburgh and that city's corresponding lead in the number and tonnage of boats launched can be attributed to the eastern location. Perhaps more importantly, it was due to the early availability of iron and related products. Certainly the construction of steamboats would have benefited from this close proximity of iron and iron workers. By 1850 the yards at Pittsburgh had constructed 914 vessels of 136,881 tons, compared to the 438 hulls built at Louisville and the 628 which had been built in Cincinnati up to the same year. Reflecting the requirements of the Upper Ohio's navigation as well as the problem of the Falls already mentioned, the average hull size from Pittsburgh measured but 150 tons to the 198 tons of the Louisville average or the 181 tons of the Cincinnati boats.[30] In Pittsburgh, with the construction of the *New Orleans*, small machine shops early turned to the building of steam engines while near-by forges, foundries, and rolling mills turned out the heavy shafts, pitman arms, chains, and boiler plate. But Louisville and Cincinnati were not tardy in turning

[30] Hunter, *Steamboats on the Western Rivers*, p. 106.

to such trades either. Up to 1820, in fact, Louisville had built more steamers than Pittsburgh, but she lost the lead badly in the next decade.[31] So here, too, in the matter of engines and boilers, the Howards were at no disadvantage in their location. The Louisville firm of Ainslie, Cochran and Company and the New Albany company of Charles Hegewald did nearly all the Howards' boiler and engine work until the era of the diesel engine arrived. An occasional owner contracted for a Cincinnati engine or, in later years, for one from St. Louis foundries. In 1860, machine shops and foundries supplying the steamboat trade numbered 70 in Pittsburgh, and they employed over 4,000 men. In Cincinnati, the firms numbered but 18 with about 2,000 hands employed; in Louisville 21 firms existed in this industry and employed 1,333 men. St. Louis listed 58 firms with employment numbering some 3,000.[32]

If the Howards found no pre-eminent advantage at Jeffersonville in the selection and the cost of timber, *the* raw material for steamboats, and if they were at no serious disadvantage vis-a-vis the thousands of machine shops and foundries around Pittsburgh or Cincinnati, they likewise found neither great advantage nor hindrance in the supply of shipwrights, carpenters, joiners, and unskilled labor from the pool that had grown up with the yards and the population of Louisville. If the thirty-five wage earners paid on April 23, 1853, represented the Howards' usual work force, it accounted for about 10 per cent of the hands employed by all the shipyards around the Falls.[33] In summary, then it seems evident that the success of the Howard Ship Yards, apparent by 1850, could not be attributed to the uniqueness of the yards' location and the sources of their raw materials, machinery, or skilled, competent labor to which they had access. Jeffersonville did possess the advantage of a deep pool of water. However, even that blessing was somewhat diminished by being located above the Falls.

CRAFTSMANSHIP

THE success of the Howard Ship Yards is no enigma. In the earliest years,

[31] Hunter, *Steamboats on the Western Rivers*, p. 106.
[32] *Ibid.*, p. 654.
[33] Cash Book, week of April 23, 1853, Howard MSS. The total for the Louisville area is computed from Hunter, *Steamboats on the Western Rivers*, p. 654.

price might have been a factor. The Howards recorded a price for the hull of the *Glendy Burke* of $4,778, or $11.24 per ton.[34] Such a price was well below the average cost of a hull built in the Louisville area, as the Louisville *Courier* reported the average price that year at $16.00 or $17.00 per ton.[35] In 1854 the cost of the hull for the *Marion* was $27.00 per ton, and in a letter to Captain John C. Sinnott of New Orleans, February 12, 1854, the Howards quoted a price which was about $25.00 per ton. With the exception of the one recorded instance in 1851, the *Glendy Burke*, prices quoted by the Howards were in line with the known costs of other builders of the time. Hunter reported that hulls were usually contracted for at $25.00 to $30.00 per measured ton in the thirties and forties.[36]

From one fragmentary page in a Howard journal that survived fire and flood it appears that wages paid were also in keeping with the area and the times. For the week of April 23, 1853, for example, $10.00 was paid to M. Winslow for five and three-quarter days' work. James Lee received $8.00 for five and a quarter days' work, while William Collins was paid $6.00 for six days' work. Henry Eversole got $3.00 for four days' work, while James Howard drew out $2.00 for the week, Daniel drew $5.00 and John Howard, their young brother, drew $3.00. The total number of workers paid that week, as recorded on the page, was thirty-eight. For a total of 169¼ days' work, the amount paid out equaled $1.44 per day. If M. Winslow was a shipwright or a nautical carpenter, his daily rate of $1.75 would have been 25 to 35 cents higher than the average carpenter's pay in the United States in 1850.[37] The $1.00 a day to Bill Collins contrasts with the daily wage for nonfarm labor of 90 cents for the United States generally or $1.05 in New England for the

---

[34] Appendix A, pp. 193–229, and Savage, James Howard of Jeffersonville, p. 52.

[35] The Louisville *Courier*, January 17, 1852, reported the average cost per ton of the boats built in 1851 as $84.00. This was for the completed vessel, including hull, cabin, and machinery. Since the hull usually accounted for 20 to 30 per cent of a completed boat's cost, the average cost of hulls per ton was thus computed to be $16.80.

[36] Hunter, *Steamboats on the Western Rivers*, p. 111.

[37] National Bureau of Economic Research, *Trends in the American Economy in the Nineteenth Century* . . . (Princeton: Princeton University Press, 1960), pp. 457, 462.

De Glendy Burk is a mighty fast boat
Wid a mighty fast captain too.
He sets up dar on de hurrican roof,
And he keeps his eye on de crew.
The Glendy Burk(e), a side-wheel packet, was launched in 1851.

same labor that same year.[38] Only seventeen men were paid for the week that followed, however, and no more entries were recorded until November 26, 1853, when but five men were paid. There are no more recorded entries for the year. It would appear, though, that wages were in accord with the prevailing levels of the times. Thus, barring a windfall in the purchase of timber, there would be little allowance possible for any great variance in the cost of hulls. In a labor-intensive industry before the days of the steam-powered saw, one builder would not be likely to get much greater output per man hour than the next. It is possible, of course, that the Howards arranged their work more systematically or pursued specialization to a greater degree than their competitors. But we only conjecture. Their costs seemed to be identical with those of their competitors, and yet there is the price for the *Glendy Burke* fully a third below the average.

Perhaps Howard hulls were built differently than the others if they were able to attract new customers so quickly in competition with a dozen local yards and fifty more along the Ohio. Their hulls were not radically different in design, or surely some record would have been left. The bid to John C. Sinnott in 1854 mentions "good substantial hog-frames," which were in use in the West by 1848 at least.[39] It is significant, however, that the fifty-five Howard-built hulls from 1834 through 1850 had an average life span of seven years compared with a five-year average for the industry. The Howard average includes the short life span of the *Louisiana* and the *Falcon*, both of which existed for a year or less.[40] A boat that could endure two more seasons than the rest of the fleet would certainly be attractive to a hard-pressed, profit-seeking river captain. Given a prevailing annual rate of return to capital invested in steamboats at that time, 30 per cent before allowance for amortization and depreciation,[41] a boat with a life span of seven rather than five years could alter the profit-and-loss statement significantly and allow an owner to recoup

[38] *Ibid.*
[39] Although John Howard called them hog frames, he probably meant "Sampson posts" which supported the hog chains. Hunter, *Steamboats on the Western Rivers*, p. 99.
[40] Computed from statistics in Savage, James Howard of Jeffersonville, Appendix B, pp. 119–25. See also Hunter, *Steamboats on the Western Rivers*, p. 101.
[41] Hunter, *Steamboats on the Western Rivers*, p. 386.

his capital. The net return would be increased by 50 per cent. But only the shrewder owners would be likely to figure so closely. Given the praise later bestowed on Howard-built boats, it seems highly probable that the initial, as well as the lasting, success of the Howard Ship Yards was due to the knack that the Howards had for constructing superior hulls. It was a skill not universally shared. Jim Howard and his brothers were artists and master craftsmen.

CUSTOMERS

LOUISVILLE's location at the Falls of the Ohio did provide an opportunity on which the Howards were able to capitalize. The importance of Louisville as a river-trade center continued to grow during the last antebellum decade and at the expense of Cincinnati. The growth of trade in Louisville and, particularly, the growth of the southern trade provided a market for hulls and customers who cared to go no farther up the Ohio. They contracted for their new boats at Louisville. Throughout the last half of the forties and the decade of the fifties, the number of boats built at and around Louisville slowly increased until it virtually equalled the number launched in Cincinnati. From 1836 through 1840, Louisville built 40 boats to Cincinnati's 136. From 1851 through 1855, however, it was Louisville 144, Cincinnati 160. And for the five-year period 1856–1860 it was Cincinnati 128, Louisville 122.[42]

Louisville itself proved to be a ready market for the Howards, and from 1834 through 1858, some 30 per cent of their boats recorded Louisville as their home port. The southern location and orientation of Louisville also determined to a large extent the nature and the location of the rest of the Howards' customers, with 18 per cent of the hulls destined for New Orleans and 15 per cent for Mobile, Alabama. Ten per cent were berthed at St. Louis, where they could engage in the southern trade to New Orleans also. A few were destined for the Missouri River trade out of St. Louis.[43]

These customers proved to be loyal. But to judge from their suc-

[42] Purdy, "Report on Steam Navigation in the United States," *Tenth Census* (1880), IV, *Transportation*, p. 672.
[43] Appendix A, pp. 193–95, 222.

cesses, it was a loyalty strongly based on economics. By 1858 the company's records show that there were nine men or companies who had contracted for more than one Howard-built hull. Between them they accounted for twenty-four of the recorded 118 hulls launched during the life of the various Howard shipyards up to that time. While it seems that only one customer in five returned, bear in mind the average life-span of a Howard-built hull was seven years and the fact that the yards and most of these customers were dated after 1847. So in a decade the Howard Ship Yards had made a successful impression.

These two-or-more-boat customers were an interesting cross section of the river trade and the Howard customers. They ranged widely in location and in type of trade. Each, in short, had his own particular specifications and requirements to which the Howards were able to build not one but two or more successful hulls—without plans, drawings of more than a most rudimentary nature, towing-tank tests, or any of the other myriad tools of today's naval architect.

One of the earliest Howard purchasers had been the Louisville and Jeffersonville Ferry Company, which in 1834 had contracted for the *Black Locust*. In 1852 they ordered the larger *Athey Watchen*. J. B. Walker of Mobile, Alamaba, ordered three hulls: one, the *Emperor*, in 1848; another in 1849; and again in 1852. They were intended for the Alabama River and the Mobile–New Orleans trade. One of the first corporations on the Ohio, the Louisville and Cincinnati Mail Line Company, ordered two hulls from the Howards, the *Southerner* in 1853 and the *Ben Franklin*, 300 feet long, in 1854. Benedict and Carter of New Orleans ordered nine boats from 1849 to 1856 for the Louisville–New Orleans trade, the largest of which, the *Empress*, was 285 feet in length and 692 tons. Captain Cannon replaced the *Louisiana* with the *S. W. Downs*, and Captain J. M. White ordered the *Glendy Burke* and returned later for another. These men would surely attest to the superiority of a Howard-built hull, at least for their particular purposes.

The Howards were receptive to new ideas, too. They had the experience, curiosity, and the skill to innovate successfully. On the *C. D. Jr.* in 1853, for example, they installed the first freight-hoisting steam engine for Captain Dalferes of Bayou LaFourche. There must have been other such incidents too small to merit recording by modest men.

With the ability to build superior hulls well demonstrated, the Howard firm was able to survive the financial strains of 1857 and its aftermath. They, too, were inconvenienced, if not actually embarrassed, by the shortage of money and the plethora of paper. The Howards had to write to one of their creditors in 1857:[44]

> We intended to have paid most of the money due on the Ship yard this fall but since the commencement of this Panic in money matters we have found it almost out of the question to raise money in any way. Although we have got along extremely well with our business and are now very busy finishing off two large class Boats which will make twelve Boats built this year. We think now that the crisis in money matters is pretty well past. Business is resuming & everything wears a Better aspect, & it is our intention to pay most of the money due on the Ship Yards early in the spring. We have plenty of good paper maturing & apprehend no difficulty in collecting.

Once again price cutting on freight rates became rampant. From 1856 to 1858, the Cincinnati–New Orleans rates were cut in half, but trade with New Orleans did not fall off. Indeed steamboat arrivals in Cincinnati and New Orleans actually increased.[45] Whether the boats were all as fully loaded as formerly is not known. But the Panic of 1857 did not cause another retreat from the river for James Howard. Although output dipped to but five hulls in 1858 from the twelve of 1857, the Howard Ship Yards were on their way to becoming one of the most renowned of all the Western yards.

[44] Letter of November 26, 1857, to John Zularef, Zurich, Switzerland, in Howard MSS. Zularef owned property that was bought by the Howards, presumably the site of the Yards themselves. Another letter subsequently refers to the transfer of deeds to the Howards.

[45] Berry, *Western Prices before 1861*, p. 557; Hunter, *Steamboats on the Western Rivers*, p. 645.

CHAPTER III

The
War Years

HULL, CABIN, AND OUTFIT

NEW INQUIRIES about steamboats arrived at the Yards almost every day, either by mail or with a casual visit by a passing captain. As the inquirer described the trade he intended to run in and the rivers the boat was to ply, with a mention of the load it was to carry and the power it ought to have, Jim would set to thinking. If some feature was unusual, he would draw a little sketch of how it was to be done—using most anything that lay close to hand. In the early days most of the boats required no plans or drawings of any kind. Perhaps a model would be made for the hull, carefully carved from a block of black walnut or from a block made up of alternating strips of dark and light woods so that the shipwrights had a guide for cutting the frames and planks of the actual hull. Once the owner had described what he wanted and the two men had come to agreement on the terms, he could take off down the river knowing that on his next trip up in a month or less he would see the hull that he had asked for. No long officious list of specifications, standards, and threats for nonconformance were required. For James and his brother Daniel had already demonstrated their mastery of the art and craft of building steamboats.[1]

To an inquiry by mail, the Howards sent a one- or two-paragraph

---

[1] For a description of wooden hull construction see Savage, James Howard of Jeffersonville, pp. 43–47.

reply. While it was succinct, it sufficed for a contract between men of integrity and full understanding of boats and rivers.

From the *Hyperion* to the *Grand Duke*, the last vessel of 1858, the Howards had concentrated on building better-than-good hulls for steamboats, ferryboats, snagboats, and barges, although they had floated only seven or eight barges compared with nearly a hundred side-wheeler hulls. As was the practice of the day, the Howards themselves would make arrangements about the machinery with Roach and Long or maybe with Stuckey, Twomey Company. Hipple, Smith and Company of New Albany or McClarend & Company would then build the cabin. Occasionally the yards would erect the superstructure's framework, but generally some other specialized firm would take over from the hull builder and complete the boat from the main deck upward. Occasionally a busy master would have the Howards arrange the work with the engine builders and the cabin makers, and the Howards would then subcontract this work and arrange for reimbursement from the owner.

But in a letter to William Kay at Victoria, Texas, in December 1856, they made an estimate for a small boat that did not list separately the hull and the cabin but gave one price for the complete works, without machinery of course. And in February 1857 they again estimated the price for a complete ferryboat, ready for the machinery, at $7,000, or a slightly smaller boat with machinery installed for $5,900. Thereafter, their replies to inquiries and estimates listed with increasing frequency the cost of not just the hull, as formerly, but the cabin, the machinery, the iron work (hog chains, braces, guard supports, etc.), the painting, and the outfit as well. The outfit referred to all the equipment required in order to handle the boat—the lines, anchors, tools, shackles, bitts, etc. The Howards always arranged for another firm to install the engines, boilers, flues, and pipes, but after 1859 they apparently had a sufficiently large work force with enough carpenters and joiners that they could build the cabins, finish the iron work, and paint her themselves. Perhaps the falling off of trade after the Panic of 1857 prompted the shift, for whereas they had built twelve hulls the year before, in 1858 they contracted for but five. It would have been a logical and easy way to keep a good work crew busy. It was about 1858, too, that the more detailed estimates were made with greater frequency.

TABLE 1. *Abstracts of Replies to Inquiries and Estimates by D. & J. Howard, 1855–1862*

Date	Correspondent	Dimensions of Hull	Estimated Cost	Terms
1855				
June 20	D. H. Townsend	155 x 31 x 5.5	$ 5,600	One-half cash, balance at 4, 6, and 8 months
June 25	G. B. Weaver, Mississippi River	200 x 32 x 6	8,000	Same as above
July 7	W. T. Yeatman, Nashville, Sternwheeler, draft 24 inches, carry 700 tons, weight but 400	200 x 36 x 6	8,000	Same as above
August 1	Wm. Locke, Florida. Deck, pilot house, rooms for officers	85 x 22 x 4	2,000	Same as above
July 3	D. Cummings, Mobile	185 x 32 x 6	6,700	Same as above
July 12	Dyas Power, Aberdeen, Ohio	150 x 36 x 5.5	6,200	Same as above
1856				
March 2	E. F. Gross, New Orleans, Cabin about $5,000	210 x 36 x 8	11,500	Same as above
March 2	Jas. C. Wingard, New Orleans	130 x 33 x 4.5	4,000	Same as above
April 14	Samuel Applegate, New Orleans. If sharp, draft 4 feet, if built full, draft 3.5 feet	200 x 38 x 7	10,600	Same as above
April 15	C. P. Warner, upper Mississippi	200 x 33 x 5.5	7,000	Same as above
April 16	Capt. W. C. Wilson, New Orleans	185 x 33 x 6.5	7,900	Same as above
June 10	C. Hall	150 x 34 x 6.5	6,650	Same as above
June 16	. . . for the Red River trade	135 x 30 x 5.5	4,800	Same as above
	. . . also for the Red River trade	110 x 28 x 4	2,800	Same as above
July 7	J. E. Barrow, St. Joseph, Mo. Machinery estimated at $8,000	165 x 28 x 5.5	5,800	Same as above
July 31	J. C. Johnson, St. Louis. Estimated cabin at $5,500, H. M. McClarin & Co. Machinery by Roach & Long estimated at $9,000	215 x 33 x 6	9,000	Same as above
October	Prices for large boats about $22 per ton			
December 19	Wm. Kay, Victoria, Texas. Cabin included. Machinery estimated at $4,500	120 x 29 x 5.4	4,200	Same as above

Table 1—(Continued)

Date	Correspondent	Dimensions of Hull	Estimated Cost	Terms
1857 February 19	Mr. Ray, Hannibal, Mo. Ferry boat, double hull aft, cabin, steering, painting capstan, ready for machinery	130 x 33 x 5	$ 7,000	One-half cash, balance at 4, 6, and 8 months
	Or			
	Complete with machinery	100 x 30 x 4.5	5,900	Same as above
	Or one just like Porter's at Boonville, Mo.	90 x 30 x 4	8,199	Same as above
April 13	T. R. Bowman, Memphis	150 x 28 x 5	6,600	Same as above
			5,000	Same as above, plus 90 days to build
April 17	Railroad Company at New Orleans, Barge with cargo box extra		9,400	Same as above
	Quoted price of $22.75 per ton for 413 tons		2,200	
1858 January 13	Capt. J. Kinney, St. Louis	240 x 36 x 6	9,800	Same as above
		245 x 37 x 5.6	10,500	Same as above
March 30	Capt. Thos. Peacock, Galveston, Texas	150 x 33 x 5.5	5,000	
	Machinery		5,500	
	Cabin		1,675	
	Painting		900	
	Iron Work		800	
	Outfit		1,000	
	Total estimate		14,875	
April 1	Capt. Applegate	215 x 38 x 7.5	10,500	Same as above
May 4	Capt. W. C. Hite	175 x 35 x 6	6,500	Same as above
May 27	J. C. Reeves, Blackhawk, Miss.	180 x 35 x 6	6,400	Same as above, 60 days to build
June 12	Capt. Livingston, Louisville, Hull and outfit	175 x 35 x 6.5	6,600	Same as above
July 18	Capt. Cotton, Louisville, Hull and outfit	210 x 37 x 8	12,200	Same as above

TABLE I—(Continued)

Date	Correspondent	Dimensions of Hull	Estimated Cost	Terms
1859				
February 18	Capt. E. E. Saunders, Franklin, La.	150 x 30 x 5.5	$ 4,700	One-half cash, balance at 4, 6, and 8 months
	Cabin extra		1,300	
March 11	Capt. W. S. Mathews, Mobile	180 x 32 x 6	6,500	Same as above
	Machinery		13,600	
May 16	S. E. Walsh, St. Louis, Hull and outfit	260 x 38 x 8	14,000	Same as above
May 16	Capt. Hooper, stern-wheel, scow bow	85 x 36 x 3.5	2,000	Same as above
June 3	. . .	230 x 34 x 6.5	9,800	Same as above
June 21	Capt. Bill Snyder, stern-wheel	155 x 32 x 5	5,500	Same as above
June	George Kinney	230 x 37 x 6.5	12,000	
	Outfit, additional		1,800	
July 30	Capt. E. Bernard, stern-wheel	160 x 30 x 5	4,600	Same as above
September 5	Capt. Henry McPherson	230 x 38 x 6	10,800	Same as above
	Outfit		1,800	
1860				
January 20	W. C. Hite, ferry	155 x 39 x 6.5	6,800	Same as above
	Machinery		6,900	
	Cabin		900	
March 14	Holmes and Wilson	200 x 37 x 8	14,600	Same as above
	Machinery		14,000	
	Cabin		6,250	
	Painting		2,600	
	Iron work		1,800	
	Holmes and Wilson	225 x 37 x 8	16,000	Same as above
	Machinery		18,500	
	Cabin		7,250	
	Painting		2,800	
	Iron work		2,000	

TABLE I—(*Continued*)

Date	Correspondent	Dimensions of Hull	Estimated Cost	Terms
March 20	Capt. J. W. Cannon, New Orleans, including outfit	160 x 35 x 6.5	$ 8,800	One-half cash, balance at 4, 6, and 8 months
March 21	Capt. E. Lanone	170 x 35 x 7	9,700	Same as above
		180 x 36 x 7.5	10,900	
	Both together		20,400	
March 22	Capt. J. M. White, Hull and outfit	225 x 37 x 8.5	16,000	Same as above
	Machinery		18,500	
	Cabin		7,500	
	Painting		2,800	
	Iron work		2,000	
April 16	Capt. Puckett, Hull and outfit	120 x 28 x 5	4,600	Same as above
April 23	Capt. J. J. Atkinson, Hull and outfit	140 x 30 x 5.5	5,000	Same as above
April 23	H. H. Beard, Hull and outfit	170 x 35 x 7	9,700	Same as above
May	Tom Buckley, stern-wheeler	140 x 30 x 4.5	3,900	Same as above
		150 x 32 x 4.5	4,500	Same as above
May 16	Gasvin Bell and Company	100 x 22 x 3.5	2,000	Same as above
	Machinery		900	
	Cabin		500	
	Painting			
June 2	Capt. A. Hooper, Hull and outfit	230 x 38 x 8	14,000	Same as above
1861				
January 7	Capt. John Porter	110 x 32 x 4.5	3,300	Same as above
January 8	Capt. Z. M. Shirley, Hull		12,075	Same as above
	Machinery		9,700	
	Cabin		6,090	
	Painting		890	
	Complete boat, duplicate of the *Superior*		28,755	
	Duplicate of the *Major Anderson*		28,755	

TABLE 1—(*Continued*)

Date	Correspondent	Dimensions of Hull	Estimated Cost	Terms
March 15	Capt. Bill Snyder	182 x 28 x 6	$ 7,800	One-half cash, balance at 4, 6 and 8 months
May 3	Saml H. Lambdin Ferry Co., Natchez, Miss.			
	Hull		2,500	
	Machinery		5,500	
	Cabin		1,000	
	Painting		600	
	Wheels		150	
	Steering apparatus		100	
	Iron work		150	
	Complete boat		10,500	Same as above
1862				
April 3	Capt. Williamson, Cincinnati, Hull only, no outfit	250 x 41 x 7	12,900	Same as above
March 22	John Watson, Hull, painting, iron work	150 x 30 x 5.5	6,400	
	Cabin		2,000	
	Machinery		5,300	
	Complete boat, duplicate of the *Dove*		13,770	

SOURCE: Howard MSS. Brown leather-bound journal identified as Cash Book, 1851–1853, and Letter Copybook, 1855–1862.

So in January 1859 the *D. F. Kenner* was launched for George Cotton in the Bayou Sara and New Orleans trade. The recorded cost of $12,200 was for both the hull and cabin, and the Howards noted that this was the first boat actually to be built under such a contract. For the Howards this first cabin simply meant an expansion in their gross revenues of some 28 per cent, and, perhaps, a more fully employed crew and yard. The *J. D. Swain*, launched in September for E. E. Saunders in the Red River trade, was the result of an estimate written on February 18, 1859, with the hull $4,700 and the cabin $1,300. The *LaFourche* and the *Laurel Hill* were the only other boats of 1859 noted as having gone out as "hull and outfit."

TABLE 2. *Steamboat Construction on the Western Rivers, 1834–1870*

Year	*Industry Total*		*Howard Yards Total*		*Howard Tonnage as Percentage of Industry*
	Number of Hulls	*Measured Gross Tonnage*	*[1]Number of Hulls*	*[2]Measured Gross Tonnage*	
1834	62	8,263.31	2	231.13	2.8
1835	51	5,718.35	1	98.00	1.7
1836	107	14,478.85	2	280.49	1.9
1837	115	21,500.09	2	250.80	1.2
1838	66	12,626.27	0	0	0
1839	108	14,454.61	3	463.70	3.2
1840	63	9,223.86	1	98.40	1.1
1841	90	15,870.52	0	0	0
1842	102	16,794.88	0	0	0
1843	55	9,385.82	1	140.00	1.5
1844	129	25,395.24	0	0	0
1845	119	20,104.70	0	0	0
1846	150	25,560.32	6	1,169.06	4.6
1847	120	22,438.82	0	0	0
1848	120	27,271.03	5	1,151.57	4.2
1849	139	28,353.24	5	1,521.75	5.4
1850	109	20,910.87	12	2,460.24	11.8
1851	132	26,711.10	9	2,823.93	10.6
1852	155	35,259.24	12	3,409.34	9.7
1853	126	33,452.44	12	2,989.19	8.9
1854	142	33,805.39	7	2,799.58	8.3
1855	116	30,926.03	9	2,273.81	7.4
1856	138	32,632.65	12	3,519.79	10.8
1857	163	37,080.30	12	3,620.65	9.8
1858	127	31,481.40	5	1,183.70	3.8
1859	85	13,838.52	7	2,616.26	18.9

TABLE 2—(*Continued*)

| | Industry Total | | Howard Yards Total | | Howard Tonnage as Percentage of Industry |
Year	Number of Hulls	Measured Gross Tonnage	[1]Number of Hulls	[2]Measured Gross Tonnage	
1860	162	32,432.03	8	3,206.64	9.9
1861	146	30,459.57	1	435.72	1.4
1862	49	6,653.34	4	1,693.10	25.4
1863	118	21,721.76	5	2,352.81	10.8
1864	206	44,656.06	4	3,529.41	7.9
1865	187	50,081.84	2	1,062.56	2.1
1866	153	46,755.49	8	3,065.40	6.6
1867	63	18,551.74	4	2,329.75	12.6
1868	93	20,742.46	5	2,219.81	10.7
1869	79	21,022.75	7	2,986.93	14.2
1870	116	35,506.15	14	8,244.92	23.2

[1]Included here are the relatively few hulls for unrigged vessels.

[2]For a hull for which measured gross tonnage was not available, tonnage was estimated by comparison with a similar-sized vessel.

SOURCE: For industry total, Appendix B, pp. 231–232; for Howard Yards total, Appendix A, Tables 1 and 2, pp. 193–223; Baird's *History of Clark County Indiana*, pp. 331–38; William M. Lytle (comp.), *Merchant Steam Vessels of the United States 1807–1868*, "The Lytle List," edited by Forrest R. Holdcamper (Mystic, Conn.: The Steamboat Historical Society of America, 1952); and Savage, *James Howard of Jeffersonville*, pp. 120–32. See also note regarding tonnage measurement following Appendix A, Table 3, p. 224.

The *Isaac Bowman* left the ways in March 1860, the third ferry for the Louisville and Jeffersonville Ferry Company which the Howards had built. They contracted for the job with an estimate for the hull and cabin at $7,700. Machinery, installed by another contractor, was $6,900. The hull for the *Mary T* followed in March that year, with the stern-wheeler hull of the *Little Sallie* down the ways in April. The *Acadia* in June was priced at $9,800 for hull and outfit. In July, the *Memphis*, hull only, slid into the Ohio. In their record for the day, the brothers noted that this was the first boat they built for the Memphis–St. Louis trade. She was a big one, 263 feet long and measuring 645 tons. At the price quoted for the hull, $14,000, the cost per ton was but $22.00; the *Mary T*, 185 feet in length and measuring 373 gross tons, had cost $27.00 per ton. The boats that year ranged between these two extremes, reflecting differences in requirements and construction costs, as seems likely, or possibly just skillful bargaining and sizing up a fellow.

The year 1860 was a good one. The eight hulls launched marked a near record in gross tonnage for the Yards, with only the twelve in 1856 measuring larger. Of the boat yards along the Ohio, the Howard Yards had few peers, for in the decade of the fifties it had launched 10 per cent of all the steamboat tonnage built on the Western Rivers. And 1860 had continued the trend. Ten years earlier the Howard brothers still owed $4,000 on the Yards themselves plus another $3,500 for the sawmill and machinery.[2] But 1860 saw the brothers debt free, or virtually so. Wages paid had grown. In 1858, the figure amounted to $21,700.75, less than the $24,288.75 paid in 1853 to be sure, but 1858 was an off year. In 1859, however, wages had totaled $27,145.78 paid to some sixty men and a few boys. Wages in 1860 totaled $32,752.79. The flow of cash from the steamboat captains through the Howards' books to the shipwrights and sawyers and to the machinists and merchants had grown from $61,011.86 in 1858 to $86,393.16 in 1859 and to $89,527.73 during 1860.[3] The decade just past had been favorable for the Howards, and they had been rewarded for their enterprise and their skill.

AFTER THE *Major Anderson*

THE year 1861 came in with the usual accompaniment of steamboat whistles and bells along the river. The Yards commenced work on a good-sized hull for the Louisville and Cincinnati Mail Line Company that was to be 245 feet overall. But business was slow and the Mail Line people got a good price for her 436 tons. With an $8,600 estimate for the hull, she cost them but $20.00 per ton. She was launched in April.

The Howards had sent out the usual replies and estimates during the winter, but no other boats lay on the ways when April 12, 1861, dawned. After the fall of Fort Sumter, the new Mail Line boat was called the *Major Anderson* after the Fort's commander at the time it was attacked. By the first of May, the Yards employed only the watchman! The war years had begun.

It should not be surprising that the ways were idle after April, for trade had been disrupted with increasing frequency and severity in the months between South Carolina's secession and the seizing of Fort Sum-

[2] Cash Book, 1851-53, p. 68. Howard MSS.
[3] *Ibid.*, 1858–63.

Major Anderson, side-wheel packet launched in 1860. She was named for Major Robert Anderson, commander of Fort Sumter at the time of the Confederate attack. She ran in the Louisville–Cincinnati and Cincinnati–Wheeling trade and burned at Cincinnati in 1872.

ter. Southerners tried to take Northerner's property when it was within their borders. Likewise, Northerners took powder and shot, at least, as it passed down the rivers to Memphis or New Orleans. A well-organized force of secessionist vigilantes could effectively commandeer a vessel, appropriate her cargo, and leave the crew and passengers to drift or swim to shore. And they did it! For example the folk of Napoleon, Arkansas, will do. With two six-pounders and more bluster and bravado than skill, they successfully intimidated the *Ohio Belle* early in April 1861. Next they tried their hand with the *Westmoreland*, bound up to Pittsburgh from New Orleans with a full cargo and passengers. A shot across the bow brought the Yankee boat to the Napoleon shore, and the Captain of the Infantry accosted the Captain of the *Westmoreland*. The word Pittsburgh on her papers was enough and surrender was ordered. But the *Westmoreland* in the interim had slipped her moorings and was moving out into the current as serenely and quietly as only a boat can do. As the gulf between shore and ship widened, the outmanned and outmaneuvered infantry had to retreat, presumably by swimming. Moreover, the nearest cannon failed to fire when the wet infantrymen pulled the lanyard, and by the time the company had raced up to the second, the *Westmoreland* had paddled out of range. The town's suddenly commissioned naval fleet could not pursue, for want of fire in the boilers. So the *Westmoreland* made good her escape. However minor or ludicrous the incident appears in hindsight, it cost the life of one man and the wounding of at least one woman and child.[4] Thereafter, trade became even more hazardous, although magnificently rewarding to the successful few.

The dilemma of the Howards in May 1861 is reflected in their transactions with the Samuel H. Lambdin Ferry Company of Natchez, Mississippi. Although an estimate was made on an inquiry from that company and posted on the 3d of the month, that ferry was never built. Of 1860's eight boats, only two rested in Union waters, although the *Memphis* plied between St. Louis and Memphis. If all had scrupulously adhered to the Howards' usual terms—one-half cash and the balance in good New Orleans acceptances at four, six, and eight months—some $4,300 would

[4] A. Clarke Denson, *Westmoreland. Secession Ferocity at the Breaking Out of the Rebellion* (1865), quoted in H. Allen Gosnell, *Guns on the Western Rivers* ... (Baton Rouge: Louisiana State University Press, 1949), pp. 26–30.

have been due in April 1861, and about $6,000 would have come due in the following three months. Some $10,000 would have fallen due in the interim months following South Carolina's secession. At worst, all these accounts receivable could have been lost, or only a portion, perhaps those falling due after April. At best they might have been fulfilled as specified, but what discount did New Orleans paper require in May or June 1861? In August the year before, Tennessee notes had required $14.00 discount per $100, the cash book recorded. Whatever the unrecorded outcome of the accounts receivable, the Howards were somewhat prepared for the worst and as early as the previous November the bookkeeper had noted a "balance of $400 in gold at James Howard's house," and again in March 1862, that "$300 gold and $64 notes" was there in safekeeping.

The impact of the War would have been more evident in the Yards that continued quiet and empty throughout the remainder of the year. The chirp of the caulking mallet, the saws' heavy breathing, the pounding and shouting of the men were all ominously absent. The Howards had built big boats (290 tons was the rule); the mean for the rest of the Western Rivers builders was but 210 during the past decade. The big boats of the Howard Yards were meant for the deep waters of the Lower Mississippi or the Alabama—the Southern trades. Half of their total production had gone to either New Orleans or Mobile, Vicksburg or Franklin, or west to Galveston. From the South had come the inquiries; to the South had gone the replies, the estimates that created all the activity in the Yards. It was well that James and Daniel were known in Louisville, Cincinnati, and St. Louis, too, for from these cities were to come their only customers during the Civil War.

The Louisville and Cincinnati Mail Line Company put the *Major Anderson* in service late in 1861 and forthwith ordered another boat like it, named the *General Buell*. Early in 1862, about the first of March, the Yards got busy on this big packet. They had a $27,425 contract for the works, although two thirds of it was to be subcontracted. The $8,600 for the hull was the same as that paid for the *Major Anderson*, although the new hull was three feet longer and in other ways measured 515 tons to the *Anderson's* 436.[5] Such differences in measured tonnage crop up to

[5] For explanation of how tonnage is computed see Appendix A, Table 3, Note 1, p. 224.

Home of James Howard, the founder, 1021 East Market Street, Jeffersonville. Built in 1856, it still stands today.

plague any comparison between equally dimensioned craft. They are unavoidable because of minor or major differences in the construction of the cargo space on board. Yet the measured gross tonnage is the only consistent standard available. As a result of the tonnage differences, the *General Buell* cost but $16.70 per ton as opposed to the $20.00 of the 1861 boat. Yet the total sum paid for each hull was the same.

The faithful Louisville and Jeffersonville Ferry Company was next to order a boat in 1862, and the Yards launched a side-wheeler ferry in June. In July they had the hull for the *Wren* ready, while on the other grade the frames were taking shape for a titan 273 feet in overall length, with a beam of 46 feet. Boats of that size and with an eight-foot hold ran only on the Mississippi—to Memphis or New Orleans. That was the trade George Pegram from St. Louis had in mind for his first *Ruth*. Launched in October and in service early the next spring, she ran only six months until, as the result of the Confederate losses at mid-year, some sympathizers set her afire six miles below Cairo. She was completely destroyed. But in the six months of her running, the Howards noted, she made $110,000 over her cost, including the insurance.

While the runners on the rivers reaped the War's profit or its havoc, the yards were having a hard time of it. Total production in the Ohio River yards stopped almost as completely in 1862 as in the Howard Yards in 1861. Total output equaled but 49 hulls during the entire year—a precipitous decline from the 162 and 146 hulls in the preceding two years. Competition between builders for the remaining business must have been intense, for the prices quoted by the Howards reached a new low during 1862. In 1860, it will be remembered, the cost per ton had ranged from $27.00 to $22.00. But in 1862, the only price above $20.00 per ton was the $23.00 paid for the *Wren*. The *General Buell* brought but $16.50, and the ferryboat but $17.00 or $18.00 per ton. Since 1860, furthermore, the cost of building material had increased by 10 per cent.[6] Nationally, wages had increased by 7 per cent in the construction trades.[7] For the Howards in 1862, however, wages might have been even below the 1860 levels; the poor year in the other yards along the river would

[6] U.S. Bureau of the Census, *Historical Statistics of the United States, Colonial Times to 1957*, p. 15.
[7] *Ibid.*, p. 90.

have contributed to such a wage level. The total paid in wages by the Howards reflected the times. In 1860, $32,753 in wages had been paid for the year's output of 3,207 gross tons. In 1861, wages were but $6,631 for the *Major Anderson* and whatever other work overlapped the ends of the years. For 1862, wages paid totaled $17,258 for four boats with gross tonnage of 1,693. The wages paid per ton of output, thus, were $10.21 for 1860 and $10.19 per ton for 1862. Apparently no records were kept on the cost of construction for each vessel, nor on the hours put in on each until early in the twentieth century. If such matters were recorded, the records were subsequently lost. But from the total wage bill it is possible to see the reflection of the ebb and flow in the Yards' overall business. Clearly, 1862 was not the banner year that 1860 had been. Even the poorest year in the fifties, 1858, resulted in total wages paid of $21,701 out of a cash flow through the firm of $61,102.

By sampling the wages paid and the daily rate for each year's period of peak employment, usually near the end of June, it is possible to obtain a consistent indication of the year's maximum wage rates. This measure indicates that the cost of labor per day declined by 15 per cent by 1862. If so, then the decline in the revenue received for each ton built would have had less drastic impact on the Yards' income despite the rise in the cost of timber. Clearly, however, 1862 was a poor year even though it was an improvement over 1861.

Wages climbed in 1863, both nationally and for the Howards. War prosperity began to permeate the country, and it served to overcome the loss of the traditional markets. The rivers began to reflect prosperity, too. The Howard Yards' daily wages rose 23 per cent from 1860 through 1863, compared to the national rate of increase of 18 per cent for the construction trades.[8] In 1864, the wages the Howards paid rose again till the level was fully 35 per cent higher than in 1860. But thereafter, the Howards' time and cash books imply that their wage rates did not increase in concert with the rest of the nation. Their price per ton for the one recorded instance in 1863 was $24.00 which was back to 1860 levels. In contrast to the many nouveau-riche of the war, the Howards continued to operate as before. The fantastic profits of the merchants and the blockade runners did not show up on their ledgers.

[8] *Ibid.*

TABLE 3. *Wages Paid at Howard Ship Yards*
(*Last Week in June for Selected Years*)

Year	Total Wages Paid	Number of Men Paid	Average Weekly Take-Home Pay	Total Man Days Worked in Week	Total Payment on Daily Basis	Average Daily Rate
1839	$ 54.00	17	$ 3.17	62.25	$ 54.00	$ .86
1843[1]	85.50	18	4.75	65.75	85.50	1.30
1846[2]	124.25	25	4.97	89.75	124.25	1.38
1851[3]	747.00	64	11.67	. . .	. . .	. . .
1852	701.64	66	10.63	. . .	. . .	. . .
1853	769.00	56	13.73	186.00	279.00	1.50
1858	73.00	. .	. . .	. . .	. . .	. . .
1859	695.65	. .	. . .	. . .	. . .	. . .
1860	967.87	62	15.61	247.00	439.00	1.78
1861	131.74	17	7.75	. . .	. . .	. . .
1862	600.90	57	10.54	257.00	386.90	1.51
1863	980.50	65	15.08	246.00	539.00	2.19
1864	1,004.00	63	15.94	288.00	691.31	2.40
1865	50.00	4	12.50	24.00	50.00	2.08

[1]Last week in August, 1843. June data not available.
[2]Last week in September, 1846. June data not comparable.
[3]Last week in July, 1851. June data not available.
EXPLANATION: The last week in June represents the pay period for peak employment in each year. It thus gives a consistent, representative estimate of the year's maximum wage rates.
SOURCES: Howard MSS, Time Book, 1839–1846; Cash Book, 1853–1855; Cash Book, 1858–1863; Time Book, 1863–1865.

The war years wore on, and one was not measurably better than the rest. Although 1863 saw the Yards busy turning out five boats, it had its debits, too. News of the skirmishes and battles were carried back to the Valley, naturally, for their papers posted correspondents everywhere and especially with the rams and gunboats on the rivers. In March the Valley papers carried the account of Admiral Porter's stealthy move up the flooded bayous to surprise Haine's Bluff on the Yazoo and thus allow a rear attack on Vicksburg. The Valley folk cheered him on that venture even though he had to withdraw because of the willows. The feats of the *Queen of the West* when still a Union gunboat would have been equally exciting to people reared on the rivers. Such accounts would have brought notice of how the older Howard-built boats were faring. The *Mary T* was a gunboat for the Confederacy by then, as was the *Jno. A.*

Cotton; both skirmished with the *Queen of the West.* The *Grand Duke* was also in on that fracas as a Confederate transport. The roll of Howard boats would show the *J. F. Pargoud* sunk in service as a transport, Confederate of course. The *Alonzo Child,* built in 1857, also a Confederate transport, was captured by Union forces in 1863. There were Howard-built boats on the Union side, too, but they played a more prosaic role of carrying stores and mules and army men. The *Tarascon,* however, which slid down the ways in October 1863 had a notable history. After Mobile surrendered on April 14, 1865, the *Tarascon* went there and plied the Alabama River until the following fall. She was said to be the largest boat ever to ascend that river.[9]

For the Howard Ship Yards 1864 was about as slow as 1863. Up and down the river a tremendous expansion in steamboat construction was under way, which was to extend over the next three years. But the Jeffersonville Yards launched only four hulls in 1864 and only two in 1865. The *Ida Handy* was first down the ways in April 1864, another big boat for the St. Louis–New Orleans trade now that Vicksburg had fallen and the river was open. She was the fourth vessel that George Pegram had bought from the Howards since 1861. Pegram's second *Ruth* went down the ways late in December. Truly a giant for her day, she was 300 feet overall, a 49-foot beam, and a 9½-foot hold. While the beam of the flat-bottomed hull measured but 49 feet, at the main deck her true width was nearly 90 feet. On either side of the hull extended the paddle wheels with a 15-foot width. Since the guards forward and aft of the wheels made her whole main deck 300 by 90 feet in dimensions, when the *Ruth* floated down the river, her main deck covered nearly two thirds of an acre. Her measured gross tonnage of 1,681 made her by far the largest vessel thus far turned out by the Howard Yards.

The *Ruth* also suggested the manner in which the Howards combatted the loss of their southern customers and thus survived the war years. For with the *Ruth,* George Pegram had built five boats with the Howards, beginning with the first *Ruth* in 1862, the *Julia* and *Olive Branch* in 1863 and the *Ida Handy* and the second *Ruth* in 1864. Pegram

[9] Frederick Way, Jr., *Way's Directory of Western Rivers Packets* ([Pittsburgh] 1950), p. 285.

The second Ruth, side-wheel packet launched in 1864, the last boat constructed by the firm of D. & J. Howard. Built for Captain George Pegram of St. Louis, she is remembered for making the run from New Orleans to St. Louis in 4 days, 9 hours, and 54 minutes. She was destroyed by fire at Pawpaw Island, thirty miles from Vicksburg, in 1869.

was a daring and successful river man before, during, and after the Civil War. His boats earned tremendous profits for him by running to New Orleans from St. Louis or Louisville during the war. He probably carried contraband as well as cotton to earn the $110,000 the *Ruth* earned in early 1863 or the $30,000 profit for a single trip which the *Olive Branch* made later the same year.[10] He ran the risk of losing all, of course, as happened with the first *Ruth*, for there were Confederate guerrillas along the river until after Lee's surrender. But Pegram was successful and he alone gave the Howards 50 per cent of the tonnage they constructed from 1861 to 1865.

The Louisville and Cincinnati Mail Line Company ordered three hulls from the Howards during the war, while the Louisville and Evansville Mail Company had two steamers built. The John Watson Company had the *Wren* and the *Blue Wing No. 3* built for the Kentucky River. There were but four other customers during the war. All in all only eight customers called on the Howard Ship Yards during the five years of the war.

When the second *Ruth* slid down the ways, she became the last boat built by the firm of D. & J. Howard. Daniel retired that year, although he retained ownership of some of the Yards's real estate and lived off the rent. James reorganized and took as a partner his younger brother John, who had been in the Yards or on a steamboat for most of his life, too. The third partner was James's son, Edmonds J. Howard. The new firm became James Howard and Company and work went slowly on.

The year 1865 saw the *Virginia* down the ways followed by the *North Missouri*. The *North Missouri* signaled the changes awaiting the steamboat and the steamboat builders after Appomattox. The hull, 160 feet overall in length by 30 feet in beam, was designed especially as a single-track railroad transfer steamer. She was launched on November 11, 1865, for the railroad at St. Charles, Missouri, and the Howards recorded that she was the first railroad transfer steamer in the West.

---

[10] Key Book, Howard MSS. The Key Book is a compilation, "A Record of the Boats Built by the Howards," edited through 1884 by John C. Howard, younger brother of James Howard, and in later years, through 1932, by others.

CHAPTER IV

Different Whistles

In the Aftermath of the Civil War

THREE STROKES on a steamboat's big bell were the signal for a land-ing, alerting the deckhands to ready the stage planks and to start hustling up the cargo. For the passengers intending to debark, the sound was the signal to congregate at the head of the grand staircase with luggage and wait until the packet had touched the bank and the stage planks were laid to shore. Since the steamboat could stop almost any place along either bank, the passenger could easily find himself spanning a century as he walked down the stairs, across the main deck to the stage planks and to shore. The carved and chryselephantine splendor of the cabin, the ruddy fires of the boilers, the sound of steam gently hissing in the engine room, these could give way in a few paces to primeval dark-ness and silence only punctured by the blast of the departing steamboat's whistle and the panting of her exhaust.

To bring a steamboat to the bank took only a signal from a would-be customer. To be sure, the faster and regularly scheduled packets might not see the beckoner, but with a little prearrangement or a plainly visible sign, such as a torch at night or a pile of cotton by day, the passing steamer would draw up. At the town wharf, the crowd of passengers would have collected along with the freight as soon as someone had spread the word at first sight of the plumes of smoke and steam rising over the willows. Or else the sound of the boat's whistle would have preceded her—by as much as ten miles on a good day. And as the boat drew near the land-

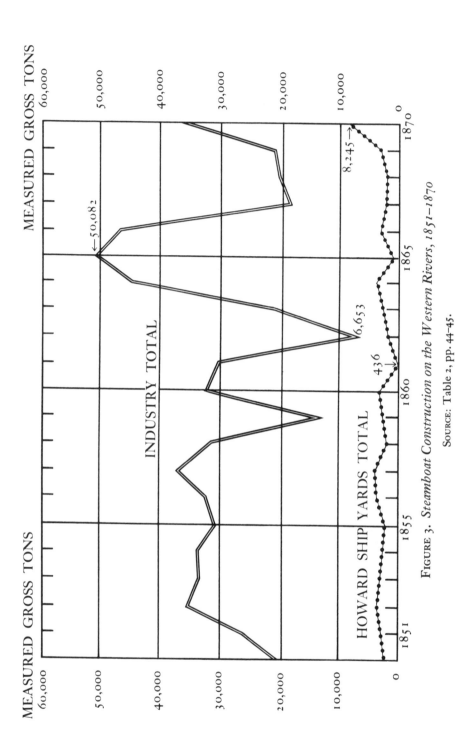

FIGURE 3. *Steamboat Construction on the Western Rivers, 1851–1870*

SOURCE: Table 2, pp. 44–45.

ing, she would call the tardy with another blast, the puff of steam announcing the notes well before the sound reached the shore.

Steamboat whistles made a beautiful noise. Each vessel had her own more or less distinctive notes, and each hand upon the rope could pull forth a different voice: now a friendly nod of the head; a full tip of the hat; a screaming blast of annoyance punctuated with short silences; or a long, stentorian call that ranged and echoed o'er the valley. To the uninitiated, such as a visiting backwoods cousin, the sounds of river commerce were startling: sudden, shrill, felt as well as heard. Even a blasé pilot could start with surprise at a quick, powerful blast.

When the *New Orleans* disturbed the flocks of carrier pigeons with her hissing steam in 1811, Nature's cacaphonic silence in the West was forever broken. To some, it was at first a sound of the supernatural; to others, it was an upsetting of the Infinite plan and surely the cause of the great earthquake in that year. But in time steamboats' whistles were but the sound of commerce and enterprise. They promised excitement enough to call out a whole town and the somnolent would be energized to lift a bale, roll a hogshead, tote a bag or two, and catch a bit of gossip if not news. The young would gawk and find their ideal, a cub pilot, lolling against a gilt pillar, twenty feet or more above the hubbub on the main deck. Then the engine bells would sound, the paddle wheels would revolve and roil the water, and majestically the river between boat and bank would widen until in mid-stream, with a puff of steam and a whistle blast, the vessel would set her course and disappear slowly, tantalizing those who remained on the humdrum shore. Up and down the meandering Western Rivers whistles were the sound of civilization.

By the end of the Civil War, the whistles of the steamboats were a prosaic noise, probably heard only by those especially listening for them. The awe the steamboat had created a decade or more before was quelled by the knowledge the War's disruptions had dissipated. To those who had known only a log cabin, mud-chinked, earthen-floored, cold and silently lonely, the white and gold steamboat with its lights, its fires, its heat, and crowds was the epitome of civilization. A steamboat was everything the hand of man had hewn out of the wilderness. Its ostentation, its gewgaws and curliques masking and excusing its flimsiness, were but an honest expression of skills and craft. From the hog-chains through the engine room to the black walnut bar and the cabins with every door an oil painting, the steamboat echoed the small boy's honest boast, "Hey, Ma, look at me. See what I can do!" But having pioneered and captured the pioneers' spirit, when the frontier moved on and civilization filled the banks of the rivers, when the log cabins were finally replaced with brick and frame houses, the romantic appeal of the steamboat declined.

A different steam whistle was heard then, and not only in the valleys. Already the locomotive on rails had illustrated Doppler's principle with its whistle, something the stately steamboat could never do. For the train's whistle as it approached at thirty miles an hour or more would change in pitch when it passed, the speed of the locomotive first increasing and then decreasing the apparent frequency of the whistle's sound. With its greater speed and the comparative ease with which the rails could be laid to almost all points, the railroad became the new Pied Piper, hooting his way westward and southward and then back again, crisscrossing the nation. To the pioneers moving onto the plains of the Dakotas or Kansas, this new whistle became the sound of civilization bringing succor and commerce to the dry and silent prairie. But back in the river valleys the boat and train whistled in competition, each drumming up trade thereby. Each hand upon the whistle rope was sure of his own manifest destiny, each certain of his own invincibility, for the one was armored with speed and the other was shielded with comfort and economy. So by 1866 the contest was set and the Midwest was its arena. The Titans struggled, as they struggle still, though whistles no longer exhale white steam. They use air horns now.

In the first years of the post-Civil War era it seems doubtful that steamboat men knew who their new competitor was; accustomed only to fear and battle the exploits of the new steamer that disrupted their own trade, if they heard the railroad whistle, they dismissed it and made little change in course. At first! The reconstruction of the war's damage in the South required more boats. The rising crescendo of trade in the North also needed more steamers, and so the pace of construction on the Ohio picked up after the first postwar lull. The chirp of the caulking mallets, the saws' whine, the hammer blows, all reached their greatest intensity during the year 1871 when 155 steamboats hit the water. The gross tonnage of the year's vessels exceeded by the smallest margin the

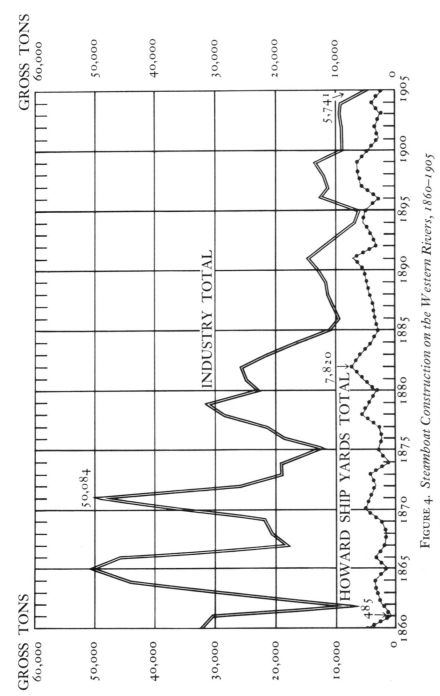

GROSS TONS

60,000

50,000

40,000

30,000

20,000

10,000

0

INDUSTRY TOTAL

HOWARD SHIP YARDS TOTAL

50,084

7,820 ↓

485 ↗

5,741 ↓

1860 1865 1870 1875 1880 1885 1890 1895 1900 1905

Figure 4. *Steamboat Construction on the Western Rivers, 1860–1905*

Source: Appendix A, Table 3, pp. 224–225 and Appendix B, pp. 231–232.

tonnage of any preceding year. In 1865, 50,081.84 gross tons were the total, while 1871's mark was 50,083.72. The 1871 steamers were larger, averaging 323 gross tons to the 267 mean for the earlier year.[1] The year turned out to be the all-time high-water mark for the construction of steamboats on the Western Rivers.

As early as 1875, the depression in steamboat construction could not have escaped general notice. Around Pittsburgh only five vessels were built during the year, compared to 66 a decade before. Cincinnati likewise found her yards less active than formerly, for only 16 steamers were launched there that year whereas 51 had been the number in 1865. Louisville and its environs—New Albany, Silver Creek, Clarksville, and Jeffersonville on the Indiana shore—were not in as depressed a state. Some 20 vessels were built there in 1875, 14 of them by the Howard Yards. For all the yards on the Western Rivers, only 91 boats were launched that year; and although there followed a small boom during the next eight years, the peaks of output no longer exceeded one another and the trend was clearly downward. Ten years later, in 1885, but 81 steamers of 11,220 gross tons were launched and a decade still later, 1895, only 60 boats of 7,240 gross tons were built.[2]

By 1895, the side-wheeler era in Western American history was all but dead. Many of the grand old steamers lay dying at the wharf, and as they rotted, or burned, or were destroyed in a spectacular "ice gorge," they carried with them to the bottom the last remnants of steamboating as it had been in its prime: the days of spectacular profits and gaudy profiteers, of ostentatious gilt and stained glass and a sumptuous board that beckoned a corn- and salt-pork-fed populace. Anything as aristocratic as a full-fledged Western Rivers packet was almost inevitably destined to an early death in such a competitive, and egalitarian therefore, society as was the West. So that phase sank into the rivers and left only enough superstructure exposed to whet a later generations' curiosity and admiration. The artifacts of that age turn up now and then—a chandelier from the *Rob't. E. Lee* in a Louisiana church, the *J. M. White's* bell on a sugar plantation, the *Kate Adams'* whistle on a lowly towing steamer.

[1] Appendix B, pp. 231–232, and Purdy, "Report on Steam Navigation in the United States," *Tenth Census* (1880), IV, *Transportation*, p. 680.
[2] Appendix B, pp. 231–232.

Ice in the Ohio River at Jeffersonville, 1918(?).

Though these classic steamers and their era sank into ignominy in the years following the Civil War, there were other, less pretentious, steamers built. They, too, carried whistles and commerce.

With the demise of the romantic packet, the Western Rivers steamboats slipped downstream into a fog of obscurity and a limbo of humbler means. They were scarcely known and seldom thought of beyond the range of audibility of their whistles. A whistle, wailing in the distance, was for most people by 1890 simply another railroad locomotive, and, if they heard it at all, they probably stopped and tried to estimate its speed —45, 50, 60 miles an hour and more. It took one's breath away. And so a new generation congregated around the depot to see Number 7 come in, gawk at the passengers, catch a glimpse of their new ideal sitting in the cab all powerful, and shudder with joy at the whistle's reverberations and the sight of power in a slipping driver. But, of course, the race is not always to the fleet. There is something to be said for the sure. Although the railroad clearly dispatched the packet, the railroad never silenced the riverboat's bell.

For the changes in river commerce and thus for the changes in boat construction, the Civil War must be reckoned as the greatest initiating factor. The eventual eclipse of the Western Rivers packet was partly an inevitable matter of geography as well as a change of heroes in the public's eye, but the economic disruptions of the war and the altered postwar economies of the rivers' contiguous regions clearly hastened the packet on its way to oblivion and greatly altered the means of survival for those boats and trades that remained viable.

Perhaps the most momentous incident in the Civil War that so drastically altered the course for the steamboat was the early closing of New Orleans as an internal port for transfer of goods to the East Coast or for export abroad. Although the river was opened again after the fall of Vicksburg in 1863, guerillalike tactics of the Confederates, such as the burning of the *Ruth*, and actual armed attacks on boats in the bayou country served to discourage river trade until the complete ending of hostilities. But by 1865 the damage had been done. More direct and faster routes to the East had been devised. In this, of course, the steamboat was caught up in the net of geography and climate as well as the disruptions of the Civil War. Yet the very success of the steamboat in transporting goods at lowest cost had virtually forced the building of railroads as either feeders to the rivers or else as tenuous overland routes for high-priced freight and passengers. Thus by 1860, rails connected the cities of the South, but not the South with the North although a passenger could buy a through rail ticket from New Orleans to Bangor, Maine, and check his baggage the entire distance.[3] The entire southern railroad network had not a single rail-to-rail connection with the North. The Cairo–Columbus connection required a two-hour steamboat trip, and Louisville did not achieve a rail connection with Indiana until the completion of the bridge over the Ohio in February 1870. The bridge at Washington, D.C., was too weak for trains in 1860.[4] But the East Coast cities of Baltimore, Philadelphia, and New York were linked with Chicago.

The forerunners of the North's four great trunk lines were in operation by the Civil War—the Pennsylvania, the Erie, the New York Central, and the Baltimore and Ohio.[5] Whereas not a single rail connected the Midwest with the East Coast in 1850, save the Baltimore and Ohio track from Wheeling to Baltimore, the construction of 21,000 miles of track in the 1850s created the trunk lines by 1860 and created them precisely where the steamboat could not go—across the isthmus of lower Michigan and Indiana and through or around the Appalachians. They were new, untried, and often composed of disparate parts, but they were in existence in time for Lincoln's inaugural trip, and they could serve. In 1860, furthermore, the canals of Illinois, Indiana, Ohio, Pennsylvania, and New York were still in commission. So there existed in 1860 a ready alternative route to the steamboat ride down the Mississippi to New Orleans and thence around to New York City. Such alternative routes were natural and inevitable, awaiting only the arrival of technology and capital. Indeed, the steamboat itself owed much of its meteoric rise and success simply to the fact that technologically it was simpler and preceded the railroad; it was less capital-consuming, using as it did a natural waterway, and it was more easily constructed and adapted to an early pioneer region.

[3] John F. Stover, *The Railroads of the South, 1865–1900* (Chapel Hill: The University of North Carolina Press, 1953), pp. 11, 12.
[4] *Ibid.*, p. 11.
[5] MacGill *et al.*, *Transportation in the United States before 1860*, p. 500.

Not only was an alternative to the river route available by 1860, but there also occurred at the time the settlement of lands farther and farther away from the navigable waters and in a direction contrary to the flow of the rivers. The settlement of Indiana, Illinois, Wisconsin, and Iowa in the 1850s and 1860s upset agriculture in the older, eastern states—if not during the Civil War, then in the decades following it. As the cheap lands of the Midwest were opened and settled, emigration from New England and New York occurred, as well as from Germany, Sweden, and England. The inevitable result was a gigantic growth in agricultural output of the Midwest and at the same time its growth in importance as a market area for Boston, New York, Philadelphia, and Baltimore. The wool Ohio once sent to Cincinnati and thence to New England moved after 1860 via Albany or New York. The salt pork Cincinnati once shipped to New Orleans and then to Baltimore went by rail if it went at all, for Chicago outstripped Cincinnati in pork packing during 1862.[6]

With the stage thus set, the Civil War saw the easy toppling of the northern half of the steamboat's old empire. It was not a knockout blow delivered by the railroads but a simple, almost inevitable, transfer of passengers as well as freight to a faster, if not more comfortable, more direct route between markets that had changed drastically in their relative importance. Higher-valued freight moved by the quicker route. But where the speed of transit was less important than the cost, barring cut-throat competition, the river route always was shown to be the less expensive. In 1880, for example, rates on bulk corn from St. Louis to New Orleans from April through July were but 7 to 7.5 cents per bushel. Added to this rate were charges at the port of one-half cent per bushel for transfer to an ocean vessel and one-tenth of a cent for inspection. The total was 8.1 cents per bushel on board an ocean ship in New Orleans. From there to Liverpool was but 16 cents per bushel, or a total of 24.1 cents per bushel from St. Louis to Liverpool. Insurance was perhaps 4 cents per bushel more. Such a rate compared with a rail rate through New York to Liverpool of 36.25 cents per bushel.[7] Though the grain traffic fluctuated greatly

[6] Emerson D. Fite, "Agricultural Development of the West during the Civil War," *Quarterly Journal of Economics*, XX (February 1906), 259–76.
[7] Purdy, "Report on Steam Navigation in the United States," *Tenth Census* (1880), IV, *Transportation*, p. 695.

in response to variations in supply, in demand, and in the railroad–river rate wars, the 1880 rates fairly represent the economic cost differences of the two modes of transit.

The Success of the Howard Yards

If the Civil War only precipitated and hurried a bit changes in Midwest transportation which were well-nigh inevitable anyway, the War between South and North had a more direct and responsible role in determining the part the steamboat and river trade played in the Old South during the three decades following Appomattox. The Civil War devastated and retarded southern agriculture for more than a decade. It destroyed capital, both real and financial, and seriously crippled the ability of the region to generate, accumulate, or attract savings for the financing of reconstruction and growth in the postwar years. Some of the factors fostered the lingering on of the grand old packet, while others prevented the emergence of a river trade that was adequate to allow the growth of a river transport technology that could capitalize on the peculiar economic advantages of water transportation. Because a majority of the purchasers of Howard-built boats were from the Old South or traded with it, the post-Civil War achievements of the Jeffersonville yards succinctly summarize and point up the era's changes in transportation on the Western Rivers. Although the output of all the other boat yards along the Ohio trended downward from the peak years of 1865 and 1871 to the nadir of 1906, the output of the Howards was steady if not even on a slight upward trend until the end of the century. While such a phenomenon reflects the workings of a competitive market and the success of the Howard Yards in meeting and mastering their rivals, it also reflects the transport needs and fortunes of the Old South. They were served by the steamboat. While the railroad scored an easy supremacy in transport north of the Mason and Dixon line, it fared far differently in the South. For a long time, long enough to give the Howard Yards their finest years, the only whistle heard along the bayous of the South was that of a steamboat.

The gross tonnage of boats that slid endways or sideways down the bank to the Ohio at Jeffersonville did not again equal the annual average output of the decade of the fifties until after 1878, excepting the three years of 1870, 1871, and 1873. Thereafter, until the end of the nineteenth century, the Howard's annual gross tonnage constructed averaged some 40 per cent greater than in the golden prewar decade. Of course, the actual volume of work at the Yards, the man-hours put in, the lumber used, was greater than the comparison of gross tonnage indicates. For throughout the 1850s until 1859, Jim and Daniel Howard had concentrated on building steamboat hulls only, leaving the rest of the boat to other, specialized contractors. Beginning in 1859, however, they had commenced building the cabin and, in general, completing the whole boat, excepting the machinery, of course. After the war the practice continued. Within a few years the other specialized contractors had been decimated by the general blight that hit the industry; the Howard Yards had no alternative but to build a boat from keel to pilot house, stem to stern.

In brown leather-bound journals the Howards recorded pertinent data for nearly every vessel they built from 1877 to 1918. By adding the contract price for each vessel together with all others launched in the same calendar year, some idea of the gross revenues for the firm can be gained and utilized to judge its growth. In a prewar year for which comparable data were found, 1860, the total cash flow amounted to $89,528.[8] By using the current dollar data, the growth in activity at the Howard Ship Yards would seem to have been almost five times the 1860 level by 1882. The gross tonnage data, on the other hand, had indicated only a doubling of output in the same period.[9]

The Howards' postwar prosperity was established on the same foundations that had propelled the yards so rapidly to a foremost position in the industry in the decade preceding the Civil War. They were skilled craftsmen and artisans still, with a knack for making a boat that pleased the eye as it filled the purse. As before, most of their boats went into service on the Southern trades. In the first postwar decade half the boats were built for owners in the Old South. Even excluding the thirty-nine boats built for Louisville or St. Louis, which were destined primarily

[8] Appendix A, Table 4, p. 226.
[9] Appendix A, Table 3, pp. 224–225.

Frank Pargoud, side-wheel packet launched in 1868. She was built for Captain John W. Tobin whose fortune she was said to have made. Out of her earnings Captain Tobin built the J. M. White.

for trade on the Lower Mississippi, the roll of home ports reads: New Orleans, Galveston, Houston, Nashville, and at least one boat each to Natchez, Vicksburg, and the Arkansas River. Of the 105 boats launched from 1866 through 1875, less than one fifth were built specifically for the Ohio River trade. Thus it was that the whistles of the locomotives on the B&O or the Pennsylvania so little affected the fortunes of the Howard Ship Yards for more than forty years.

TABLE 4. *Home Port or Trade of Vessels Built at the Howard Ship Yards, 1866–1875*

Arkansas River	1	Memphis, Tenn.	2
Cairo, Illinois	4	Nashville, Tenn.	5
Cincinnati, Ohio	3	Natchez, Miss.	1
Evansville, Ind.	9	New Orleans, La.	18
Galveston, Texas	8	Paducah, Ky.	1
Houston, Texas	9	St. Louis, Mo.	22
Jeffersonville, Ind.	2	Vicksburg, Miss.	1
Louisville, Ky.	17	Total	103

SOURCE: Appendix A, Table 1, pp. 193–221. Home ports of two vessels built in this period are unknown.

As before, the owners and captains that came to Jeffersonville to take their new boats south were returning for the second time, or the third, or even more. The letters between Jim and these Southern masters were not the terse notes of finance and business alone, but they were personal inquiries and reports filled with family news or gossip and an occasional aside such as, "We've had a real cold spell which will delay your boat a few weeks." Or from the other end, "I had a poor season and was wondering if you could hold off discounting my note due the first for a few weeks more." Some of the owners would even come to stay with the Howards during the construction of their new boat. While many new names were written in the daybooks and the letter copybooks, many of the old, familiar ones appeared and continued to reappear. In 1866, John Porter of Boonville, Missouri, was back for two more ferry boats. J. W. Tobin ordered the *Frank Pargoud* in 1867 and the *Trenton* in 1869. The Louisville and Cincinnati Mail Line commissioned another *Ben Franklin* that year, too, for the Cincinnati–Louisville trade. George Pegram ordered another leviathan, this time 328 feet long with a beam of 54

Ben Franklin, side-wheel packet launched in 1869. She was built for the Louisville and Cincinnati Mail Line.

James Howard, side-wheel packet launched in 1870. She was built for Captain George Pegram for the St. Louis–New Orleans trade and in 1875, on one trip, carried 7,701 bales of cotton to New Orleans—breaking all records up to that date. While loaded with sugar she burned in St. Louis in 1881.

feet and a gross tonnage of 2,321. As a fitting gesture and a suitable tribute, he christened it the *James Howard*.

Late in 1875, colorful John W. Cannon was back at the Falls with ideas about another boat. The hull under his *Rob't. E. Lee*, built originally by Hill and Roberts of New Albany in 1866, was in need of repairs or rebuilding. It had sunk once, at New Orleans in December 1870, shortly after the race with the *Natchez*.[10] He concluded a contract with Jim Howard that called for a new hull and the transfer to it of the old *Lee's* cabin and machinery. The new hull was launched on April 25, 1876, at the traditional hour of four in the afternoon, and the new *Rob't. E Lee* entered the New Orleans–Vicksburg trade on August 15. The old hull did service as a wharfboat at Memphis for many years afterwards, outliving the new *Lee* which burned in 1882.[11]

JAMES HOWARD'S LAST LAUNCHING

The *Lee's* hull had been the third launched in 1876, and the Yards must have turned full force to completing her, for the next launching was not until the *Yazoo Valley* slid down the ways on August 10. The *C. W. Anderson* was floated on August 31, and the *Alberta* on September 7. With little fanfare, the launching of the *Alberta*, only ten feet longer than the *Hyperion* had been, was the final launching that James Howard was to witness. His last hull was that of the *E. B. Stahlman*.

Late in the afternoon of October 14, 1876, Jim Howard concluded some business in Louisville and hurried his horse and buggy onto the Jeffersonville ferry. A light drizzle was falling and the driver of the rig ahead of Jim's had gone for shelter near the boilers. Jim, however, stayed in his buggy. He could see the *Ben Franklin* leaving the Louisville levee, and perhaps it was her whistle that startled the horses, but the unattended team reared and backed and made Jim's horse shy, too, so that horse, buggy, and Jim rolled backward off the guards and into the old Ohio.

The ferry was stopped immediately and the passengers saw Jim bob up once. He dived as though to release the horse from the harness, sur-

---

[10] For the race see Way, *Directory of Western Rivers Packets*, pp. 253–58.
[11] *Ibid.*, pp. 258–59.

faced, and struck out for the Louisville shore a short distance away. But half way there he stopped swimming, straightened up, and sank from sight. Thus did the Ohio claim the master steamboat builder.

Captain James Howard was buried with simple ceremony in Cave Hill Cemetery in Louisville. The Reverend James Craik of Christ Episcopal Church officiated at the services which were attended by fifteen hundred persons. Some fifty thousand, however, silently lined the road from the church to Cave Hill, and the Reverend Mr. Craik spoke for the multitude when he reported:[12]

> It was the grandest and most imposing funeral I ever witnessed. There were no societies, no music, no military display, the usual trappings of an imposing funeral, to mark the obsequies of this boat-builder. We have buried from this church the commander-in-chief of the United States [Zachary Taylor], and all that the power and majesty of the great government could do to make the occasion grand and honorable was done, but it was nothing in comparison with the funeral solemnities of the simple, untitled citizen, James Howard.

Inescapably, from the first faltering steps in 1834 to the pre-eminent position of 1876, the success of the Howard Ship Yards was a product of Jim Howard. To be sure, he had had partners. There was his brother-in-law at first, David Barmore, and then Emerson in Madison. John Enos in Louisville was succeeded by Jim's brothers, Daniel and John, and his son, Edmonds J. Howard. But what each of these had contributed, or what any of the workmen had given, was in no small measure enhanced many-fold by the skill, artistry, and integrity of "Uncle Jim." An examination of James's correspondence bears it out. And the tribute paid to him at his funeral is surely a testimony to his worth and measure as an honest, enterprising individual.

The name of *Rob't. E. Lee* graced the final side-wheeler steamboat hull that James Howard built. All the rest of the boats launched in 1876 had been of the stern-wheel design, which Jim had confided to one of his correspondents that he found less graceful and elegant than the side-wheelers.

[12] Quoted in *Baird's History of Clark County*, p. 433.

Edmonds J. Howard (1840–1919), son of James Howard, the founder.

The Howard Ship Yards were yet to launch their greatest side-wheelers. But the tides of incessant change had already signaled that the ungainly stern-wheeler and the humbler towboat were what the river needed. James Howard had succeeded during the greatest era of steamboating in establishing a record of skill and integrity of such merit that there were men with money, and some without, who would have their new boats built by no one else. To those who survived and followed him, he bequeathed this reputation. But of greater worth, this man succeeded in transmitting to his son his own skill with wood and boats and with people.

As much as historical change can be marked by one single event, the passing of James Howard served to mark the end of the side-wheeler days on the Western Rivers, the era which Mark Twain captured so well. The succeeding phase was that of the stern-wheeler; it was the era which heard a different whistle.

CHAPTER V

Cotton
and
Coal

TONS

A TON of coal weighed more than a ton of cotton, at least on a steamboat for an honest fact. The measured gross tons that have been bandied about in describing one or another steamboat refer not to the quantity of tons of 2,000 pounds avoirdupois which a boat could carry without going under, but rather the term refers to a measured volume of space on a vessel within the hull and below the deck, or above the main deck, too, with certain exceptions. A measured gross ton was 100 cubic feet that could contain about 1,200 pounds of cotton or 7,700 pounds of coal. Thus, a gross ton of coal would weigh more than the same volume of cotton. A gross ton of people would weigh hardly anything at all. As matters eventually turned out, the final fortunes of the river trades turned on such matters of weight and density.

James Howard's final side-wheeler, the rebuilt *Rob't. E. Lee*, went into the New Orleans–Vicksburg trade for Captain Cannon when she left the yards in August 1876. In two years' running the *Lee* made forty-three round trips and transported mostly cotton and people, some 124,084 bales of cotton and 103,029 sacks of cotton seed, along with smidgens of other agricultural items.[1] Such a record meant that the *Lee* could have carried some 2,886 bales to New Orleans each trip. And these bales, comprising as they did about 39.5 cubic feet each, meant the *Lee* would have

[1] Way, *Directory of Western Rivers Packets*, pp. 258–59.

carried 113,984 cubic feet of cotton. Since her gross tonnage was estimated to be 1,479, the *Lee* would have traveled three-quarters full of fleecy cotton which weighed but 721 short tons. In season though, the passengers would probably have found the cotton bales piled outside their stateroom doors—as on the *Henry Frank* when she toted a record 9,226 bales to New Orleans.[2] Pictures of cotton boats with the bales piled from the main deck to boiler deck and even higher abounded, and these examples were pointed out with pride as evidence of the steamboat's great capacity for transport. Only the pilot had a clear view of the river, but this was the way the cotton boats earned their keep, the side-wheelers like the *Lee*, the *Natchez*, the *John W. Cannon*, the *Frank Pargoud*, and the great *J. M. White*.

Despite rumors and visible signs of the steamboat's decline elsewhere on the rivers, the *Rob't. E. Lee* was earning $2,500 to $3,000 a week in cotton season,[3] enough to induce the indomitable Captain Cannon to commission another Howard boat, the *John W. Cannon*, which went down the ways on the 29th of January, 1878. She, too, was a side-wheeler. Although some fifty feet shorter than the *Lee*, she was every bit as finely fitted out. The chandeliers of crystal, the stained-glass clerestory windows of the cabin, even the chairs that graced the lounge were all specially built, and elegant. The chairs, for instance, had inlaid in the back the monogram of John W. Cannon. The wool carpet was brought especially from New York City where Captain Cannon had selected it and bought it on credit for $600. The hull cost $20,000. The posh cabin and carpet cost $17,600, and the machinery and boilers were $30,880, for a total cost of $68,480. Such a total for elegance contrasted sharply with other Howard-built boats destined for less lucrative trades. The *G. Gunby Jordan* built in 1877 for the Chatahoochie River (cotton country, too) had a cabin that cost but 16 per cent of her total $10,000 cost. The *Fashion*, for the Wabash River–Louisville trade, had a cabin that cost but $2,500 out of a total expenditure of $20,714. Even the *James Guthrie*, a side-wheeler for the Louisville and Evansville Packet Company, which also ordered the stern-wheel *Fashion*, cost but $28,250, of which the cabin was $5,000.

[2] Hunter, *Steamboats on the Western Rivers*, p. 588.
[3] Letter from John W. Cannon, November 30, 1877. Howard MSS.

John W. Cannon, side-wheel packet launched in 1878. Built for Captain Cannon for the New Orleans–Bayou Sara trade and lavishly outfitted, she was described by Frederick Way as "primarily a carriage horse for the planters of the fabled upper coast."

While there was rivalry among the captains in any trade, it did seem to reach its climax on the Lower Mississippi. Captain Cannon had been sparring with Captain T. P. Leathers since before the war. The celebrated race to St. Louis between their two craft the *Lee* and the *Natchez* was only the best-known incident and that but one of the innumerable shorter races that occurred almost daily. If the *Lee* reached a landing ahead of the *Natchez*, she might carry away all the freight, owners willing, and leave the bank bare for the next boat. Perhaps the exploit of the *Henry Frank* with 9,226 bales in one trip had the unrecorded obverse side of two or more empty steamers following disconsolately behind her.

A speedier boat would, of course, have allowed more round trips per season. Certainly the forty-three trips of the *Lee* in twenty-two and a half months is not a stupendous record upon examination. It meant that each trip from Vicksburg to New Orleans took more than two weeks: two weeks for a total mileage of 724, or fifty miles a day.[4] If she tied up for spells in the off season, her daily mileage average would increase; but nevertheless, with a staple commodity that was easily stored and would not depreciate in quality nor spoil, maybe the slowness of each trip was not of concern. Perhaps it even helped smooth out price fluctuations on the market by spreading out the time it took the year's crop to reach the cotton brokers and factors for resale.

But for passengers, even in the languid regions of Mississippi and Louisiana, a week's time to go from Vicksburg to New Orleans would have required the utmost in society's embellishments for boredom's relief. In such a context, the stories of Mississippi River gambling, drinking, gun play, and other such dalliances seem of a less depraved and sordid nature. Without a doubt, the captain and the boat that offered the most promise of a pleasant voyage was the one that attracted the most passengers. And the passengers might well consign their cotton to the same boat. Since freight was paramount in revenues, a few hundred dollars for a glittering chandelier that would attract a dozen more passengers, or an elegant and comfortable lounge that would garner fifty more passengers a year than a boat less well endowed, would have seemed worth the expenditure to

---

[4] U.S. Bureau of the Census, *Eleventh Census* (1890), XIX, *Transportation Business*, Pt. II, *Transportation by Water*, p. 422.

a prudent businessman as well as a competitive egotist. A similar phenomenon is evident today in the trans-Atlantic traffic; the *Normandie* displaced the *Queen Mary* before the Second World War, but was in turn replaced by the *Queen Elizabeth* and then the *United States* as THE boat to take to Europe. Then the new *France* displaced the last two vessels and now there is the new *Elizabeth*. The passengers and planters along the Mississippi had preferences; Captain Leathers visited certain plantation landings that denied the trade to Cannon, and vice versa. Certainly, the foremost masters of the river in those days were colorful characters, and they themselves doubtlessly attracted trade, and, in some instances, repelled it. John Howard, for one, was aghast at the tales Captain Cannon told and the tricks he indulged in during the building of the *Cannon*, and John's correspondence showed it. Edmonds J. Howard, since he was Cannon's host, presumably had a more favorable attitude.

The *J. M. White*

JAMES HOWARD's fellow partners, John, his brother, and Edmonds J., his son, continued after him to inspire and to deserve the confidence and loyalty of captains and masters, both the colorful and the more prosaic. While 1877 was a good year, with output exceeding the year before, 1878 was a climax with both quantity and quality reaching a new peak for the Howards. Old customers turned up in 1877 full of confidence and cash and contracted for eight new boats and two barges. One old customer came with the earnings of his other Howard-built boats, the *Frank Pargoud* and the smaller stern-wheeler, the *Trenton*. J. W. Tobin had switched the *Pargoud* from the Ouachita River trade to the Vicksburg–New Orleans run when that cotton trade picked up in the early seventies. He had earned good money with her, enough to order the construction of the finest and fastest steamboat the Howards were ever to build—or that anybody would ever build on the Western Rivers! The contract for the *J. M. White* was signed on June 12, 1877.

The *White's* keel, 11 by 18 inches thick, was laid on the fifteenth of September in 1877; it indicated a vessel 310 feet long between perpendiculars. With a finely modeled bow to allow a smooth easy entry through the water, the hull curved back for 80 feet before the sides became

J. M. White, side-wheel packet launched in 1878. The "cotton queen of the Mississippi" was built for Captain John Tobin for the Vicksburg–New Orleans trade. Described as "the supreme triumph in side-wheel cotton boat architecture," she burned at the St. Maurice Plantation, Point Coupée Parish, Louisiana, in 1886.

straight. The stern likewise swept gracefully back to the rudder. On deck, she was 321 feet in overall length and 49 feet in breadth to the outermost hull planks. The depth of her hold measured 11 feet and 2 inches. The Falls had seen others of her size and even larger go by. The *Richmond*, 340 feet long, was perhaps the longest Western Rivers steamboat ever built, and the *Grand Republic* was but one foot and three inches shorter. In gross tonnage, the latter boat was the greatest, measuring 2,600 gross tons and having the ability to float 4,000 short tons on a draft of 10 feet.[5] One Howard-built boat, the *James Howard* (1870), was also larger than the *White* was to be, being 328 feet in length and measuring 2,321 gross tons. But it is a measure of the *J. M. White* that even though there were others of more impressive dimensions, the contemporary newspapers generally granted that the *White* was the finest steamboat to float on the Western Rivers. While the Louisville *Courier-Journal* could be expected to take a partial view for a home-town achievement, it is a matter of maturity, sophistication, and authority to find the Cincinnati *Commercial* likewise acclaiming the *White* as greater even than the St. Louis-built *Grand Republic*.[6]

From her keel to the flaring, painted sunflower tops of her smokestacks the *J. M. White* was the culmination of the Western Rivers steamboat packet. She was a masterpiece of materials, design, and construction. Although the reporters were overwhelmed mostly by the magnificence of her cabin, her hull and machinery were no less grand; indeed, they were probably the more outstanding achievements. Her main backbone, a beam of West Virginia oak, was 11 by 18 inches and was flanked on either side by twelve parallel keelsons. The bottom of the hull was flat except for a neatly rounded bilge. Rigidity of the hull was helped by three longitudinal bulkheads, which, however, did not facilitate cargo stowage or handling.[7] Her planking was of Pennsylvania pine four and a half inches thick.

[5] Hunter, *Steamboats on the Western Rivers*, p. 608. Data on the *J. M. White* is taken from *ibid.*, pp. 609–11, and from correspondence and records in the Howard MSS.

[6] Cincinnati *Commercial*, April 4, 1878, and Louisville *Courier-Journal*, August 7, 1878.

[7] A drawing of an earlier but similarly constructed steamer is shown in Hunter, *Steamboats on the Western Rivers*, p. 98.

As with most Howard boats destined for the Lower Mississippi, this hull had about six feet of sheer in order better to adapt the boat to the swells and waves likely to be encountered on the broader reaches of the river. (For the uninitiated, this means that if a person stood squarely at the mid-point of the hull he would be six feet lower than one standing on the bow. These six feet of pointed bow would serve to deflect the majority of the waves and thus keep the main deck dry most of the time.) Despite the size of the keel and the keelsons and the longitudinal bulkheads the hull would still have been easily deflected when loaded had it not been braced further. The narrower bow and stern sections had less buoyancy than the broad, flat-bottomed mid-section, so, unchecked, a Western Rivers steamboat with its relatively shallow hull would tend to droop at the ends. Or, from a different vantage point, the mid-section would tend to rise up, like the belly of a hog floating in a wallow, as it was colloquially described. This tendency was overcome by the use of sixty tons of hog chains, which cost $6,650, and were not chains at all but iron rods connecting the ends of the vessel and running over a dozen samson posts two decks high or more and which were stepped directly on the keelsons. The effect during construction would have looked like an iron bridge of the era, with the posts fanning out from the middle, the iron rods connecting them all with the keel in a concatenation of unalterable triangles, and thus was a light girder strengthened. This hog-chain-and-post system interfered somewhat with cargo and passenger arrangements, but it was an engineering achievement that allowed the lightest weight of hull construction to carry a prodigious tonnage. A similar arrangement transversely supported the great guards. On a hull but 49 feet in breadth, the main deck was extended by hog chains and cantilevering fully 23 feet on either side for the entire length of the hull, excepting the 45 feet cut out for the paddle wheels and the narrowing at either end. Thus, the main deck was a graceful boat-shaped area 321 by 95 feet, or about the size of a modern football gridiron.

About two thirds of the way aft on the hull were located the shafts for the paddle wheels; the shafts with their flanges and cranks weighed 27 tons apiece. The wheels themselves measured 44 feet in diameter and 19 feet in width, with the buckets themselves 3 feet in width. Forward of the bulkhead which enclosed the engine room were located the ten boilers, each 42 inches in diameter and 34 feet long. They were the only all-steel boilers on the rivers at the time. The fire boxes, as always, faced the bow to take advantage of the natural draft created when the boat was under way.

The Howards' *J. M. White* was the third such vessel to bear the name. While the earlier ones had been named for a prominent merchant, J. W. Tobin apparently called his boat after a Captain J. M. White who resided in Cloverport, Kentucky.[8] The earlier boats had been famous, too, with the second one chalking up speed records in 1844. That *White* ran from New Orleans to St. Louis, 1,218 miles, in 3 days, 22 hours, and 9 minutes. Twenty-six years later the *Lee* only bettered that record by but 5 hours and 5 minutes.[9]

The designer of the second *White*, William King, introduced an innovation that for quite a long time was thought to have resulted in her great speed. He simply moved the paddle wheels aft from the then customary position about half the way along the hull so that they caught the secondary swell that followed along the hull in the wake of the primary bow waves. If one observes a modeled bow of a displacement-type hull cutting through the water, the water first climbs up the bow for a ways, and then, just aft of this, it is sucked away only to ride up higher further aft again. Thus, it would seem plausible that by placing the wheels so that they bit into the relatively deeper water of this secondary wave created by the hull's passing, they would then be able to develop greater thrust. Later, however, naval architects discovered that changes in the loading trim of a vessel, as well as the channel and depth of water under the hull would change the characteristics of these waves and would thus alter the water level at the paddle wheel. They further found that a paddle thrust too deeply into the water actually developed less thrust than one that was only partly submerged and thus exerted its energy on the surface.[10] Hence the earlier *White*, as well as the Howard-built one, must

8 Way, *Directory of Western Rivers Packets*, p. 156.
9 *Ibid.*, pp. 255, 257.
10 Hunter, *Steamboats on the Western Rivers*, p. 169 and note 193; Ambler, *Transportation in the Ohio Valley*, pp. 178–79.

accredit her speed to such factors as her lightness and trim, and her engines, of course.

The engines for the new *J. M. White* were also on a grand scale, nearly as much power as the great ocean liners of the day: 3,400 horsepower at 100 pounds steam pressure. The diameter of the cylinders was 43 inches, and the engines developed an 11-foot stroke. They rested on pine timbers 18 by 26 inches in width and 82 feet long. Needless to say, these engines by Ainslie and Cochran of Louisville contrasted greatly with the ordinary run of the mill; indeed, they exceeded any others built on the Western Rivers for the next fifty years.[11] They were to drive the *White* at an easy, profitable speed, capable of bursts up to twenty miles an hour or more. Her record time was seven hours and forty minutes from New Orleans to Baton Rouge. This beat the *Lee's* time for the same trip by forty-five minutes.[12]

By the time of the April 3 launching, the hull, iron work, and superstructure's framework had cost Captain Tobin $56,500. The suspense must have been great indeed when they took her over the Falls in May. She did rub on some of the rocks, the daybook noted, but gently, however. Her machinery was installed at New Albany and required $47,000 more from Tobin by its completion date. All the while work was going on for her cabin; the cabin brought her total cost to more than $220,000, perhaps even $300,000.[13] Comprising more than half the total cost of the boat, her cabin and furnishings were elegant indeed. The Louisville firm of Bell, Coggeshall and Hillerich had started a crew of forty carpenters and joiners to work on August 16, 1877, and they labored until June 13, a year later. The main cabin, or lounge, was 19 feet wide, 233 feet long and 13 feet high. It rested on the boiler deck which covered 20,000 square feet. Flanking the lounge on each side were twenty-four staterooms which ranged from 8 by 10 feet in dimensions to the 12-by-14 size of the bridal chambers aft. The forward end of the cabin was formed by a semi-circular promenade hall 17 by 38 feet which was decked with

[11] Hunter, *Steamboats on the Western Rivers*, pp. 143–44.
[12] Ambler, *History of Transportation in the Ohio Valley*, p. 276; Gould, *Fifty Years on the Mississippi*, p. 537.
[13] Howard MSS, chiefly Daybook 6, p. 197. See also Hunter, *Steamboats on the Western Rivers*, p. 612.

HOWARD STEAMBOAT MUSEUM

Lounge-cabin on the J. M. White

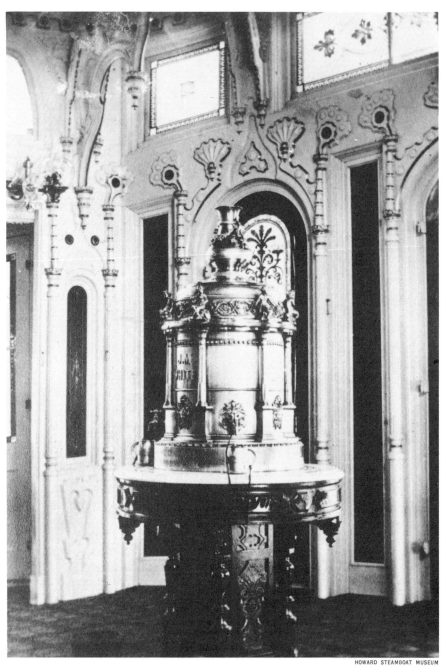

Water cooler on the J. M. White

wood mosaics. At the stern, aft of the ladies cabin, was another parlor with large windows that opened "to take a view of the surroundings." Forward of the starboard wheelhouse was the pantry with a floor, counter, and cupboards of Scott County black walnut. The port side housed a barber shop and the bathrooms and water-closets. There was hot and cold running water in the bathrooms.[14]

As the *Courier-Journal* correspondent, Will S. Hays, noted: "The style of architecture of the cabin will have to be seen to have an idea of it, as it is not taken out of the books; nor was it got up to be like anything that has ever been built before . . . . It is an original idea of Mr. Thos. Bell's." Uncontestably steamboat gothic and mid-Victorian, it was called chaste and tasteful in that day. It certainly was grand, if not grandiose, and elegant, if not purely opulent. Stained glass filled not just the skylights at the cabin's roof, but the dozen doors that opened onto the promenade as well, and the windows and doors aft of the ladies' cabin. The doors that separated the ladies' cabin from the main lounge were etched and embossed in designs representing Spring and Summer. The doors and paneling were of rosewood and walnut burl (to be sure, veneered on quarter-inch poplar wood), and gilt abounded everywhere. The seven chandeliers were of Egyptian design plated with gold. Presumably they used gas for their illumination. Counting the staterooms in the second cabin on the texas deck above, the *White* boasted twenty-two French-designed and monogrammed walnut bedroom suites, fourteen plainer double bedsteads with six more in the gentlemen's quarters, and the remaining thirty-four staterooms boasted upper and lower berths like all the other boats but with both spring and hair mattresses. For this decor, Gorham furnished the monogrammed silver, and Haviland the china. A Chickering full concert grand piano reposed in the lounge, one of the two exhibited at the Philadelphia Exposition and awarded the Centennial Prize. The *Courier-Journal* concluded:

> Her general appearance is that of ease and grace. Her beautifully modeled hull, upon which sits robed, as it were, in snowy-white, one of the handsomest and most gracefully-designed cabins we ever beheld, together with her lofty and beautiful chimneys and stately

[14] Louisville *Courier-Journal*, August 7, 1878.

wheel-houses, makes her look 'monarch of all she surveys', a thing of beauty and a proud living monument. . . .

> *Proud monster of the Sunny South,*
> *Go, bearing proud thy name;*
> *May every trip you make for Tobin*
> *Add fortune to his fame.*[15]

She was the 276th boat built by the Howards, and their crowning effort. She steamed away on the twenty-sixth of June 1878, drawing 7 feet and 3 inches and towing the *Edward J. Gay* behind her. It was a case, however, that bore resemblance to other monarchs of an earlier century, for "Apres elle, le deluge."

The *John W. Cannon,* the *J. M. White,* and the *Ed Richardson,* built in 1878 for Cannon and Tobin alone and in partnership, were three of the best, the largest, and the last of the great side-wheeler cotton boats. The *White* was specifically designed to tote 10,000 bales of cotton per trip. These two colorful captains spent between them $350,000 in a year's time to build boats for carrying cotton from Vicksburg to New Orleans. They profited, but the trend was beginning to run the other way. The rest of the boats down the ways in '78 illustrate it well. It was the year that yellow fever caught the river valley by surprise and cut short many a boat's season, as well as many a captain's. The *Laura Lee,* the *Jewel,* and the *B. S. Rhea* were smaller stern-wheelers, the *Laura Lee* barely two thirds the length of the *White.* They headed down to the Red River and the Cumberland. The *Herbert,* a small stern-wheeler for towing duty in the bayous, was followed down the ways by two barges destined for the New Orleans and Red River Transportation Company.

The Louisville newspaper that described the *White* also advertised another new boat by the Howards. In the amusements section, it was noted that the YMCA was sponsoring an excursion for eight o'clock Thursday night on the "elegant and new" *Shallcross.* Music would be by Eichhorn's orchestra and all were assured that the moon would be at its brightest. The Louisville and Jeffersonville Ferry Company had built another new ferryboat that year. Elsewhere on the page, the *Grey Eagle*

---

[15] *Ibid.*

was promised to depart at 4 P.M. for Owensboro, Evansville, and Henderson bearing the U.S. Mail and the Adams Company Express. The Howards had built her in 1871. The Shortline Excursion to Lake Chautauqua was to leave Louisville August 14 and 15. That trip or one to Put-In-Bay on the Ohio and Mississippi Railroad cost but $12.00, while to Niagara Falls the cost was but $16.75. The paper wryly noted: "In these days of excursions it is a trifle odd somebody in another city doesn't get up a party to visit Louisville."

Other than those few excitements, life seemed to go placidly and contentedly on along the river. A few gunshot wounds and beer-mug bleedings were noted and the guilty excoriated as always. A corpse or two merited explanations. Two boys narrowly escaped drowning off Two-Mile Island but were rescued and enabled to get back to their clothes by a man in a skiff. And over in Jeffersonville the Greenbackers were to meet Thursday night to elect delegates to their convention. The City Hiring Office on Fifth Street advertised for homes and work for 50 nice, industrious German girls, 250 first-class Irish girls, 300 American colored, etc. And under the City Features with pointed index finger it read: "The Kentucky Military Institute, Farmdale, Kentucky, is in the country, where the boys should be when at school." Like a steamboat steaming down the river, life went on but an era was ending.

The Next 276 Boats

The next 276 Howard-built hulls followed the *J. M. White* quickly down the ways, and from the vantage point of the 552d hull, the changes on the river were apparent. It was a strangely prophetic boat, from hindsight, for the little *Help*, built in 1893, was only 55 feet long with a beam of 14 and she had two propellers instead of a paddle wheel. James T. Duffy in Louisville ordered her to tug and tow his barges of sand and gravel about. Though the *Help* measured but 14 gross tons, she nevertheless transported as much in a year as a packet a hundred times greater in gross tonnage. She did not need to carry the load; she could push it instead.

It was but a span of fifteen years from the grand *J. M. White* to the *Help*, and but fourteen years more for the next 276 hulls, for construction methods and materials changed as well as the steamers. From 1876 through 1885, the Yards had floated 146 hulls: 31 side-wheelers of various sizes, 49 stern-wheelers, and 63 unrigged floats and barges. In the next decade, 195 hulls were numbered, with but 24 side-wheelers, 66 stern-wheelers and 98 barges. There were seven vessels propelled by means other than the traditional paddle wheel that decade, such as the *Help* with her twin screws. From 1896 through 1905, 195 vessels were launched and the side-wheelers numbered but 10 to 89 stern-wheelers. Ninety barges were built that decade.

TABLE 5. *Output of the Howard Ship Yards, Quinquennial Periods 1876–1905*
(Number of Hulls)

Years	Total	Side Wheel	Stern Wheel	Other	Unrigged
1876–80	58	13	27	2	16
1881–85	88	18	22	1	47
1886–90	80	14	31	1	34
1891–95	115	10	35	6	64
1896–00	104	8	52	1	43
1901–05	91	2	37	5	47

Source: Appendix A, Table 1, pp. 195–212.

Whereas from 1876 through 1880, the Howards built but 58 boats and barges and from 1901 through 1905 they launched 91, the total gross tonnage for the two five-year periods showed a decline of 16 per cent by 1905. Unquestionably, then, the Howards were building smaller hulls by 1905 than they had in 1875. The average gross tonnage per hull showed a decrease of 47 per cent. Just as the gross tonnage data had understated earlier comparisons with the Yards' output when only hulls had been constructed, now, too, do the data mislead somewhat. For the Yards in the seventies and eighties were engaged in building complete boats, but in 1905 over half the number of hulls were barges, that is just hulls with occasionally one decked over or built with a cargo box attached. Thus, by the turn of the century or so, the output of the Yards had exhibited a slight decline. Such is also shown by the size of the firm's gross contract revenues which had declined below the seventies' levels by 1905, and this despite a doubling or so in the number of hulls constructed.

TABLE 6. *Home Ports of Hulls, Quinquennial Periods, 1876–1905*

Home Port	1876–80	1881–85	1886–90	1891–95	1896–00	1901–05
			STEAMERS			
Evansville	2	1	..	1	1	3
Louisville	9	2	4	9	3	2
Memphis	2	..	3	2	10	5
Nashville	3	3	5	8	6	3
New Orleans	6	4	13	8	8	4
St. Louis	3	11	7	11	8	6
Vicksburg	..	..	1	1	1	..
Total	42	41	46	51	61	44
			UNRIGGED			
Evansville	1	1	..	..	..	..
Louisville	3	4	5	6	7	2
Memphis	..	5	1	4	1	2
Nashville	..	..	..	2	..	7
New Orleans	6	..	6	2	8	..
St. Louis	2	27	19	32	11	21
Vicksburg	..	..	..	3	..	..
Total	16	47	34	64	43	47
Total All Types, All Ports	58	88	80	115	104	91

SOURCE: Appendix A, Table 1, pp. 193–221.

COTTON AND RAILROADS

THE home ports listed on the registration of the Howard boats continued to be predominantly Louisville, St. Louis, and New Orleans. Memphis, Nashville, and Evansville formed a second rank. This probably merely reflected the fact that these cities were the natural terminal points for many river trades. Louisville, of course, was so because of the Falls and the Portland Canal. Cincinnati was a terminal, too, but chiefly for a smaller class of packet. St. Louis formed the upper limit for the Lower Mississippi trades and was a natural breaking point for boats from the shallower Upper Mississippi as well. At New Orleans, of course, goods were loaded into ocean steamers for export. But for the barges and other unrigged (not self-propelled) craft, the home port most frequently listed was St. Louis. There were barges built for New Orleans, but the ratio

T. P. Leathers, stern-wheel packet launched in 1891. She is shown here laden with cotton. Built for Captain Leathers of New Orleans, she was snagged and lost about forty miles above Natchez in 1900.

was 46 steamboats to 112 barges for St. Louis during the thirty-year span 1876 through 1905. Louisville accounted for even fewer Howard-built barges than did New Orleans. Thus, broadly, is the picture painted by the Howard Ship Yards in the thirty years following the death of its founder, James Howard, in 1876. It is, of course, but a part and a reflection of the larger mural painted by trade on the Western Rivers.

TABLE 7. *Cotton Production in States Contiguous to Mississippi River System Selected Years, 1870–1905*
(in Thousands of Bales)

States	1870	1875	1880	1885	1890	1895	1900	1905
Arkansas	429	551	537	611	828	521	813	619
Mississippi	830	871	906	1,019	1,262	1,013	1,047	1,199
Missouri	...	...	...	...	...	12	28	43
Louisiana	567	689	374	488	629	514	706	513
Tennessee	246	225	383	322	344	173	222	279
Total	2,072	2,336	3,200	2,440	3,063	2,246	2,816	2,653
U.S. Total	4,352	4,631	6,606	6,576	8,653	7,162	10,124	10,576

SOURCE: U.S. Department of Agriculture, Agricultural Marketing Service, *Cotton and Cottonseed . . . 1866–1952 (Statistical Bulletin No. 164,* Washington, D.C., 1955), pp. 5–19.

Part of the baleful look of the river's commerce of the period could be attributed to cotton, not its total production, perhaps, but the harvesting and processing in cotton country along the Mississippi. In 1880, there was enough cotton picked throughout the United States to fill 6,606,000 bales. This was a 15 per cent gain from 1870 and reflected the resurrection of Southern agriculture from the ravages of the war. From 1880 to 1890, cotton bales increased by 13 per cent; by 1900, 10,124,000 bales were filled at the gin mills, again a 13 per cent increase in the decade.[16] But in the cotton states of Arkansas, Louisiana, Mississippi, and Tennessee, states which are contiguous to the Mississippi or its tributaries, aggregate production in 1875 numbered 2,336,000 bales. And in 1905, the crop from these states plus Missouri filled 2,653,000 bales. (See Table 7.) The region that had produced half the nation's cotton thirty years

[16] U.S. Department of Agriculture, Agricultural Marketing Service, *Cotton and Cottonseed . . . 1866–1952 (Statistical Bulletin No. 164,* Washington, D.C., 1955), p. 5.

previously was then producing but one quarter of the total in 1905. These states contain the rivers that floated the majority of the steamers the Howards had built. The Tennessee and the Cumberland both claimed a good share of the Yards' output. The Yazoo, the Red River, the Ouachita likewise took a number for many years. And the Mississippi from Cairo to New Orleans knew the whistles of the best boats the Howards ever built. Before the war, the region had been bursting with growth and the Howards had grown with it. From 1850 to 1860, the growth in cotton production had amounted to 120 per cent—from 2,450,000 bales to 5,400,000. Furthermore, exports of cotton also increased during the same period, almost trippling in the last prewar decade. These bales first moved on their way to Boston or Lancashire by steamboat.[17] Furthermore, in virtually every decade from 1820 to 1860, the value of receipts at New Orleans from the interior had doubled. From a total value of but $12,-637,000 in 1820, by 1860 the goods were valued at $185,211,000. There had also developed concurrently with the New Orleans trade an increase in intra-valley traffic, the increase in this traffic being of such magnitude that even the greatly expanded New Orleans receipts of 1860 formed but a much smaller portion of the total than they had twenty or thirty years earlier. The total mostly moved on the decks of steamboats.[18]

After the Civil War, the South everywhere had to struggle to rebuild and recapture the war loss. Cotton production in 1870 did not equal the 1860 level. In fact, the prewar production totals were not exceeded until the harvests of 1879 and 1880 had been weighed.[19] Then after 1880, the cotton grown on the regions contiguous to the Mississippi River sys-

[17] Fite, "Agricultural Development of the West During the Civil War," in *Quarterly Journal of Economics*, XX, 262–63; U.S. Bureau of the Census, *Eleventh Census* (1890), XIX, *Transportation Business*, Pt. II, *Transportation by Water*, p. 440.

[18] William F. Switzler, *Special Report on the Commerce of the Mississippi, Ohio, and Other Rivers, and of the Bridges which Cross Them (Report on the Internal Commerce of the United States. Part II of Commerce and Navigation*, Washington, D.C., 1888), pp. 199, 209, 215. During 1819–20 western products composed 58 per cent of the total value of receipts at New Orleans. For 1849–50 they were about 41 per cent, and they remained at about this level until the Civil War. *Ibid.*

[19] Fite, "Agricultural Development of the West During the Civil War," in *Quarterly Journal of Economics*, XX, 262–63, and Table 7, above.

tem knew only a desultory increase, with a few good years and a few bad ones. Without growth, then, the need for packets after 1880 would have been but a demand geared to the replacement of the worn out or the obsolete only. But other factors influenced the development of even that demand.

The balloon-stacked railroad locomotive began to poke its cow-catcher into river business at this time. Prewar, of course, it had been more of a curiosity than a serious contender for hauling a region's freight, but it had had some value other than that of a mere novelty, to judge by the miles of track laid. In the South, over 7,000 miles were built in the fifties, which brought the total for the area—including Kentucky—to 9,167 miles by the end of 1860. While comparatively lightly built and at but half the expense of the roads in the northeastern regions of the United States, the Southern roads served to haul both passengers and freight.[20]

From Mobile to Columbus, Kentucky, by 1860, the Mobile and Ohio was aided by a Federal land grant which gave it about $2,000,000, and by loans amounting to a million and a half dollars from the states of Tennessee and Mississippi. Out of New Orleans, around Lake Pontchartrain to Jackson, a second railroad, the New Orleans, Jackson and Great Northern, and a third, the Mississippi Central, gave a through route from the Gulf to the Ohio by the eve of Fort Sumter.[21]

James Guthrie in Louisville pushed a roadbed south to Nashville by November 1859, and in conjunction with the Kentucky Central thus opened a route by rail from Cincinnati to New Orleans.[22] In 1860, then, 109,000 bales of cotton went northward by these rails. While only one eighth of the total, it was a portentous traffic nevertheless.[23] The rest of the South's roads were east-west lines. The Western and Atlantic Railroad was built westward from Augusta through Chattanooga and Nashville to Memphis by 1857. The route served to divert cotton traffic from

[20] Stover, *Railroads of the South*, pp. 3–12. Southern railways cost an average $28,000 per mile in contrast to the Middle Atlantic region's $52,000 per mile. *Ibid.*, p. 6.

[21] *Ibid.*, pp. 7–8.

[22] *Ibid.*, pp. 8–9.

[23] Taylor, *The Transportation Revolution*, pp. 168–69.

the Tennessee and Cumberland rivers to Savannah and Charleston instead, but it was unnoticed in the growth of the prewar years.[24] The Virginia and Tennessee ran from Lynchburg through the mountains to Bristol on the Tennessee state line and then into Chattanooga, also by 1857.[25] Thus Sherman and his troops found five major trunk lines, albeit a few different gauges, that gave the South a rail network connecting the major cities with their markets and providing limited access to the North by ferryboat. On this rail ran locomotives that were not numerous enough to warrant numbers, so they sported names like the steamboats. They cost from $10,000 to $12,000 and could be operated for less than $1.00 a mile. In the South, they scarcely made over twenty-five miles an hour, not counting stops for traffic or lunch. Some of the roads pulled cars made by a former steamboat builder in Madison, Indiana.[26]

By 1867, the Southern railroads were back in about as good a condition as before the war, and certainly by 1870 further construction of new lines was under way. The Federal government helped them out by selling them rolling stock on credit for less than the market prices. In the seventies, when the Panic of 1873 hit them hard, Congress relieved them of many of their obligations.[27] Rehabilitated and capable of expansion, the Southern railroads nevertheless constructed new track at a far slower pace than the Northern roads, or the Western ones in particular. Thus, 1875 found the South with a decade's increase of but 4,187 miles added to the 9,135 that had existed before. Illinois alone had seen the construction of as much track in that decade, and for the total United States, the mileage had more than doubled.[28] The Panic of 1873 crippled Southern plans and efforts and in 1874 and 1875 only 247 miles of new track were built. More importantly for the steamboat, however, was the even slower pace of construction in Mississippi, Louisiana, and Tennessee, where new construction amounted to but 658 miles out of the total of 13,322 for the

[24] Stover, *Railroads of the South*, pp. 10–11; Taylor, *The Transportation Revolution*, p. 168.

[25] Stover, *Railroads of the South*, pp. 9–10.

[26] *Ibid.*, pp. 8, 12, note 34, p. 13.

[27] Eugene M. Lerner, "Southern Output and Agricultural Income, 1860–1880," in *Agricultural History*, XXXIII, No. 3 (July 1959), pp. 121–22; Stover, *Railroads of the South*, p. 58.

[28] Stover, *Railroads of the South*, p. 59.

ten Southern states from 1865 to 1875. Only Florida scored a smaller increase.[29]

The total of new miles of track constructed hides another interesting fact that contributed indirectly to the continued success of Captains Cannon, Tobin, Pegram, and their peers. The Mobile and Ohio Railroad, probably by accident, had been built with a gauge of five feet. The Mississippi Central, which connected with it at Humboldt, Tennessee, was built of the same gauge, as was the New Orleans, Jackson, and Great Northern. In fact, most of the rails in the South had been placed five feet apart. The Southern Mississippi from Vicksburg to Meridian, Mississippi, had been built to a 4-foot-10-inch gauge, however, which corresponded to no other Southern road but matched the rails laid north of Cincinnati and a few in New Jersey. There were no equally spaced connecting links, however. Ohio's gauge of 4 feet 10 inches had been thus set by a fluke, since the Mad River and Lake Erie Railroad's first locomotive had been purchased from a New Jersey road.[30] The Montgomery and West Point had a 4-foot-8½-inch gauge, standard on the New York Central and the Illinois Central railroads. West of the Mississippi, the Memphis and Little Rock had a 5-foot-6-inch gauge. As at the Russian border today, a change in the gauge, say from 4 feet 6 inches to 5 feet, was more than an inconvenience. It was an outright obstacle. Originally devised, if devised it was, as a means for capturing or maintaining a mercantile monopoly which one city fancied it had and intended to hold at the expense of another, this mercantile monopoly argument readily overcame any foresighted objection to the differences in gauge, because in those days railroads were thought to be but short-haul, feeder-type operations. In 1861, over half the nation's rails were laid to today's standard, 4 feet 8½ inches from inside rail to inside rail—the English standard adopted by Stephenson. Twenty-two per cent of the track was 5-foot gauge, while the 4-foot-10-inch gauge formed the third largest category (10 per cent).[31]

[29] *Ibid.*, p. 61.

[30] George R. Taylor and Irene D. Neu, *The American Railroad Network 1861–1890* (Cambridge: Harvard University Press, 1956), p. 35 and Map III at back of book.

[31] *Ibid.*, p. 14. See comments on Maine railroads v. Boston on p. 19; the New York and Erie Railroad, p. 25; Philadelphia, p. 28; Pittsburgh, p. 33; and North Carolina, pp. 44, 78.

The Civil War did much to create a unified standard-gauge network in the North, as it did even in the South. But the greater shortage of capital in the South, as well as the prevalence of the 5-foot gauge and the lack of rail connections with the North, only served to foster the South's standardization attempts with the 5-foot gauge. It was, of course, incompatible with a 4-foot-8½-inch gauge. The grain trade from the plains west of Chicago did as much as any single item to foster a standardization at the 4-foot-8½-inch width.[32] As the traffic from the West gained in weight and value during the Civil War and after, the costs and inconvenience and shippers' agitation forced a gauge change. Trans-shipment services amounted to a surcharge of 20 per cent on the shipment of a bushel of wheat from the Mississippi at St. Louis to New York.[33] By gauge standardization and elimination of trans-shipment inconveniences, the rails' charges for shipments began to approach those of the all-water route through New Orleans. When added to the relative speed of the rail shipment, as well as the year-round service, the railroads began to gain traffic at the expense of the river route as well as the Great Lakes route. For competitive survival reasons, then, the railroads in the North and West of the United States had switched to one standard gauge by 1880. Eighty-one per cent of all mileage was equipped to accommodate the standard gauge rolling stock. Bothersome trans-shipments had been eliminated. But in the South, the 5-foot gauge still prevailed east of the Mississippi and comprised 11 per cent of the nation's total track mileage.[34]

As railroad bridges were built across the Ohio, such as the Pennsylvania bridge at Louisville in 1870, or the ones in Cincinnati, Steubenville, and elsewhere, the insular character of the Southern roads was ended. For survival, or at least for greater profits, they, too, needed to standardize their gauge. In July 1881, the Kentucky Central Railroad was converted from the 5-foot gauge to the standard gauge. In 1884 the Illinois Central adopted the standard for its lines south of the Ohio, and the Mobile and Ohio, of course, had to follow suit. This left the remaining

[32] Taylor and Neu, *The American Railroad Network*, p. 57.
[33] *Ibid.*, p. 67.
[34] *Ibid.*, p. 77.

competitive roads little alternative; the Louisville and Nashville and the Cincinnati Southern accordingly quickly made the change. The rest of the broad-gauge Southern lines converted on Monday, May 31, and Tuesday, June 1, 1886. When traffic was resumed at 4 P.M. on June 1, 1886, the American railroad system became a physically integrated network.[35] The railroads, of course, lost no time in whistling in their brakemen and getting under way again. In the eighties, 70,330 miles of track were laid, 14,485 of them in the South. In the state of Georgia, 2,134 miles were built, while Florida saw the construction of 1,971. Mississippi, Alabama, and Louisiana had greatly expanded their networks by 1890, the gain amounting to 4,021 miles that more than doubled the 1880 total. In Arkansas, the rail mileage increased by 1,335 to 2,195.[36] These miles of track meant that then was heard, for the first time, the locomotive's whistle along the Mississippi from Baton Rouge to Vicksburg, Memphis, and Cairo. The Ohio, likewise, was parelleled by rails and spanned by their bridges.

The standardization of the gauge not only allowed a reduction in the costs and inconveniences of trans-shipment at the gauge changes, which alone would have worked to the disadvantage of river transportation, but the creation of a unified network over which a car could be sent without further expensive unloading or loading (the roads willing), meant that now the steamboat men found the trans-shipment shoe upon their foot. It meant that with increasing frequency the riverboats were the mode of transport that required expensive trans-shipment.

When the *Rob't. E. Lee* burned on October 30, 1882, Captain Cannon's son chose not to replace her. John W. Cannon had succumbed some months earlier. But there was still river trade, and J. W. Tobin replaced the aging *Frank Pargoud* with the more economical *Pargoud*, still a sidewheeler, but on a more modest scale. Then the *J. M. White* caught fire at Blue Store Landing on December 13, 1886, and when the blaze got to the kegs of gunpowder stored in the forward hold, the magnificent *White*, too, went down. Captain Tobin seemed to lose his zest for the

[35] *Ibid.*, pp. 79–81.
[36] U.S. Department of Commerce, *Statistical Abstract of the United States, 1920* (Washington, D.C., 1921), p. 333; Stover, *Railroads of the South*, p. 193.

river after that and by September 1888, another Western Rivers pioneer had been laid to rest.

RIVER TRADE

EVEN with the sinking of these monarchs and the passing of the pioneers and some second-generation steamboat men as well, trade on the Western Rivers did not dry up. But it failed to expand in pace with the other mode of transport then developing and growing with the frontier. In the decade that saw the *Lee* and the *White* burn, total freight traffic on the Mississippi and its tributaries reached a peak, and while the censuses of the river taken in 1889, 1906, and 1916 did not always measure identical traffic or arrange it comparably, if the tonnage transported by the railway-car ferries is included as well as the lighterage or harbor work, the tons of freight handled by the steamboats continued to expand. From 1889, when 29,401,409 tons of freight were carried or towed, the total rose to 40,169,427 tons by the census of 1916.[37] The course was not without dry spells or floods, of course. But because of the changing environment and the piping of the railroads' whistles, this commendable total was viewed as but a drop in the bucket. It was! The railroads in 1905 carried 1,427,-731,905 tons of freight and generally hauled this freight a longer distance than did the riverboats. The 1905 total was more than twice the tonnage carried by rail in 1890.[38] The rivers carried 4½ per cent of the rail's total tonnage in 1890, and by 1905 riverboats transported only 2 per cent as much as the rails. By 1916, river freight amounted to less than 2 per cent of the weight of the railroad's freight pile.[39]

But to keep the data in perspective, the tons of freight hauled about on the Western Rivers in 1906 were more than fifteen times as large as the 2,033,400 tons estimated as the total river freight in 1851.[40] The 1850s,

[37] U.S. Bureau of the Census [*Special Reports*], *Transportation by Water, 1916* (Washington, D.C., 1920), p. 171.
[38] U.S. Department of Commerce, *Statistical Abstract of the United States, 1920*, p. 337.
[39] *Ibid.*; U.S. Bureau of the Census [*Special Reports*], *Transportation by Water, 1916*, p. 171.
[40] Taylor, *The Transportation Revolution*, p. 174; U.S. Bureau of the Census, *Special Reports: Transportation by Water, 1906* (Washington, D.C., 1908), p 178.

it will be remembered, were the golden days of the steamboat. To make a direct comparison, however, the freight handled solely on board packet steamers in 1906, as the freight for 1851 had been carried, amounted to but a threefold gain from 1851. Thus, whatever it was that declined on the rivers, it was not the freight that they hauled. In fifty-five years, changes occurred and the steamboat men adapted to them, grudgingly

TABLE 8. *Freight Traffic on the Western Rivers, 1880, 1889, and 1906*

Rivers	1880	1889	1906
FREIGHT CARRIED ON STEAMERS (*tons*)			
Upper Mississippi	2,698,218	2,151,624	273,362
Ohio	2,446,353	3,806,655	1,246,437
Lower Mississippi	1,276,972	4,387,215	835,587
Total Valley	6,421,543	10,345,504	2,355,386
FREIGHT TOWED IN UNRIGGED CRAFT (*tons*)			
Upper Mississippi	867,120[1]	4,108,824	1,484,739
Ohio	2,521,518[2]	11,990,303	13,980,368
Lower Mississippi	1,023,028	1,844,872	1,710,600
Total Valley	4,411,666	17,943,999	17,175,707
Total Freight	10,833,209	28,289,503	19,531,093
PASSENGERS, NON-FERRY, NUMBER			
Upper Mississippi	422,730	338,750	1,442,248
Ohio	960,936	1,506,594	1,824,180
Lower Mississippi	212,417	538,904	833,201
Total Valley	1,596,083	2,384,248	4,099,629
PASSENGERS, FERRY, NUMBER			
Upper Mississippi	958,182	1,482,084	890,836
Ohio	3,000,862	4,996,549	2,951,908
Lower Mississippi	1,172,940	1,995,113	6,179,868
Total Valley	5,131,984	8,474,646	10,022,612
Total Passengers	6,728,067	10,858,984	14,122,241

[1]St. Louis barge lines only
[2]Pittsburgh coal traffic only
The figures for the Upper Mississippi include the Missouri River
SOURCE: U.S. Bureau of the Census, *Tenth Census* (1880), *Transportation*, pp. 694–703; *Special Reports: Transportation by Water*, 1906, pp. 178 ff., and 1916, p. 171.

TABLE 9. *Freight by Commodities on the Western Rivers, 1889 and 1906*
(*Tons*)

Commodity	1889	1906
Coal	8,527,428	11,033,011
Stone, sand, gravel	321,054	4,004,259
Lumber, forest products	9,200,191	514,950
Grain	1,712,498	380,721
Iron ore	574,790	171,779
Pig iron and steel rails	7,775	55,346
Petroleum	3,534	365,479
Cotton	895,742	146,975
Cement, brick, lime	2,193	95,443
Fruits, vegetables	41,748	55,703
Flour	89,992	81,900
Tobacco	27,707	114,000
Canned Goods	. . .	63,697
Phosphate and fertilizer	. . .	44,413
Naval stores	. . .	770
Ice	91,010	17,229
Miscellaneous merchandise	6,793,841	9,291,015
Total	28,289,503[1]	26,436,690[2]

[1]Does not include 1,111,906 tons moved by ferry steamers and, presumably, comparable to the lighterage and harbor work and railway car freight tonnage reported in the Census of 1906.

[2]Includes 6,905,597 tons of railway car freight under miscellaneous merchandise. Not included in the total is that of lighterage, 5,190,291 tons. Total freight including the latter would be 31,626,981, which conforms with the data given in the text.

SOURCE: U.S. Bureau of the Census, [*Special Reports*], *Transportation by Water*, 1916, p. 171.

no doubt, but they adapted, survived, and ordered new boats from the Howards. But just because the new boats cost only one tenth the amount the *J. M. White* had cost, or just because the trademark of the golden era of steamboating, the packet, sank with the *White*, river commerce did not turn to the levee and rot away, too. The towboats and their barges were the new riverboats; if this was not clear in 1889, it was by 1906. Competition gave the towboats and barges the tonnage that had been denied to the stately packet.

COAL

THE composition of the traffic between 1889 and 1906 shows the switch from cotton to a heavy raw material, such as coal. An examination of the types of hulls turned out by the Howards during the same period also reflects the change.

Total ton miles of freight handled by the fleet on the rivers probably declined somewhat from 1889 to 1906, for the tonnage attributable to harbor and lighterage work and to the railway transfer ferries amounted to 12,095,888 tons by the 1906 Census and probably was but 1,111,906 tons in 1889, according to the apologetic report. Deleting this short-haul ferry freight tonnage and the likewise short-haul transport of sand and gravel, the resulting traffic in 1889 was 28,289,503 tons and in 1906, 19,531,093 tons. This amounted to a decline of 30 per cent in the commodities most likely to be hauled longer distances, and reflects the inroads railroad competition had made into river trade. The remaining traffic remained because it was still subject to the economic advantages which water transport enjoyed over land. The light and higher-valued commodities generally were the items showing a decrease. Conspicuously, cotton shipments declined by 748,767 tons, or by 2,995,068 standard bales. Total cotton production in the five states contiguous with the Mississippi had been 3,820,000 bales in 1906, and the 587,900 bales shipped by water were but 4 per cent of the nation's total harvest. In 1890, the riverboat had transported over 40 per cent of the country's crop. It was better, perhaps, that the *Rob't. E. Lee* and the *J. M. White* had become heroic funeral pyres in their prime rather than to have suffered the sad ignominy of a voyage without cotton.[41]

Iron ore from Missouri to Pittsburgh declined by 403,011 tons, less probably because of rail-river competition than the competition of the Lake Superior ores. But it cut off a profitable back haul for boats and barges that had carried Pittsburgh iron and steel to St. Louis or beyond. The grain trade, principally by barge from St. Louis to New Orleans, succumbed to a drastic degree by 1,331,777 tons, or almost 80 per cent. The railroads' development of in-transit privileges as well as their special export rates for grain to the East Coast were largely responsible for this

[41] U.S. Bureau of the Census, *Eleventh Census* (1890), XIX, *Transportation Business*, Pt. II, *Transportation by Water*, p. 405; U.S. Bureau of the Census, *Special Reports: Transportation by Water*, 1906, p. 178; *ibid.*, 1916, p. 171; U.S. Department of Agriculture, *Agricultural Marketing Service, Cotton and Cottonseed . . . 1866–1952*.

phenomenon. The grain traffic did pick up again in the next decade, however. Ice, as a commodity of course, melted away because of the invention and proliferation of the icemaking machine.[42]

The decline of lumber shipments by river reflected primarily the depletion of the virgin stands in Pennsylvania and along the Ohio. On that river system, the tonnage of lumber declined from 3,812,013 tons in 1889 to 279,436 in 1906. A similar phenomenon also occurred along the Upper Mississippi River, although the rails were there probably more important in causing the decline of 4,636,754 tons, or virtually the entire 1889 tonnage.[43]

The traffic that gained from 1889 to 1906, however, was in those commodities that were peculiarly susceptible to barge transport, such as coal or sand and gravel. Oil, also, commenced to grow in importance as a river commodity, for Louisiana was producing oil by 1902. The decrease in traffic least affected the Ohio and its tributaries, for in their regions were found the commodities which could still sustain economic water transportation. On the Upper Mississippi on the other hand, as the lumber disappeared, along with grain and ice, the tons carried declined from 1889's 6,260,448 tons to 1,758,101 in 1906. Along the Lower Mississippi, coal from the Ozarks went by rail, as did cotton, and the grain trade declined precipitously. The tons of freight carried on the Old Mississippi fell from 6,232,087 to 2,546,187 by 1906.[44]

Oddly enough, however, while the light-density and higher-valued traffic such as cotton was being pirated away from the riverboats by the railroads, the riverboats experienced an increase in their passenger trade. Per ton carried, passengers were probably more remunerative than the cargo the boats were steadily losing; and they had the further advantage, as someone has noted before, that passengers generally will load and unload themselves. From the Census of 1880 to the one in 1906, the number of passengers (nonferry) transported increased by more than two-and-

---

[42] U.S. Bureau of the Census [*Special Reports*], *Transportation by Water*, 1916, p. 171.

[43] U.S. Bureau of the Census, *Eleventh Census*, 1890, XIX, *Transportation Business*, Pt. II, *Transportation by Water*, pp. 436–37; U.S. Bureau of the Census, *Special Reports: Transportation by Water*, 1906, p. 179.

[44] U.S. Bureau of the Census, *Special Reports: Transportation by Water*, 1906, pp. 179–80.

TABLE 10. *Fleet of Merchant Vessels on the Western Rivers, 1880, 1889, 1906*

	1880	1889	1906
	NUMBER OF HULLS		
Total	5,052	7,453	9,622
Steam	1,198	1,114	1,435
Unrigged	3,854	6,339	8,187
Upper Mississippi	696	613	846
Steam	410	265	417
Unrigged	286	348	429
Ohio	4,041	6,245	8,104
Steam	473	537	700
Unrigged	3,568	5,708	7,404
Lower Mississippi	315	580	672
Steam	315	308	318
Unrigged	119	272	354
	GROSS TONS		
Total	1,286,537	3,381,974	4,411,967
Steam	251,793	210,337	146,227
Unrigged	1,034,744	3,171,636	4,265,740
Upper Mississippi	254,790	213,547	46,112
Steam	96,018	32,964	21,313
Unrigged	158,772	180,583	24,799
Ohio	858,525	2,920,468	4,238,373
Steam	107,472	107,195	81,645
Unrigged	751,053	2,813,273	4,146,728
Lower Mississippi	173,222	247,958	137,482
Steam	48,303	70,178	43,269
Unrigged	124,919	177,780	94,213

SOURCE: U. S. Bureau of the Census, *Tenth Census* (1880), IV, *Transportation*, pp. 695–705; *Eleventh Census* (1890), XIX, *Transportation Business*, Pt. II, *Transportation by Water*, pp. 425, 448; *Special Reports: Transportation by Water*, 1906, pp. 164, 173.

a-half times—from 1,596,083 to 4,099,629.[45] These were the longer-haul traffic, too—the drummers headed for river towns, the planters on their way to market and back again, some were on excursions, many just took the boat for its comparative comfort over the rails' best offering of the time.

Passenger traffic along the Lower Mississippi saw the greatest increase, rising nearly fourfold in twenty-six years. The Upper Mississippi

[45] See Table 8.

River system, which would include the Missouri, the Illinois, and half a dozen smaller rivers of that region, saw at least a doubling of passengers between 1880 and 1906, although the trend was not always steadily upward. The Ohio River system passenger traffic, by far the largest, witnessed an expansion in the same period of some 863,244 passengers carried by water.[46]

The ferry business likewise experienced a good increase; although not quite doubling in the number of passengers carried in the years from 1880 to 1906, the total in the latter year amounted to 10,022,612 people ferried across some river somewhere.[47]

The tides of business on the rivers thus waxed and waned and never remained the same. Although the decade of the eighties saw the grand old packet and the humbler tramp steamer carry more goods than ever before or since, the rivermen were neither supine nor struck dumb by the effects of competitive modes of transport when they were finally hit. The growth in freight towed in barges shows the nature of their response; likewise the change from the opulence of the side-wheeler to a less ostentatious stern-wheeler which sometimes carried more staterooms. The decline in the size of the steamboats, too, was an obvious economizing and accommodating step. The number of vessels of 1,000 gross tons or larger, twenty-three in 1889, had declined to but eight by 1905. At the same time, the number of boats of but 5 to 49 gross tons increased from 24 per cent of the fleet to over half the total. The average gross tonnage of the steamboats built from 1901 to 1905 was but 59, and the gross tonnage for the Western Rivers steamboat fleet declined by more than 40 per cent from 1880 to 1906, totaling but 152,592 on June 30, 1906. The number of steam or power vessels, however, had never been greater, as 1,451 boats were registered. Part of the gain, as part of the gain in traffic tonnage, too, must be attributed to the growth of small, gasoline-powered boats used for harbor work or on runs to the smaller river towns with insufficient trade to support the landing of a large steamer.[48]

Throughout this whole period, Louisville and its environs continued

[46] U.S. Bureau of the Census, *Special Reports: Transportation by Water*, 1906, p. 186.

[47] *Ibid.*

[48] *Ibid.*, pp. 165–67.

Home of Edmonds J. Howard, 1101 East Market Street, Jeffersonville. Built about 1892, the house is presently the Clark County Historical Society Howard Steamboat Museum.

Music Room, Edmonds J. Howard home

Dining Room, Edmonds J. Howard home

to rank as the leading port in new steam vessel construction, not in number but in gross tonnage.[49] Of the ninety-one boats built around Louisville from 1901 through 1906, 51 of them came from the Howard yards. The twenty-five years from 1880 to 1905 were the zenith for the Howard Ship Yards of Jeffersonville throughout the 108-year span in which they were owned by the Howard family. Ed. J. Howard was able to build, in 1891 and 1892, a mansion that rivaled the *J. M. White* in its elegance. The music room, though sadly shorn of its artistic gilt by the flood of 1937, is perhaps the only surviving indication of how grand a cotton packet once looked, although the salon of but thirty some feet can only suggest the dazzling sight which a similarly executed cabin 233 feet long would have presented.

But more important than the embellishment of but a house or a boat were the yards across the street, noisy with busy men and the third generation of Howard boys carrying water, steaming a plank, or learning how to rivet. So the Howard Ship Yards could build in their first 276 hulls the grandest boat on the Mississippi, and in their next 276 the smallest but prophetic propeller-driven towboat. Where once a Howard had built boats to carry cotton, now was there a Howard or two learning how to build boats to carry coal.

[49] U.S. Bureau of the Census, *Special Reports: Transportation by Water*, 1906, p. 169.

CHAPTER VI

The
Evolution of
the Steamboat

Paddle Wheels

T HE FIRST PADDLE WHEEL was very likely only that—an axle with paddles radiating outward and adequately braced to exert thrust when the axle was rotated by any suitable means.[1] It was an improvement on the method employed by John Fitch about July 20, 1786, which moved the first steam vessel in the United States—six paddles on either side of the boat which were worked perpendicularly in a canoe-paddle manner. The paddle wheel's innovation may perhaps be credited to Samuel Morey of Connecticut, who certainly used one in 1797 on what was probably the eighth steamboat built in the United States. Robert Fulton, with the *Clermont* in 1807, constructed the twelfth steam-propelled boat in America and utilized two paddle wheels—the first of the side-wheelers that moved the world.[2]

By 1830 the days of rapid innovation and alteration in the river steamboat had about ended. The major changes had been made that had turned an ocean-going sailing vessel into the practical Western Rivers

[1] The definition given for paddle wheel in *Webster's New International Dictionary* (1934) reads: "A wheel used to propel a steam vessel, originally having long paddles arranged about a hub or shaft end, but later having floats or boards on its circumference, and revolving in a vertical plane parallel to the vessel's length."

[2] The early evolution of the steamboat is covered in James Thomas Flexner, *Steamboats Come True: American Inventors in Action* (New York: The Viking Press, 1944); see also Gould, *Fifty Years on the Mississippi*, pp. 3–10, and Purdy, "Report on Steam Navigation in the United States," *Tenth Census* (1880), IV, *Transportation by Water*, pp. 659–62.

side-wheeler. It was by then a shallow-draft, flat-bottomed boat, with boilers and engines on deck and not in the hold as on an ocean-going steamship. Above the boilers, engines, and woodpiles was placed the cabin with its flanking staterooms, and on top of that a pilot house surmounting the officers' cabin. The cargo was carried in the hold where it had to be placed by deckhands in and around the structural timbers that the shallow hull required—the keelsons, longitudinal and transverse trusses, the poles for the hog chains, and the bulkheads. Cargo was also carried on the guards, those huge aprons that were cantilevered out from the hull and that carried the main deck to just beyond the paddle wheels and their housings. The boats young Jim Howard was set to working on were like these; with only minor changes Jim Howard made his name building them.

While the basic technology of the pioneering side-wheeler was unchanged after the decade of the 1830s, continual improvements were made in the hull's construction as well as in the boilers and engines. While the boilers on Howard-built hulls blew up also—the explosion of the *Louisiana* in 1848, described earlier, was perhaps the most spectacular—the output of the Howard Yards attests to something unique about their craft. In the absence of direct evidence, and since extant photographs cannot tell all, it can only be surmised that Howard-built boats did not leak as much, did not vibrate as much, floated with less draft, were faster, or lasted longer. Only the last factor is demonstrable today and must bear the entire weight of explaining the early success of the Yards. As was stated earlier all the boats built by James Howard, including those lost by boiler explosion, ramming, and grounding, averaged a life span of seven years. The life span of all other steamboats on the Western Rivers averaged but five years.[3] Accordingly, a Howard-built boat for the same money would provide a useful life 50 per cent longer than that of most competing boats. Or, with everything else equal between a Howard boat and one built elsewhere, a $40,000 investment with the Howards was the equal of a $60,000 investment elsewhere. A longer life span is testimony enough, perhaps, to explain why the Howard Ship Yards in Jeffersonville survived and grew.

[3] See also pp. 21, 33–34, above.

Not all the boats that Jim Howard built were side-wheelers. In fact, his second hull, the *Black Locust*, was a catamaran with a single paddle wheel recessed in between the twin hulls. It was a practical arrangement for a ferry in that it allowed a reversal of direction without any impairment of efficiency for the wheel and engine. Jim built many like it. The Yards also turned out occasional barges, which were nearly identical to steamboat hulls in those early days and posed no problems in construction. The first stern-wheeler the Howards built was the small *Terrebonne* packet that left the Towhead Island yards in 1850. After the Civil War the stern-wheeler arrangement was built with increasing frequency. Although once again there are no records, patents, or even legends to tell how the Howards helped or hindered the evolution of the stern-wheeler, their records of boats built indicate that they constructed stern-wheelers in compliance with the general trend of demand after the Civil War. By 1880, the stern-wheelers outnumbered the side-wheelers, and a similar trend was found at the Howard Yards.[4]

The change in the Western Rivers steamboat from side-wheelers to a single, stern-mounted paddle wheel was not revolutionary, although it posed certain problems for the builder of the hull. At first the stern-wheeler was a small, light, shallow-draft boat, probably a packet, intended for the headwaters of the Mississippi's tributaries. The stern-wheeler seemed to work better in shallow water than the side-wheeler, which could encounter difficulty and even lose propulsive thrust in a river too shallow.[5] At first, the stern-wheeler used but one engine and consequently a smaller number of boilers. The machinery, accordingly, weighed less than for a comparable-size side-wheeler, but it was, of course, less powerful. It posed problems for the hull builder, however, in that the weight of the machinery was concentrated at the stern, and custom placed the boilers at the bow to catch the natural draft when the boat was under way. Such a concentration of weight on the extreme ends of the hull, where it was least buoyant, aggravated the tendency for the

[4] Appendix A, Table 1, p. 200, and Charles E. Landon, "Technological Progress in Transportation on the Mississippi River System," in *The Journal of Business*, XXXIII, No. 1 (January 1960), pp. 45–46.

[5] Hunter, *Steamboats on the Western Rivers*, p. 85; John H. Morrison, *History of American Steam Navigation* (New York: W. F. Sametz & Co., 1903), p. 245.

middle to "hog-up." This problem was overcome by increasing the strength and number of the hog chains and braces as well as by using internal stiffeners and trusses in the hull. Such efforts, however, contributed to reduce the hull's available storage space. But the advantages of lightness, shallow draft, lower investment cost, lower operating costs, and an extended trading sphere and trading season as well, all combined to make it an economical boat. Thus it shouldered the side-wheeler slowly off the tributaries and finally off the Mississippi itself. It was a slow process, however. River men everywhere, from Mark Twain and John Morrison to Jim Howard himself, sorrowed at its passing, for they all loved the side-wheeler. Stern-wheelers were to them always the "Mosquito fleet" or the stripped-down, economy model that the competition dictated.[6]

It was with the side-wheeler packet that James Howard learned his craft, built the yards, and left his name on the Western Rivers. The elegant side-wheeler which George Pegram ordered in 1870 and named the *James Howard* was admirable testimony to its builder's skill. It was one of the river's true queens, 330 feet long with a beam of 56 feet; only a few others—the *Eclipse*, the *Grand Republic*, the *Richmond*—were longer, and none were ever better built.

The stern-wheeler was for another generation, another job and the result of another environment. So it was when Edmonds John Howard, Jim's only son, took over the Jeffersonville yards when his father died in 1876. Though Ed. J. turned out elegant side-wheeler packets in his father's pattern, such as the *J. M. White* in 1878, *City of Louisville* in 1894, and the *City of Cincinnati in* 1899, his forte and reason for survival were his skill and success in building the stern-wheel packet and then the stern-wheel towboat.

Under Ed. J. Howard's direction the Jeffersonville Yards turned out boats in about the same volume that Jim Howard had attained in the 1850s and then again after the Civil War. In the decade of the fifties an average of nine or ten hulls left the ways each year, displacing a total of about 2,680 tons. In the seventies the number of hulls built increased to an annual average of twelve, with each year's total tonnage approximately

[6] Morrison, *History of American Steam Navigation*, pp. 242, 244. James Howard's preferences have been reported by the Howard family and deduced by imputation from his correspondence in the Howard MSS.

City of Louisville, side-wheel packet launched in 1894. She is shown here at the Howard Ship Yards after her trial run. Built for the Louisville & Cincinnati Packet Company, she had seventy-two staterooms and could carry 1,500 passengers. Immediately after her trial run she made a record run from Louisville to Cincinnati of 9 hours, 42 minutes.

City of Louisville, *lost in the ice at Cincinnati, January 1918.*

City of Cincinnati, side-wheel packet launched in 1899. She is shown here at the Howard Ship Yards new and being towed to mooring. Built for the Louisville & Cincinnati Packet Company, she has been described as "one of the best-proportioned side-wheelers ever built."

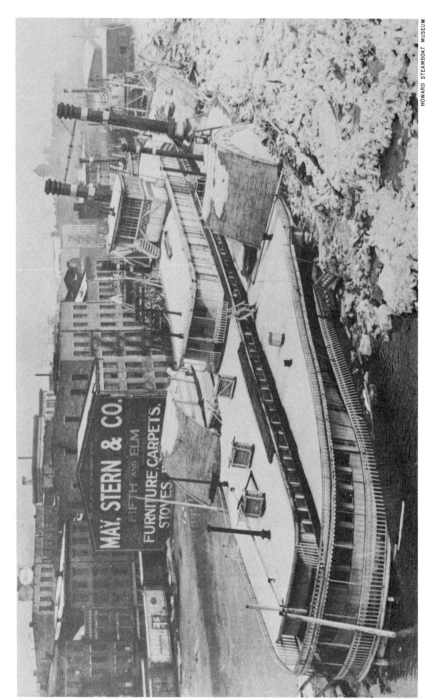

City of Cincinnati, *lost in the ice at Cincinnati, January 1918.*

4,300 at the beginning of the decade and 3,600 at the end. The yards launched at least eleven or twelve hulls annually for the forty years following 1870.[7]

However, the annual tonnage constructed from 1875 to 1915 reflected the shrinking in size of the Western Rivers steamboat during the period. It was a response to the drastic change in the economic role the steamboat was forced to play after the advent of other modes of transportation. Nevertheless, for the Howard Yards, the maintenance of annual output on a scale nearly equal to their best decades, either 1850s or 1870s, in the face of a steadily contracting steamboat building industry is indicative of the Howards' ability to build a better steamboat, whether it was a side-wheeler like Jim built or a stern-wheeler that was the mark of Ed. J. It is possible, then, that if quality of materials and construction allowed Jim Howard to forge so rapidly ahead in his industry, garnering a tenth of the industry's output by 1850, then similar factors must have been responsible for the continued high output by his son. As industry output declined, the Howards' share increased from a tenth to one half or more, and this decline in alternative boatbuilders whom captains and masters could find might have allowed the Howards' greater latitude with a poorer quality boat the result. But at least while wood was the principal boatbuilding material, there is no indication in correspondence or the sparse records of the boats' longevity to indicate that a Howard-built boat was ever anything but the best built on the rivers.

For three quarters of a century, then, father and son achieved an enviable place in the Western Rivers steamboat industry. They were virtually without peers in the construction of wood-hulled side-wheel and stern-wheel steamboats. A historian could write of the Howards' "reputation of long standing for the excellence of their products."[8]

METAL BOATS V. WOODEN BOATS

WITH such a record in building wooden-hulled boats and barges, it is not surprising that the Howard Ship Yards did not pioneer in the construc-

[7] Appendix A, Table 3, pp. 224–225.
[8] Ambler, *Transportation in the Ohio Valley*, p. 426.

tion of iron or steel hulls. In general, all American shipyards lagged behind the British and continental builders in experimenting with hulls of material other than wood for reasons that were clearly the result of relative resource scarcities in Europe and America. Thus, while an iron-hulled canal vessel was built in Yorkshire, England, in 1777, and an iron-hulled steamer, the *Aaron Manby*, was assembled in London in 1821, the earliest such ship built in the United States was recorded to be the *United States*, constructed in 1838 by the West Point Foundry, in New York.[9] An iron-hulled steamboat, *Valley Forge*, was built by the steam-engine builders, Robinson and Minis, in 1839 at Pittsburgh, and the second iron-hulled steamer on the Western Rivers was assembled at Jeffersonville in 1840. John Laird, pioneer builder of metal ships of Birkenhead, England, sent the material for this hull from England and the *W. W. Fry* was erected within hailing distance of the Howards.[10] The *Fry* served in the Mobile trade until about 1860. There were apparently no other iron-hulled steamers built in the West for commercial service until after 1870, although the United States Navy constructed an iron steam frigate, the *Allegheny*, at Pittsburgh in 1847,[11] and several iron snagboats were constructed in St. Louis.[12]

On the Eastern sea coast, following the strides of the British, iron hulls began by 1870 to supplant wooden ones, particularly for the larger oceangoing steamships. An iron-hull shipbuilding industry began to emerge, centered around the iron works on the Delaware. As the knowledge of building iron ships increased, debate about them spread down the western valleys. Iron steamboats were in the newspapers constantly.[13] Then Captain Boardman had an iron-hulled steamboat built in Cincinnati. Intended for the snag-infested Red River trade, the *John T. Moore* went into service during the season of 1871 and sparked an even livelier debate over iron v. wood.[14] Iron vessels did cost more; some said an iron

[9] *Encyclopaedia Britannica* (1968 ed.) XX, 406–407; Morrison, *History of American Steam Navigation*, pp. 253–54.
[10] Morrison, *History of American Steam Navigation*, p. 254.
[11] *Ibid.*, p. 254.
[12] Hunter, *Steamboats on the Western Rivers*, p. 115; Gould, *Fifty Years on the Mississippi*, p. 357.
[13] Hunter, *Steamboats on the Western Rivers*, p. 115.
[14] *Ibid.*

hull cost double a wooden one.[15] But against the inescapable higher first cost were ranged the minuscule maintenance expenditures. A Federal iron-hulled snagboat, the *J. N. Macomb*, in six years service had incurred annual hull maintenance charges of but $500 for painting. A similar wooden-hulled snagboat would have incurred annual hull maintenance of from $5,000 to $6,000. In addition, a wooden-hulled boat had to be replaced for certain at the end of ten years, whereas an iron-hulled boat could last as long as five to seven wooden hulls.[16] But, of course, in 1871 experience had yet to convince the rivermen that a higher first cost was really less expensive in the long run.

With the inescapable advantages of iron, the practical rivermen had already made their working agreement. They built what were called composite boats, which were simply wooden-hulled boats as before with the bows clad with strong, protective iron plates. Perhaps the practice was a lesson learned in the Civil War. Whatever its source, it was a low-cost attempt to gain some of the advantages of a metal hull. The change to a complete metal boat with keel, frames, and hull plating all of iron or steel was nearly fifty years in the future. For by 1870 it was already apparent to some that the lush days of steamboating were at an end.

The year 1871 saw the peak tonnage of steamboats built on the Western Rivers, with an uneven decline thereafter. With the falling off in demand for boats, yards everywhere in the seventies and eighties faced increased competition for the dwindling number to be built each year. The result was, of course, that anyone wanting a boat could get it built at a low price, lower than ever before certainly. Such price cutting by competitors in wooden-hulled boats reduced the demand for metal hulls.[17] In addition, the small capitalization of most river entrepreneurs meant that the majority could not afford the greater first cost of an iron hull.[18]

The consequence was that only two yards on the Western Rivers were capable of building metal-hulled steamboats during the seventies and eighties. They were not competitors of the Howards then, for in

[15] Gould, *Fifty Years on the Mississippi*, p. 357.
[16] Hunter, *Steamboats on the Western Rivers*, pp. 115–16.
[17] Gould, *Fifty Years on the Mississippi*, pp. 358–60.
[18] Hunter, *Steamboats on the Western Rivers*, p. 116.

truth they were building virtually a different product. Indeed, up until 1881 only one iron-hulled packet, the traditional western steamboat, was built. In that year, however, the firm of James Rees and Sons of Pittsburgh built the first steel-hulled steamboat for use in the United States, the *Chattahoochee*. The total number of metal-hulled steamboats built in the West up until 1882 was but thirty. The Rees firm and the Western Iron Boat Building Company at St. Louis survived and grew on orders from the Federal government for snagboats and on orders from South American and other foreign rivermen.[19]

The first steel hull that the Howards built was the *Josie*, in 1891, a radical departure from the stately, wooden side-wheelers and stern-wheelers the Howards had built up until then. The *Josie* was not only a steel-hulled ferryboat, built as far as the records tell with steel keel, frames, and hull, but she was also a twin-propeller boat. As such she represented but the second propeller-driven boat to leave the Howard Yards. She was followed down the river in a month or two by the steel-hulled stern-wheeler, *Santa Fe*, destined for service in South America. Both the pioneering *Josie* and the *Santa Fe* were small vessels, the *Josie* 74 gross tons and 95 feet long, the *Santa Fe* but 27 gross tons and 65 feet long.

However pioneering the two vessels were for the Howards, or for the Western Rivers for that matter, they were but two small drops in the expanding bucket of American metal shipbuilding of the 1890s. With the advent of steel in the eighties, another revolution in shipbuilding occurred nearly as great as that of the original introduction of iron. For malleable steel could be shaped cold with greater ease than iron. With the use of appropriate machinery, steel significantly lowered the price of steamships. It permitted new hull designs of greater length and capacity, too. Significant improvements in propulsion machinery and boilers followed.[20]

The behemoths constructed on the Atlantic had little in common with the lilliputian *Santa Fe*, except that steel was used and formed in much the same way for both. Of more importance for the Howards was the establishment and rapid growth of a metal shipbuilding industry

[19] Hunter, *Steamboats on the Western Rivers*, p. 116.
[20] John G. B. Hutchins, *The American Maritime Industries and Public Policy, 1789–1914* (Cambridge: Harvard University Press, 1941), pp. 456, 460.

on the Great Lakes. With a total of 6,459 gross tons and but three steel ships in 1886, by 1891 output reached 48,000 gross tons. At that level, the Great Lakes industry began to exceed the peak 1871 output of the Western Rivers builders. Thereafter the Great Lakes industry overshadowed the rivers completely until after World War II. In fact, in the nineties the Great Lakes builders accounted for 60 per cent of the commercial vessels constructed in the United States.[21] Most important, the Great Lakes developments led to the creation of a trained labor force and a steel industry that was accustomed to turning out and forming the frames and plates peculiar to shipbuilding. A flat-bottomed, shallow-draft stern-wheel riverboat was of a relatively simple shape compared to the lakes or oceangoing, propeller-driven ships. But in time the riverboats grew more complex and required compound curves to shroud the propeller that replaced stern-wheels. By that time (the 1920s) the Howards and their competitors found a source for steel with the equipment and skill needed for shipbuilding in Chicago, in Cleveland, and in Pittsburgh. But until that day, the Howards made do with local machine shops and boiler works and in the nineties began the slow change-over to steel. It was so slow, hindered by the economic malaise everyone said hung over the rivers, that by 1906 only 5 per cent of Western Rivers boats were built with hulls of iron or steel.[22]

In the Howard Yards during the decade of the 1890s, steel hulls accounted for but 30 steamboats and barges out of a total of 219 built. The orders were principally for specialized boats such as ferries, snag and survey boats for the Federal government, or smaller towboats and barges for South American rivers. In 1894, however, the Yards contracted to build the *E. R. Andrews* with a steel hull and a conventional stern-wheel and designed to be a towboat for use by the Kanawha and Ohio Transportation Company. One-hundred and sixty-five feet long with a beam of but 32.5 feet and a hold of five feet, the *Andrews* hull and cabin cost $25,000. The machinery was installed by the Frisbie firm in Cincinnati under a separate contract. The first steel towboat constructed by the Howards, her cost was considerably above that for similar size and pur-

---

[21] *Ibid.*, p. 461.
[22] Hunter, *Steamboats on the Western Rivers*, p. 116.

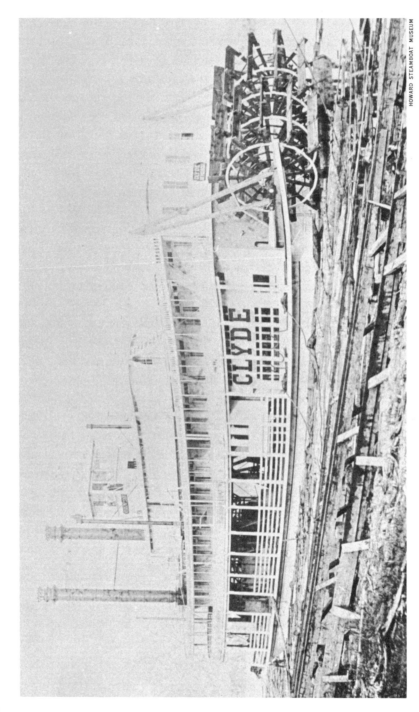

Clyde, stern-wheel packet launched in 1894. Built for the St. Louis & Tennessee River Packet Company, she is shown here at the Howard Ship Yards.

pose wooden hulls. The wooden-hulled *Clyde*, for example, although destined to be a packet, cost but $11,500 for a hull ten feet longer and one foot greater in beam; the *W. T. Scovell*, a wooden-hulled towboat 160 feet long, cost but $12,500, without machinery. For the Howards, as for their competitors, a metal hull at first cost approximately twice as much.

THE DEMISE OF WOOD

THE first steel-hulled packet was a memorable ship. The Memphis and Arkansas City Packet Company contracted with James Rees and Sons of Pittsburgh for a side-wheeler packet in the grand old manner, only she was to have a hull of steel. Rees in turn subcontracted the boat with the Howards. It was then in 1898 that the *Kate Adams* took form on the ways at Jeffersonville. For such a monumental boat, however, the records are sparse. Her cabin cost $11,000; the machinery and boilers were apparently installed by Rees; and the rest of her, the hull, wheels, and outfit, cost $32,750. Her total cost then would have approximated $58,000. At such a price she was twice the cost and more of the *James Lee* which had been launched the year before. Only ten feet shorter, the *Lee* was the equal of the *Adams* in all other respects except that the *Lee* had a wooden hull. Her price? $27,000.

The utilization of steel for Western Rivers steamboats thus had significant economic barriers to cross. As long as wood was readily available and maintained a price advantage over steel, the pace of construction of steel-hulled boats and barges was very slow. At the Howard Yards only one or two steel boats were launched each year until 1912. But the slow pace allowed a careful appraisal of the relative advantages of each material. In small hulls there were fewer gains from using steel than in the ocean-going giants of 2,000 gross tons or more or in the Lakes cargo vessels. Although wooden sailing ships in excess of 2,000 gross tons were built in Maine, with keel lengths up to 300 feet, draft of 25 feet or more, and a carrying capacity of 5,000 tons,[23] the limits of wood construction had been reached, and iron and steel were the only economical solution for larger, lighter, and stronger ocean ships. But in a river towboat of

[23] Hutchins, *American Maritime Industries and Public Policy*, p. 379.

James Lee, side-wheel packet launched in 1897. Built for the Lee Line of Memphis, she later became an excursion boat and was renamed the De Soto. She was lost in the ice in January 1918.

Kate Adams, side-wheel packet launched in 1898. She is shown here new at the Howard Ship Yards. The Howards' first steel-hull packet, she was built for the Memphis and Arkansas Packet Line for the Memphis trade. She burned at the Memphis wharf in 1927 after a long service.

perhaps 150 feet in length, a hold of 5 feet, and a beam of 30, the weight saving gained by using iron or steel rather than wood was of less importance. In a packet of 250 feet, a metal hull would have weighed 125 tons less, floated on a draft six inches shallower, and carried 125 tons more, but by 1910 the days of the packet were numbered. Towboats were the riverboats then, and they were smaller and for pushing not for carrying.[24]

The slow transition also allowed the Howards to acquire a labor force accustomed to building steel hulls. Not the least important was their association with a marine engineer from James Rees and Sons Company. Thomas Dunbar was the superintendent and inspector for Rees when that company contracted with the Howards for the *Kate Adams* in 1898. After that he was variously a superintendent or consulting engineer for the Howard Ship Yards for the next twenty-two years. J. M. Sweeney was also employed as an engineer during the period. In addition the Yards were able to explore working arrangements with several iron and steel fabricators, using the Marine Iron Works in Chicago in 1904, the Portsmouth Steel Company at Portsmouth, Ohio, for a ferry boat in 1910, and the Illinois Steel Company predominantly thereafter.

In 1912, five steel boats were launched, and they presaged the days ahead. Two of them were special ferryboats for the Wiggins Ferry Company of St. Louis, a steady patron of the Howards. The other three were towboats for the Mississippi River Commission. The gross sum paid for all five vessels was $256,000. The two ferryboats were exceptionally fine boats, and they received notice in the river-marine press.[25] They indicated then that the Howard Yards were as able to turn out exceptionally designed and built steel-hulled craft as they had always done with wood. The Howards were ready, willing, and able to build in steel. The demise of wood hulls now depended on other factors.

Back in the days when Jim Howard was first struggling along, he got his lumber from the knolls and river bottoms of Clark County, Indiana, or the neighboring country in Kentucky. Then in the seventies he began to buy from lumbermen in Pennsylvania along the Allegheny

[24] Hunter, *Steamboats on the Western Rivers*, pp. 115–16, 653.
[25] *Waterways Journal*, April 2, 1912.

River; some white pine came from the Clarion River. The Kanawha and Big Sandy river banks provided the hardwood needed until the very end; but good, knot-free pine began to be scarce and orders were sent as far as Alabama, Georgia, and Florida by the end of the century. In 1902 a carload or two of lumber from the state of Washington came in. Then came World War I with its inflation and increased demand for wood—hardwood, soft wood, any would do—and by 1915 Southern pine had increased 40 per cent in price. The impact on boat building was immediate, for in 1910 tank steel for boats was $35.10 per ton. By 1915, it had increased but 7 per cent.[26] Virtually overnight, then, wood was supplanted entirely by steel. In 1916 only one wooden hull was launched; in 1917 one 60-foot wooden-hulled towboat. The last wooden hulls to leave the Jeffersonville ways, save for some motorboats and a barge, were the towboat and a dozen barges for the Kentucky Rock Asphalt Company in Louisville in 1918. All were but ninety feet in length. For commercial use, no one mourned the passing of wood; steel was simply superior. In fact, the steel-hulled *A. Baldwin*, launched by the Howards in 1905, served as a ferryboat until 1958, and still floats at the levee in New Orleans. So do countless other Howard-built steel hulls twenty to forty years old. All the wooden hulls have by now left their bones on the bottom of a river or are bleaching gray on a bank.

The Last Packet

The stern-wheel *Cape Girardeau* went down the ways in 1923. She was built for the Eagle Packet Company of St. Louis. Steel-hulled, of course, 210 by 38 by 6.5 feet, she required a crew of forty-two, her engines developing 900 horsepower. Her significance lay not in her specifications but in the fact that she was the last packet ever built by the Howards. Her life as a packet, that glorious combined passenger and general freight boat of the West, lasted a dozen years. In 1935 she was bought by the Greene Line, her name changed to the *Gordon C. Greene*, and she was converted into a strictly passenger boat. Later, for a time, she served as a

---

[26] U.S. Bureau of the Census, *Historical Statistics of the United States Colonial Times to 1957*, pp. 123–24, 316–18.

floating museum and restaurant, gracing the levees in Florida, at New Orleans, and at Hannibal. She ended her days by sinking near the Eads Bridge in St. Louis in 1967. Change came to the rivers. But no change made so visible a mark as that of the change from genteel packets to the snorting towboats laboring antlike with a tow far larger than they.

TOWBOATS

JIM HOWARD built barges from the first. The *Natches* and *Hard Times* were launched at Madison in 1837. But the first Howard-built boat actually labeled a towboat was not launched until 1877, when the *Delner* hit the Ohio. She was an elevator boat for the Missouri Sand Company and probably not a true towboat as we would use the term today. Other steamboat builders, primarily around Pittsburgh, had built and registered towboats twenty-five years before the Howards. But the Howards' customers were primarily from the Deep South, and they were chiefly interested in packets for passenger and light-freight use. Not until this traffic began to wane did the Howards turn to towboats.

The first captains that ordered a towboat from the Yards were a varied lot. After the *Delner* came James T. Duffy, who ordered three towboats from 1882 to 1885. A few foreign buyers appeared, and a small stern-wheeler sixty-five feet in length went to the Honduras Land and Navigation Company for use in the Ulna River in Honduras. The next year a towboat was sent to Pharr and Williams for the Red River trade. The *E. B. Wheelock* and the *C. E. Satterlee* were labeled towboats when they were launched and registered in 1889, but their owners, the Texas and Pacific Railroad, appear to have used them principally as tugboats rather than as tow or push boats. A few other towboats came down the ways between packets and barges.

The first steel-hulled towboat was the *Santa Fe*, which went to Tabasco, Mexico. But the first boat built with today's familiar, square scow bow and pushing knees was the *Colbert*, built for the Engineer Corps at Florence, Alabama, in 1891. The scow bow was a significant development in the long tows of barges as we know of them today, for it allowed a smoother passage of closely tied together barges. Unlike the finely modeled and V-shaped bows of most steamboats, the scow bow was blunt, rectangular and only slightly angled to push the water down and away from the barge.

Barges began to outnumber packets coming down the ways in the decade of the nineties. In 1903 only twelve steamboats were built, but a total of sixteen barges and other unrigged hulls were launched. A decade later there were eleven barges and floats to five steamer hulls. In 1918 only one steamboat hull was built, but twelve wooden-hulled barges left the ways. Thereafter, steel-hulled barges far outnumber the rigged hulls, be they packet, towboat, or ferry.

Change stripped the Western Rivers steamboat of nearly all its unique features—features that had in turn been the result of its slow evolution from oceangoing ship to riverboat. The lofty smokestacks were lowered when the railroads bridged the Ohio and then the Mississippi. The glorious pineapple tops disappeared, followed by the stained-glass and cut-glass windows—all replaced with more utilitarian materials. Gradually even gilt and fresh white paint were seen less frequently. When the Western Rivers steamboat was no longer the packet but the ubiquitous towboat, even the guards were reduced to a narrow, protruding rub rail. Of course, they served no guarding function for the stern-wheelers as they had for the side-wheelers, but tradition was strong and guards had appeared on stern-wheelers, too, for a time. But a letter to Ed. J. Howard in 1898 pointed out that guards were no longer being used, and they, too, disappeared. Up in the cabin, except for the line boats between Louisville and Cincinnati or St. Louis and New Orleans, the elegance of the eighties gave way to practical plainness. The sumptuousness of board and bar likewise evaporated.

PROPELLERS

THEN another change began. Small boats left the Howard Yards with no visible means of propulsion, once they were afloat. Only the "chuffing" of the steam engine's exhaust and the quiet roiling of the water marked these craft in their departure. The majesty and awe which the mighty paddle wheels had evoked was displaced by a deeper mystery for the uninitiated. A propeller lay buried in turbid water, and it worked most efficiently unseen.

The propeller was a technological improvement over the paddle wheel. But once again, as with the metal hulls, the initial margin of superiority for use on the unimproved Western Rivers was small, so small as to delay the use of propeller-driven craft on the rivers for fifty to seventy years after they were first introduced on the ocean and the Great Lakes. Although the Howards had built a propeller-driven craft in 1868, the *Trade Palace*, in a letter of April 28, 1871, in answer to an inquiry, Jim Howard pointed out the propeller's disadvantages for river use. It needed deeper water than a paddle wheel. Propellers created excessive vibration, he said, and the smaller, higher-speed engine was prone to more breakdowns. For those reasons, as well as a higher construction cost, he counseled against a propeller-driven boat at that time.

The troubles that plagued the Confederate gunboat, the *Arkansas*, typified some of the troubles of propeller-driven riverboats. The *Arkansas* was the Confederate fleet on the Mississippi after the fall of New Orleans and during the battle of Vicksburg. The crude hull was equipped and armed literally in the backwoods of Greenwood and Yazoo City, Mississippi, with improvised materials and inexperienced men in about five weeks' time. She was powered by two steam engines in the hold driving two propellers and had a speed of perhaps seven or eight miles an hour in slack water. While she handled herself well enough in running through the Union fleet above and below Vicksburg, on the subsequent trip from Vicksburg to Baton Rouge her engines began to balk, resulting in the ship's grounding out of control. Hastily repaired, the engines were in operation in time for battle despite a broken wrist pin, but the battle had not begun before the port engine failed, irreparably damaged. With the enemy at hand, the ship was scuttled. Her career had lasted but twenty-three days.[27]

A propeller needed a faster-turning engine than did a paddle wheel. The *J. M. White*'s paddle wheels turned nineteen revolutions per minute, while a propeller would need to turn perhaps ten times as fast. Western engine builders in the nineteenth century were not able to build higher-speed engines at a competitive price, nor were there enough engineers able to maintain them. The builders of steamboat engines were

---

[27] "The Arkansas Saga," in Gosnell, *Guns on Western Waters*, pp. 101–35.

practical mechanics with skill, ingenuity, and enterprise, but once each builder succeeded in building a workable engine, further change seems to have been limited. Built "by guess and by golly" and achieving a measure of creditable, economic performance within the first quarter century of steamboating, few significant changes were made in Western steam engines for the next three quarters of the century.[28] But by the time the rivers could use propellers in the twentieth century, the engines were available.

Other factors limited the use of propellers in the first century of the river steamboat. The rivers were shallow, and the boats were of shallow draft as a result. The size of a propeller would thus have been strictly limited. The result would have required an even faster turning engine to achieve the same propulsive thrust. A paddle wheel, on the other hand, could transmit increased power simply by increasing the length and width of the buckets without the necessity of increasing the engine's speed or increasing the depth of the paddles' immersion. A propeller under water was subject to damage by the flotsam of the river as well as the mud and sand of the shallow bottom. If damaged, repair required a dry dock or a marine railroad. So a paddle wheel could be more easily serviced, and with a stern-wheel the likelihood of damage was significantly reduced anyway. Consequently, the paddle wheel reigned supreme for nearly a century. But when sizeable craft with propellers began to leave the Howard's ways and those of their competitors, it marked a significant change in Western Rivers steamboating. Not only had technology improved, but the river, too, had been changed, for the river depth was increased by the canalization of the Ohio and the Mississippi.

So propeller-driven steamboats slid down the ways at Jeffersonville. Experimental and small in the nineteenth century, like the *Trade Palace* in 1868, the *Wash Gray* in 1879, and the *Josie* in 1891, the *Inco No. 1* in 1915 with its four screws and hint of lower costs served notice to the rivers that propellers were to be the means of locomotion thereafter. In 1920, the Howards won the contract to build three tunnel-type propeller-driven towboats for Warrior River service (the *Cordova*, the *Demopolis*, and the *Montgomery*, the latter launched in 1923). The tunnel-type of

[28] Hunter, *Steamboats on the Western Rivers*, pp. 175–76.

hull design was the best adapted for river use, for it allowed a shallow-draft hull to shroud the propellers within a tunnel. At rest, the large propellers were not all submerged, but once under way water flowed to them and excluded air so that a larger propeller could be used. A larger propeller, could, of course, turn at a slower speed and still transmit the same power; so the tunnel arrangement allowed the maximum propulsive thrust per inch of draft. The tunnel-type hulls first appeared in the nineties, and once the rivers had the depth, they came to be the predominant type on the river. The Howards built them, too—not the first, but among the best after the refinements in design and the depths of the rivers increased.

Only one more change remained to transform the steamboat into today's towboat and that was to replace the boilers and steam engine with an internal combustion engine. The Howards built some of these craft, too, commencing with a small freight boat for the Cumberland River in 1905. Only 90 feet in length and measuring 34 gross tons, the *White Oak* was propelled by a gas-driven screw. The largest such vessel the Howards built was undoubtedly the self-propelled barge named the *Inco No. 1*, built in 1915. This boat, powered by four early marine oil engines with propellers, was 240 feet in length and had a gross tonnage of 1,473, which made it the equal of the *Rob't. E. Lee* in capacity, if not in speed. The famous racer was able to make twenty miles per hour at times, but the *Inco No. 1* made it upstream in June 1916 at but four miles per hour with a load of 1,000 tons.

Steam remained economic until after World War II when fuel costs and labor costs finally tipped the scales in favor of diesels, which were better able to drive a propeller than a paddle wheel.

From the side-wheeler *Hyperion* with its crude steam engine to the *Costanzo* with its diesel-powered propellers, the Howard Ship Yards of Jeffersonville spanned a century with the rivers and, like the water that crossed the Falls of the Ohio, the change was continual. Nothing remained the same for long.

Letters and Contracts

CHAPTER VII

The Flood of Changes

OUT IN THE YARDS, change was slow and imperceptible from day to day, like the old Ohio on an August afternoon. Even when the river was on the flood, the creeping waters might not seem to rise at all as they stole across the flats inch by inch, and from one minute to the next it might all look the same—just the Ohio a little more muddy and riled up than usual. But if you chanced to look away, or tend to your ploughing, your sawing, or your whittling, the next thing you knew you'd be standing in the Ohio. And change was all about you. The seasoning logs would be bumping up the ways. A willow tree would be slowly submerged, then slowly roll over and over, limbs a-waving. The newly launched hulls took on life and jealous airs as they rudely shoved their neighbors and tugged at their moorings, snapping one now and then. And when such a flood came, all that could be done was prepare for it, endure it, and then go back to work just the same even though everything was changed. But some floods came unannounced. They often wrought the greatest change.

In a decade James Howard could not have seen much change, except hard times give way to good. But in a quarter century, or in forty-two years, the flood of change and his part in it had inundated the whole Valley. His son, Ed. J., in a day or a year knew only that another boat had left for Bayou Sara and a new keel had been laid. But he, too, with the focus of age could see the change that the flood of steamboats had

Howard Ship Yards in foreground during 1913 flood, with Edmonds J. Howard's home in the background.

wrought. He could see that flood recede—not day to day but year by year. And life in the Yards went on, some would say miraculously, within earshot of different whistles, different exhausts.

The women across Market Street, if they gave a thought to sounds other than their infants' crying, could have heard in a decade the chirping, caulking mallets give way to the staccato rivet guns. Or in the lull between launching and keel laying, perhaps they heard a new sound that forecast a new flood of change—a sound difficult to transcribe into words. For how would one fully describe in words the sounds of a typewriter? But typewriters appeared and they foretold a change as great as the first screw propeller or the first little steel hull had. And that change, too, crept slowly and unrelentingly down the Valley, covering all within a certain high-water mark. There were some who changed with it and there were some who did not.

The pigeonholes in the old roll-top desk could hold a typewritten letter as well as a hand-written one. But the old letter copybooks were closed once the Howards bought a typewriter and hired a typist at the turn of the century. Within the old copybooks had been recorded through fire and flood, in the dim ink transferred from the originals, the letters the Howards had written in a fine, bold style. Therein was held unchanged John C. Howard's displeasure with his nephew, Ed. J., as well as his feelings on Captain Cannon's buying carpeting on credit. Therein were recorded the character, determination, dreams, and defeats of the Howard clan which built steamboats. In 1885 typewritten letters first appeared in the files. At first only the legibility of a letter appeared to change, but in a score of years or so, an era had closed as surely as the covers of the old letter copybooks.

Jim Howard obtained his first contract by talking with Captain Leonard of Apalachicola. That talk gave birth to the *Hyperion* and the Howard Ship Yards. Subsequent boats were built as a result of conversations, too, and as likely as not only a handshake and a steadfast gaze closed the deal, built the boat, and paid for it. The era and these men were characterized by integrity, simplicity, and action.

As the Yards prospered in the 1850s and the Howard name spread down the river, inquiries for boats arrived by letter, delivered either by the post office or a passing steamboat captain. The letter usually stated that the writer wanted a new boat to carry a certain trade, say cotton from Memphis to New Orleans. Jim Howard immediately knew a deep-draft side-wheeler was what was needed and he would reply accordingly. For example, he penned the following in 1854:

> Sir:
>
> We will build a steamboat hull of the following dimensions, say 200 ft. straight keel, 35 ft. floor, 38 ft. beam and 8 ft. hold with good substantial hog frames, for the sum of twelve thousand dollars. Payments: one-half cash and the balance in good New Orleans acceptances at 4, 6 and 8 months.
>
> *Respectfully,*
> D & J Howard

James Howard had all the information he needed when he knew the river, the cargo, the man. He knew the boat best suited for them, and he built it. It would carry the desired cargo on the designated river with a longer life and at lower cost than almost any other builder's boat in the West. The steamboat owner did not have to specify the size and quality of timbers to be used, nor did he need to check the workmanship. He had made a deal directly with James Howard, and Jim always delivered.

In the plush fifties when the steamboat's fortune seemed at a crest, boatmen and builders could afford to be leisurely and lenient. If one master declined to take a hull once ordered, the builder could manage to dispose of it anyway, and as far as the Howards were concerned, legal action to secure payments, foreclosures, and the like were rare. For example, Jim wrote on October 31, 1856, the following vignette of the era:

> . . . we have a Hull Here that will just suit you for the McRea's machinery. She was commenced for Capt. Applegate but when he bought the Duke he declined building and she is now on our hands. . . We will finish her for the sum of ($10,500) Ten thousand five Hundred Dollars. Terms One half Cash and Balance at 4, 6 and 8 months. Let us hear from you Soon for She is on our Best grade and we are anxious to get her out of the way.

Since two years later the yards launched a larger boat for Captain Applegate, the incident apparently left no rancor and may have been typical of the relaxed business climate between gentlemen in that day.

With orders from the Government, formal contracts were required. Perhaps the first such government contract that the Howards completed was for two survey boats built in 1850. When Federal money ($52,000,-000 between 1866 and 1886)[1] again was being spent for improvement of the Western Rivers, the Howards received contracts for snag boats and derrick boats. In 1880 the Howard Yards won a contract for the side-wheeler, the *Joseph Henry*, from the U.S. Lighthouse Establishment in St. Louis and in 1882 they built a towboat and barges for the U.S. Mississippi River Commission. Each Government boat was built under contract with detailed specifications and government inspectors to insure their fulfillment. But in the eighties, contracts, like typewritten letters, were not yet common.

The candor of the parties to the oral contracts was not solely because steamboats were built for individual proprietors and entrepreneurs. There were several corporations in the roster of Howard customers. The earliest such corporate customer was the Louisville and Portland Canal Company which ordered a dredge boat in 1848. That company had been chartered by the Kentucky legislature in 1825, and while its stock was held only by its directors, a few individuals and trustees for the Federal government in 1848, it was a private corporation in fact until 1874.[2] There were other corporations with hired managers dealing with the Howards. The Anchor Line Company, actually the Memphis and St. Louis Packet Company, incorporated in 1859, was one. The general manager of that line, John P. Keiser, knew the Howards and obligated his company on the basis of a letter a paragraph long because he knew any problems would be taken care of. For example, he wrote on June 4, 1871:

> I forgot to mention to you . . . an error in your guard chains. It is that the middle swivel has 2 nuts instead of one head and one nut or they should be right and left so that both would screw up together or unscrew. As they are now the middle swivel is of no benefit. As you turn it one screws up and the other unscrews, consequently they are of no service. Please rectify it in new boat.
>
> The decks of the City of Chester are scaling badly in consequence of wind-shaken lumber, and the heart of the plank turned

[1] Hunter, *Steamboats on the Western Rivers*, p. 192.
[2] *Ibid.*, pp. 183, 373.

up. Please select the best lumber for forecastle and alongside boilers and if possible turn heart down.

Other corporate buyers of the Howards included the prominent packet companies, the barge lines such as the Mississippi Valley Transportation Company, and the railroads.

CORPORATIONS

THE change from a candid letter to a detailed contract was the result of more than just the typewriter, of course, or even incorporation. Rather, incorporation followed first on the heels of the change in steamboats' fortunes following the fruitful fifties and the decades of the postbellum readjustment. Steamboat ownership by corporations increased from but 6 per cent of the total number of boats in 1860 to 36 per cent in 1880 and remained at the latter percentage through 1900. Partnerships on the rivers declined while boats owned by individual proprietors increased. But, more significantly, the percentage of Western Rivers steamboat *tonnage* owned by corporations increased from but 7 per cent of the total in 1860 to 73 per cent by 1906. Proprietors, on the other hand, owned 25 per cent of the tonnage in 1860 but only 19 per cent in 1906.[3] The larger boats, obviously, were owned by corporations after the decade of the seventies.

The flamboyant days of partnerships and single proprietors on the Western Rivers were the days when the *Ruth*, in 1862 admittedly, ran but six months and earned $100,000 over her cost, or the *Olive Branch's* making $30,000 in one trip to New Orleans.[4] Such days drew speculators like molasses drew flies. In St. Louis, as in Cincinnati or Memphis, it was said that

> [Steamboat men] often speculate just as merchants speculate and not unfrequently negotiate bills of exchange "to raise the wind" or to make ends meet under circumstances that would make a levee merchant blush. I have known a man to purchase a steamboat without a dollar in hand, drop her down to the wharf, stick up his

[3] Hunter, *Steamboats on the Western Rivers*, pp. 311, 632–33.
[4] Key Book, data for 1862. Howard MSS; Hunter, *Steamboats on the Western Rivers*, p. 386.

"shingle" for New Orleans, get a full cargo, step into one of our offices, effect an insurance on his freight list, negotiate a bill of exchange on his agent in New Orleans to pay charges and outfit here, make a successful trip or two, pay for his boat and in sixty days be on the lookout for a similar speculation.[5]

TABLE 11. *Distribution of Steamboat Ownership on the Western Rivers, 1830–1906 (in per cent)*

Year	1 Owner		2–4 Owners		5 or More Owners		Corporation Ownership	
	Number	Tonnage	Number	Tonnage	Number	Tonnage	Number	Tonnage
1830	18.9	14.9	56.8	55.0	24.3	30.1	...	...
1840	17.3	19.6	51.2	48.2	31.5	32.2	...	...
1860	27.4	25.2	51.8	52.3	14.3	15.3	6.5	7.2
1870	23.0	15.9	47.0	40.6	9.6	15.8	20.4	27.7
1880	29.8	19.9	32.2	20.0	2.1	2.1	35.9	58.0
1890	25.8	19.8	38.4	31.5	1.0	1.3	34.8	47.4
1906	47.9	18.8	15.6	8.2	...	...	36.5	73.0

SOURCE: Louis P. Hunter, *Steamboats on the Western Rivers* (Cambridge: Harvard University Press, 1949), p. 311.

These were the men who casually, or flushed with excitement, ordered their boats from Jim Howard by letter. And when the good old days were followed by bad, when the ante for the steamboat game was raised, the marginal players dropped out.

But a raise in the ante did not increase the pot. Incorporation flourished generally after the Civil War as a result of the change in incorporation procedures among the states which, in turn, allowed and resulted from the growth of the railroads and larger industrial enterprise. The limited liability features doubtlessly attracted many steamboat masters who sought its protective umbrella while remaining the sole owner of the boat's stock. Many other steamboat corporations resulted from the owners' reluctant realizations that the river passenger and small freight business required a curtailing of intra-industry rivalry. In this way workable combinations of individualistic owners of packets were made and some survived in corporate form until comparatively late. Such were the

[5] Gould, *Fifty Years on the Mississippi*, p. 729.

Anchor Line, the White Collar Line, and the Lee Line. These corporations were not the ones that initiated the change from letter copybooks to typewritten letters, from letters to contracts. Rather, that change occurred as river traffic came to be towing traffic.

Meanwhile, the journals and daybooks at the Yard's office recorded the changing business arrangements that indicated ownership of the ways. Originally, as related above, in 1834, as far as is known, James Howard built his first boat as a single proprietor. Then together with David Barmore he built the *Black Locust* and the *Tecumseh*. In Madison in 1836 he went into partnership with P. Emerson. In 1846 at Louisville, he joined up with John Enos. But this partnership expired when John Enos died early in 1848, and Jim Howard began again in Jeffersonville in partnership with his brother, Daniel.[6]

The partnership of James and Daniel Howard purchased the land of the present yards from John Zularef of Zurich, Switzerland, and built the boats that built the Howards' reputation. After the Civil War, Daniel retired from active partnership with his brother, only retaining ownership of part of the real estate and living off the annual rent. The Yards at this point were reorganized as the firm of James Howard and Company which was, in fact, a partnership between James, his son, Edmonds J., and James's younger brother, John C. Howard. This firm lasted even after James's death in 1876 when Ed. J. Howard purchased the heirs' share. But, if a few letters in the old letter copybooks are indicative, the remaining two owners were not the smoothest working partners. So, in 1884 on May 10, the daybook numbered 8 on pages 170 and 171 duly recorded the dissolution of James Howard and Company. John C. Howard deeded certain real estate, the circular saw, and planing mills to Ed. J. Howard for a consideration of $3,000. For John's share of the old firm's inventory and other assets, Ed. paid $11,500. Then, the sole owner of the yards, Ed. renamed the firm the E. J. Howard Company, but it was known popularly, simply as Howard Ship Yards whatever the official recorded title the owners chose.

Steamboat men had done their business with a Howard regardless of the partnerships. But as the day of the single entrepreneur on the rivers

[6] Baird, *History of Clark County*, pp. 330–31.

dimmed, as partners were replaced with shareholders, the Howard Ship Yards responded with a change in its form of ownership, too. Doubtlessly the coming of age of Ed.'s sons, Clyde and James E., helped hurry them into incorporating, but the increasing pedantry of steamboat-building contracts and business in general also played a part. And the Howards were dreaming of new boats to be built, new business to be won. They dreamed big! Already the builder of half the Western Rivers' annual tonnage, at the turn of the century the family had even grander ideas. So did some promoters of the day.

The American Rivers Shipbuilding Company

Late in the 1890s files, letters began to appear that talked of marine ways and boat yards. The files filled with letters that complained of lumber prices, and the ignominy of shipping lumber all the way from Washington or Alabama by rail, letters that asked randomly about a "pleasure yahct (*sic*) 65 or 70 feet long," letters that were gloomy about the rivers, letters that were optimistic.

Optimistic was the correspondence of Cave Thompson who was busy gathering support for his new incorporation of the Anchor Line Company and he wrote proudly in January 1904, of the *Wall Street Review* article about it. His letters were especially enthusiastic and helpful about incorporation and stock sales. Pessimistic was the correspondence from the Red River Line as it passed into receivership in April 1904. Then, out of nowhere, there appeared in the files letters on blue stationery —typed—and signed W. W. Hazzard. He wrote of "deals" and "stock sales" and prices for marine ways and boat yards. He wrote from the Union Club in Cleveland and the Pendennis Club in Louisville; he wrote from Wall Street and Pullman cars and he was always about ready to make a deal, a big sale of American Rivers Shipbuilding Company stock. He wrote petulantly in 1902 of how he had been dealing with the owner of the Mound City Marine Railway and had been about ready to close the transaction at a good price when the owner suddenly was approached by another and promptly sold to him. Imagine Hazzard's dismay when the buyer turned out to be Ed. J. Howard himself. These letters merely recorded the birth pains of the first incorporation of the Howard Ship Yards.

Handwritten minutes recorded the pertinent data for the new corporation which filed and received its charter from the State of Arizona on November 24, 1902, at 3:50 P.M. The charter named three directors (they could be increased to fifteen), and they were duly listed as Edwin D. Wheelock of New York, Ed. J. Howard of Jeffersonville, and W. W. Hazzard of Cleveland. The authorized capitalization was to be $5,000,-000: one half common shares of $100 paid-up par value and one half par value cumulative 6 per cent preferred stock. The first meeting of the stockholders was held at 11:00 A.M. on December 3, 1902, for the purpose of acquiring the following property:

Howard Ship Yards in Jeffersonville, Indiana
The Marine Railway, Madison, Indiana
Queen City Marine Railway and Dock Company, Marengo Street, Cincinnati, Ohio
Mound City Marine Railway and Dock Company, Mound City, Illinois

In return for these properties the corporation transferred to Ed. J. Howard 6,500 shares of 6 per cent preferred and 6,500 shares of common, both with a par value of $100 per share. There is no record of any stock transferred or sold to the other directors or, indeed, to anyone else. Thus the Howard Yards in Jeffersonville became the American Rivers Shipbuilding Corporation and Jeffersonville was the home office for an empire of yards and ways from Cincinnati to Mound City.

The next minutes recorded the directors meeting of June 20, 1903, when the corporation acquired the Mississippi Valley Marine Railway and Dock Company in Mound City and the Paducah Marine Railway as well. Ed. Wheelock resigned as a director and James E. Howard replaced him. On June 27, in return for the new properties, Ed. J. Howard was issued additional stock which increased his holdings of both common and preferred stock to a paper total of $1,540,000. Since no other stock was listed as having been issued, apparently Ed. was the sole owner of a corporation generously capitalized on paper. But his investment of property was apparently the only tangible investment made, no new capital having been obtained despite the promotion efforts of Wheelock or Hazzard.

How realistic was the capitalization? Not very. The revenues of the branches are not known, and they would have been much smaller than the gross receipts of the Jeffersonville Yards inasmuch as only repair work was generally done there. The Jeffersonville Yards in 1902 had total recorded sales of $174,492. This was a representative revenue figure over the next decade and a half. The total assets for the Jeffersonville Yards are not truly known, but in Daybook 9, a list of monthly balance sheets shows total assets for January 1, 1894, of $201,285.79 and for January 1, 1895, of $179,656.93. No other indication of the financial size of the Yards has been uncovered, but these sparse entries would indicate that stock for par value of $1,540,000 was overstated and the total authorized capitalization of $5,000,000 was ambitious to an extreme. But it was an era of optimism, often wild promotions, and speculations. And Ed. apparently sought to combine yards so as to limit competition on repairs and expand to meet his competition in construction from the vigorous Dravo Corporation and James Rees and Sons Company in Pittsburgh as well as firms in St. Louis and Dubuque, Iowa. If so, it was a plan grandly conceived but never consummated.

THE HOWARD SHIP YARDS COMPANY

ACCORDINGLY, the minutes record the next meeting on December 30, 1903, which wound up the affairs of the American Rivers Shipbuilding Corporation. Its assets were transferred to the new, Indiana-chartered corporation entitled the Howard Ship Yards Company for a consideration of $1.00. The capitalization of the new corporation was $200,000 with 118 shares to Ed. J. Howard, 40 shares each to Clyde and James E. Howard, and one share each to James H. Armstrong and James W. Baird. W. W. Hazzard's name was missing, as a director, a stockholder, an officer, or even as a correspondent. His name next appeared in the correspondence files after his death in 1916 when a note of his countersigned by Ed. was taken to court to secure payment. Thus, the Howard Ship Yards first bid for survival in the emerging world of big business ended and it remained still a company of men, all Howards, who built steamboats.

At W. W. Hazzard's death from influenza in January 1916, the

Cleveland *Plain Dealer* noted only that he lived at 79th and Euclid Avenue (a fashionable neighborhood then), sold real estate, and was buried in Riverside Cemetery. There was no mention of the American Rivers Shipbuilding Company or of his interest in marine ways and shipbuilding.

THE *Inco No. 1*

STEAMBOAT men continued to deal directly with a Howard whether by letter, by contract, or by a casual conversation. Yet the flood of change inched up the Howard ways and inundated the Yards, the office, and even Ed.'s red-brick walled mansion. Corporations, hired managers, contracts came on apace, legibly typed. By 1915, changes from but a decade earlier were everywhere evident. Thus, on October 12, 1914, Daybook 9 laconically notes a new boat for the Louisville and Cincinnati Packet Company; initially a "telephone contract for $4,350," it was followed by a typed document listing such minutiae as "3,610 lbs. of wheel and other chain, bolts, ect. (*sic*) as per list; cost 5¼ cents per lb."

The following page, 427, in Daybook 9 in some fourteen lines compressed the events and contract that signaled the end of the grand old days—with fireworks. The files of typed correspondence and replies began to refer to the Inland Navigation Company early in 1915. By June, a contract appeared.

> This contract entered into this day, June 7, 1915, between the HOWARD SHIPYARD COMPANY of Jeffersonville, Indiana, hereafter called the builder, and the INLAND NAVIGATION COMPANY, of Wilmington, Delaware, hereinafter called the owner.
>
> The owner is desirous of having built for him a steel barge 240 feet long, 42 feet beam, six feet depth, and one-half foot camber, as per general design prepared by John H. Bernhard, and attached to this contract.
>
> The builder is agreeable and able to build such barge.
>
> Now, therefore, the following agreement is reached between said parties. . . .

The barge, the company, the man differed from the usual run of the river. The barge was of generous dimensions, larger than the usual hull of 1915.

Inco No. 1, diesel-propelled barge launched in 1915. Built of generous dimensions on order of the Inland Navigation Company of Wilmington, Delaware, she was equipped with a crane for loading and unloading cargo. She is shown here at the Howard Ship Yards.

It was a size equal to a Mississippi River packet, say the *Peoria* launched in 1913. In fact, the ways had not carried that large a hull in any quantity for over a decade. It was a typical barge hull, too, having a blunt scow bow rather than the finely modeled bow of a packet. But it was to be self-propelled, not by steam with machinery taking up hull and deck space, but by four diesel engines located in a small compartment at the stern with the oil tanks tucked in the bottom. Not only that, the barge was also to have covers built on deck over the holds and so arranged that over these side-opening hatch covers could pass a crane capable of unloading the holds and setting the cargo down on the wharf alongside.

It was unusual to be sure, but in many ways it made sense. Self-propelled by diesels, it gained considerably more cargo space. The *Kate Adams*, for example, built of steel in 1898 with similar hull dimensions but as a grand old packet measured only 595 gross tons compared to 1,473 for the Inland Navigation Company's barge. Of course, the covers over the hatches added some eight feet of enclosed space to the hulls, but then portions of the *Kate Adams's* main deck were covered, used, and measured for cargo, too. All in all, the barge could carry much more than the self-propelled, packet-type riverboat.

Not only was it designed to carry more, but the barge was self-loading and unloading. A packet, of course, could carry some freight on the forward or aft portions of its main deck and these areas were easily loaded, but its greatest carrying capacity was usually the hold where the internal structure of the hull, as well as the machinery and boilers on the main deck, seriously impaired loading except by use of highly flexible carrying units—such as roustabouts. Thus, the Inland Navigation Company's self-propelled barge smote at two shortcomings of the typical Western Rivers commercial boat.

The ideas for this unusual craft sprang from the imagination of John H. Bernhard. A Dutch engineer, he was able to draw on the West European experience with waterways where self-propelled barges and small, family-operated boats are still extensively used for inland transportation. Rather than trying to speed up packets to compete with railroads, or instead of concentrating on the transport of bulk commodities in strings of barges, he conceived of the self-propelled, self-unloading barge as a profitable way of tapping the Mississippi and Ohio waterways. He succeeded in getting backing. He picked the Howard Yards as the place for constructing his barge. But the ink was scarcely dry on the contract before trouble commenced.

The Inland Navigation Company had inserted a time clause in its contract anticipating completion in about ninety days with the barge ready to operate on the river for the fall trade. But the plans for the barge submitted by Bernhard were faulty, or at least indicated potential weak spots which were pointed out, re-engineered, and the changes then incorporated in the barge. The steel for the barge was being fabricated and molded by the Illinois Steel Company in Chicago. Any change would have taken time, but Bernhard procrastinated on some important changes. One, for example, concerned the structural integrity of the barge itself with the Howards wanting to reinforce it with the Western Rivers hog chains and posts. This was not acceptable to Bernhard; indeed it brought forth a sharp retort of how the old river ways must be changed. But steel had been already fabricated and shipped only to be sent back for modifications. Another vexing change at the end was needed when it was found that the diesel engines' vibration caused the riveted tanks to leak so that they would not pass inspection. Ed. Howard noted as they installed welded tanks that "I tried to tell him all along." And so it went.

The barge, named the *Inco No. 1*, was launched on November 16, 1915, and left the Yards on April 5 the next spring. A friend noted in a typed letter in July of that year that he saw the *Inco No. 1* on the Mississippi making about four miles per hour with 1,000 tons.

But the letter of the original contract had not been fulfilled and the Inland Navigation Company filed suit to recover boat earnings and damages in June 1916. The matter was not settled until May 19, 1920, when the management of the Howard Ship Yards settled out of court with the representatives for the by then defunct Inland Navigation Company.

The *Inco No. 1* ultimately was sold and shipped to Europe.

The *Minnesota*

PAGES 428 and 429 in Daybook 9 contrast significantly with the preceding pages, for the *Inco No. 1* was followed down the ways by the *Minnesota*.

Minnesota, steel-hulled, stern-wheel passenger boat launched in 1916. Built for the Drs. Mayo of Rochester, Minnesota, for a pleasure craft, she later became a towboat and then was converted into a storehouse at Joliet, Illinois.

In response to a telegram early in October 1915, Ed. Howard took passage for St. Louis where he went aboard the steamer *Oronoco*, a pleasure boat of the Drs. Mayo of Rochester, Minnesota. He had been summoned by Dr. William Mayo to consider a plan to build a new steel hull 145 feet long with a beam of 34 feet and move the cabin of the wooden-hulled *Oronoco* onto it, using even the old engines, light plant, boilers, etc. But after the initial conference and exchange of letters, even after the price was set and agreed upon, Ed. J. succeeded in persuading Dr. Mayo that a whole new boat would serve his needs better. Appropriately, the general plans for the cabin were sketched on a scrap of paper, the overall dimensions written in the daybook, and a good round figure of $30,000 agreed to on November 13, 1915. On these two pages were listed all the specifications and details Ed. Howard needed to build a steamboat.

The Mayo's boat, the *Minnesota*, was virtually the last Ed. J. was ever to build in the grand old manner. World War I with its Federal regulation of transportation hastened the change to typewriters. Ed. grew old and suffered a stroke. His boys after 1916 gradually took over the Yards, and when Edmonds J. Howard died on January 20, 1919, another era ended. The flood of changes obliterated all but the highest and mightiest marks of the old steamboating days. But yet, the Howard Yards in Jeffersonville continued to launch boats and barges.

James E. Howard (1875–1956), son of Edmonds J. Howard and the last owner of the Howard Ship Yards.

The
Wet
Phoenix

CHAPTER VIII

A CHANGE IN COURSE

CHANGING THE watch on board a ship under way may be a prosaic procedure, with just a quiet change in the hands on the wheel and in the eyes watching the gauges, or it may be formal and dramatic. At the Yards after Ed. J. Howard died, his sons, James and Clyde, simply and without fuss tackled their own old tasks and new ones besides. Instead of consulting their father with problems and plans, they now consulted each other. So the helm changed hands in 1919.

A change in course was soon to be made, but first the unfinished odds and ends of business that Ed. J. left had to be tended to. The revenues of the Yards had declined during the previous decade and the company was in a vulnerable position by 1919. From gross revenues for hulls launched in 1914 of $184,091, the company skidded to revenues of but $46,650 in 1917, $39,076 in 1918 and none in all of 1919.[1] There had been undercurrents of problems and trouble in the Yards for the past five years or so but nothing came of them, probably out of deference to Ed. J. Yet at his death, Clyde and James Howard found creditors proceeding in court against the Yards.

There had been several financing plans and talks of selling in the correspondence files after the end of the grand American Rivers Shipbuilding Corporation. When the trouble over the *Inco No. 1* com-

---

[1] See Appendix A, Tables 1 and 4, pp. 193–221, 226.

menced in July 1915, originally perhaps but a matter of personalities and differing business backgrounds, several people took the opportunity to give their opinion of the Yards, business potential, and personalities. Thus, one anonymous and disgruntled riveter wrote Bernhard of slipshod riveting and substandard inspections. This was subsequently disproven, and letters of that nature were rare in the Howard files, but one anonymous letter probably indicated a simmering kettle of other troubles. A consulting engineer for the Howards at the time, J. M. Sweeney, pointed out some of the troubles in a penciled letter to Clyde in September 1915. In essence, Sweeney felt that the Yards needed an injection of about $250,000 capital, to be spent on maintenance, modernization, and installation of more of their own steel fabricating facilities to reduce their dependence on such distant suppliers as the Illinois Steel Company in Chicago or other fabricators the Howards used in St. Louis or Pittsburgh.

River shipping had reached its nadir and bank attitudes toward river shipping and building were conservative, cautious, and penurious. In 1916, though, Clyde and friends of the Howards believed that they had secured several war contracts with a potential of two to three million dollars in gross revenues. With this business backlog, Clyde and Sweeney approached a Mr. Hone about selling the Yards. He was given the terms for purchase of $100,000 in cash, $300,000 in bonds and $300,000 in common stock for the Howard's interest. But nothing came of it after the war contracts were let to others.

Overhead was cut in several ways. In Mound City, Illinois, the Mississippi Valley Marine Railway and Dock Company was dissolved on March 21, 1918, since there was no longer enough shipping to warrant its continuance as a repair yard. The Cincinnati ways had been closed before, though the machinery was not sold until November 1919, when Dr. J. F. York bought it for $3,000. But when the payment for the *Inco No. 1* was held up from 1916 to 1920 and there were no contracts for boats in 1918, the company found itself in an illiquid condition. The Ripley Boat Company of Grafton, Illinois, and Rohan and Son of St. Louis initiated civil proceedings which James and Clyde had to attend to after their father's death. That trouble was settled out of court for $7,000 in March 1919. Apparently, though, there were still other bankruptcy proceedings or suits which were not dismissed until early in December

1919. The company was granted an extension on its income tax in March 1919, too. But while all these matters large and small were being tended to, the third generation of boat-building Howards were taking over the helm of the Howard Ship Yards in Jeffersonville.

James and Clyde quickly put their own mark on the Yards. They started with a bid for three tunnel-type towboats for the Warrior River to be let on March 11, 1919, by the Inland Waterways Corporation of Mobile. When opened, the successful bid of $411,000 was from the Howard Ship Yards and Dock Company. James was vice-president and buyer and Clyde the secretary and treasurer. The chair of president remained vacant.

Clyde was positive about the company he wanted, even down to little details—such as ordering the company which supplied the gauges for the boilers to imprint the Howard name upon them. A little matter, but one that identified a Howard-built boat again. His grandfather's boats had been distinctive, beautiful, and finely modeled. River men knew a Howard-built boat whenever they saw one and such distinction —product differentiation—was the source of the Howards' success then. In a day of contracts and building to the designs and specifications of others, who built the boat was almost of no consequence to all but those who built the boats and hoped to survive. So the Howard name on the gauges and the successful Howard bid for the new Warrior River towboats were ways of announcing to the world that the Howards were still in production, still building steamboats.

THE TUNNEL-STERN TOWBOATS

THE *Cordova*, the first of the boats for the Warrior River, slid down the ways April 17, 1920. She was a steel towboat 140 feet by 28 feet with an 8-foot hold. New, unique at the time, she was a foretaste of boats to come. She was even, perhaps, twenty years ahead of her time. What made the *Cordova* new, along with her sister ships, the *Demopolis* and the *Montgomery*, was her system of propulsion. Compound, reciprocating, steam engines of 400 horsepower each turned propellers as tall as a man. More importantly, though, was the hull design surrounding the propellers and guiding the flow of water to and away from them. A

Cordova, tunnel-type, screw-propelled steam towboat launched in 1920. Built for the Inland Waterways Corporation of Mobile, she and her sister ships, the Demopolis and the Montgomery, forecast the re-emergence of the Western Rivers as commercial arteries.

tunnel in effect, the result was an increase in propulsive thrust from a given shaft horsepower engine. Additional beneficial effects were an increase in rudder response due to the increased hydraulic pressure of the restricted and directed water flow and an increase in power available on a given draft. Or put another way, the *Cordova's* design foretold the end of the paddle wheel, be it on the side or stern of a shallow-draft hull.

It was not solely a matter of technological breakthrough, for the propeller had been around for years—principally on the oceans and the lakes with their deeper-draft hulls. Nor was it a matter of complex hull curvatures too difficult or expensive to build until the 1920s. A cross section of the *Cordova's* hull a few feet forward of the stern would have resembled the letter "m" upside down ɯ. Steel ocean and river hulls alike had been compoundly curved for years.

It was partly a matter of getting more horsepower out of a given boiler and engine combination, more horsepower per pound of vessel weight. In a measure this was facilitated by using the compound steam engine. The universal adoption of the tunnel-type propeller-driven hull awaited the development of lighter machinery than the complex of steam engines and boilers was ever able to achieve, however, and thus the steam stern-wheeler continued until more powerful diesel engines became available after World War II.

As much as anything, though, the new boats for the Warrior River were the result of the increased and stabler drafts coming to be available then on the Western Rivers. A decade later hindsight showed the wisdom of the *Cordova's* design. Theodore Brent at the Thirty-sixth Annual Convention of the Ohio Valley Improvement Association (1930) noted:[2]

> . . . Each stream presents a different problem—frequently the several divisions of a single stream require special treatment. Power boats of 2,000 indicated horsepower can be utilized on nine-foot streams, but for a stream of six feet or less it is difficult to design a tow-boat which will produce 1,000 horsepower. This disparity is one of the strongest arguments favoring the deeper stream. Heavy power machinery

[2] Ethel C. Leahy, *Who's Who on the Ohio River and Its Tributaries* (Cincinnati: The E. C. Leahy Publishing Co., 1931), p. 789. Brent, at this time president of the Redwood Steamship Line, was engaged in research relating to improvement of inland waterways.

requires a strong, deep hull to support it. The shallower hulls for six-foot streams will not support the greater weight of such machinery. So lighter machinery must be substituted. The propulsive power of machinery is roughly proportionate to its weight. Altogether too much time and energy has, in our judgment, been expended upon the perennial controversy as to the relative merits of propeller versus radial wheel tow-boats. Both have their uses. Unquestionably both are good.

It is doubtful if in river practice there have ever been produced tow-boats which have approached those of the Federal Barge Line on the Lower Mississippi River. These boats, with eleven-foot depth of hold, support twin screws 9 feet 6 inches in diameter, operating in tunnels, propelled by reciprocating engines using steam produced with crude oil as fuel. Over a period of more than ten years these boats have propelled loads, particularly upstream, greater than ever before regarded as possible and much in excess of the expectation of the designers. They are, however, difficult of operation in times of low water and their repair cost is comparatively high. There are sections on the Lower Mississippi where shallower draft radial wheel boats doubtless could be substituted to advantage when the water is low.

As we approach more nearly to the ultimate nine foot channel, we shall expect to see heavy duty propeller boats come into very general use, because of their manifest advantages and economies. For the present both types will be used, and rightfully.

New Channels

The *Cordova* was thus a significant boat not only for the Howard Ship Yards but for the Western Rivers, too. Indeed, the screw-propelled tow-boat with the tunnel-type hull was as great an adaptation of available technology to existing rivers for the third generation of Howards as the paddle wheel and hog-chain-and-brace design had been for old Jim Howard in 1834. The old-time builders such as Jim used to boast of how their steamboats floated on the dew. Because they had to! No other transport was readily or economically available in the mid-nineteenth century except that provided by man's ingenuity and a free, natural waterway. Steamboat men took the rivers as they found them. The Ohio was then a river with a low-water stage from July to November, obstructed by snags, rocks, gravel, and sand bars. The channel meandered and was of variable and uncertain width, though not as bad in this respect as the Mississippi and Missouri. During extreme low water the worst shoals between Pittsburgh and Cincinnati offered but one foot of water and below Cincinnati one would find but two feet over the shallowest bars and rocks. Between the shoals, however, were pools with thirty feet of water or more, but they were short in length in the upper river where the rate of fall was eleven inches or so per mile. From Cincinnati to Cairo the fall was more gradual, four inches per mile, and the pools of easy navigation were correspondingly longer. It was a similar story for the Kentucky, the Cumberland, the Tennessee. Below the Des Moines rapids the Mississippi offered deeper water than the other Western Rivers, but it was a changing channel and infested with snags.[3]

To folk like Jim Howard who had walked from New York to Wheeling it was a wonder indeed to put one's goods on a boat and go like the wind (four or five miles an hour). It beat walking, or packing, or wagoning in terms of physical exertion and in costs. So Jim Howard and his competitors built boats to float and work on shallow rivers. The paddle wheel and shallow-draft hull which gathered its strength from braces and chains were thus man's initial response to the challenge of the Western Rivers.

Attempts to improve the rivers themselves were late in coming and were meager in scope or accomplishment until after the Rivers and Harbors Congress of 1909 and its resultant legislation in 1910. This does not belittle the efforts of Henry Shreve in removing snags, nor James Eads's ingenious removal of bars and shoals by use of dikes, wing dams, and the river current itself. But even the $17,000,000 spent on the Upper Ohio and its tributaries in an attempt to provide a dependable and adequate stage of water was but a piecemeal approach which could only favor local interests. Of what real value was a low-cost navigable waterway if it ended at a shoal just a few miles short of a market? With competition, the savings might well be dissipated in a single trans-shipment. Prior to the Congress' recognition of the rivers' problem in 1910, the millions

[3] U.S. Army, Chief of Engineers, *Annual Report*, 1930, Pt. 1, pp. 1209–1373 *passim*.

spent on improving the channels of the Western Rivers had created but 2,500 miles of six-foot channel. The rivers themselves flowed for tens of thousands of miles.[4]

The *Cordova* was a thoroughly wet phoenix, then, foretelling the re-emergence of the rivers as economic arteries of commerce. The eight-foot hold was the key, for towboats leaving the Yards but a few years before were seldom deeper than six feet and frequently but three feet in depth. They had been meant for shallow and obstructed rivers. Barges became a different breed, too. For small barges, an increase in channel depth, and thus the depth to which they could be safely loaded, was a gratuitous increase in capacity and earning power. Barges which could carry 20,000 bushels of grain on five feet of water could carry three times that amount on eight to nine feet of water.[5] Deeper water was also translated into a saving of time, as a St. Louis barge official noted a tow of barges laden with 3,953 tons of cargo and drawing five feet required thirty-three days for passage from St. Louis to New Orleans. Later with deeper water, 10,000 tons was taken down in but thirteen days.[6] Increased capacity, decreased time for passage with no delays due to a lack of water—all these had to come to pass before the *Cordova* could be translated from the dream to reality. But in 1920 she left the Yards for the Warrior River.

The *Cordova* and the hopes of the Howards rode on the rising pools of water being created on the Western Rivers. Nearly a century after the first dams for slack-water navigation on the Kentucky or the Monongahela, 1920 found half the proposed dams and locks on the Ohio open to navigation—principally on the river above Portsmouth, Ohio. The principal tributaries on the Upper Ohio, the Monogahela and, in particular, the Allegheny were further along in the process of canalization than the main river itself. Nevertheless, the improvement of the Western Rivers with a channel depth of at least nine feet which the Rivers and Harbors Act of June 25, 1910, contemplated was in sight by 1920.

[4] *Ibid.*, p. 1310; *Report of the Commissioner of Corporations on Transportation by Water in the United States, Part I. General Conditions of Transportation by Water* (Washington, D.C., 1909), p. 4.

[5] *Report of the Mississippi River Commission, St. Louis, January 8, 1881* (House Executive Documents, 46 Congress, 3 session, *Document 95*), p. 6.

[6] Hunter, *Steamboats on the Western Rivers*, p. 213.

THE *Cape Girardeau*, the last packet the Howards built, as noted earlier, followed the *Cordova* and her sister ships down the ways. So 1923 gave way to 1924, and 1925 was even better yet—seven towboats and ferryboats were built then, plus seven other hulls and a barge. Trade on the rivers was picking up. The Howard Ship Yards prospered.

At this point Clyde Howard retired and the Howard Ship Yards Company as an operating corporate title was allowed to expire. Business was transacted through the Howard Ship Yards and Dock Company, which had been incorporated in 1912. Originally capitalized with 8,000 shares of $100 par value common stock, by 1925 it had been reduced through successive special stockholders meeting to but 1,500 shares of $100 par value. Annual corporate reports for the company were filed with the Secretary of the State of Indiana whereas the Howard Ship Yards Company reports ceased after 1918. The Dock portion of the title apparently referred to the marine railways and repair yards which Ed. J. originally purchased for the American Rivers Shipbuilding Company in 1903. But after Clyde's retirement from the management of the Yards, Jeffersonville was still the home office for the Madison Ways, under the management of J. L. Heatherington. The Mound City Yards also continued in operation with their old manager, Dan O'Sullivan, reporting to Jeffersonville. The new principal owner and president of the company was James E. Howard. His wife, Loretta M. Howard, served ably as secretary and treasurer of the corporation.

As incorporated partners and managers, Clyde and Jim had brought the Yards a long way. Their father had been successful; he was in fact the epitome of the nineteenth-century businessman complete with a baronial and crenellated mansion. But the steamboatin' that Samuel Clemens knew passed into the mists along with Ed. J. Howard. His sons inherited the name, the trade, the river frontage; from a payroll of $60.00 for just three watchmen in 1919, by June 26, 1925, they hired 145 men with a payroll that week of $3,582.14.[7] The Yards did not resound to the shouts and labors of four hundred workmen as they had in old Jim's days,

[7] Time Book 45. Howard MSS.

Cape Girardeau, steel-hulled, stern-wheel packet launched in 1923. She was the last packet ever built at the Howard Ship Yards. Ordered by the Eagle Packet Company of St. Louis for the St. Louis–Cape Girardeau trade, she was sold to the Greene Line in 1935 for a passenger boat and renamed the Gordon C. Greene.

nor did the ways often again slide twenty-eight craft into the Ohio in a single year. But Clyde and Jim were no less successful. The game and the rules of the game had changed. Clyde and Jim had changed along with them. They survived. They prospered.

THE McALPINE DAM

ON July 14, 1925, the plan for the improvement of the Ohio River was modified by eliminating Dam 40, which was to have been built fifty-two miles upstream from Louisville. The existing Dam 41 at the Falls in Louisville was to be raised to provide nine-foot channel depth all the way to the Markland Dam sixty-four miles upriver. This project added another nine feet to the thirty-foot channel depth in front of the Howard Ship Yards[8] and it was a contributing factor to the reorganization of the company. The new dam when completed would permanently inundate the lower end of the ways, and in order better to adapt the ways for service as a marine railway hauling out boats and barges for repairs, Jim Howard wanted to extend them, firmly anchor them, and protect the bank against erosion. He had other ideas for remodeling the yards, too, and he sought the money for all of these plans in the stock market. At a special meeting of the stockholders on June 15, 1927, the capital stock of the company was increased to $150,000 common stock of $100 par-value and $75,000 preferred stock in shares of $25.00 each. The ledger listed sales through September 1928, of 855 shares of the preferred.

Output continued to grow and 1927 was a peak year—four ferries, a car-carrying barge 285 feet long, and thirty barges under contract for the Corps of Engineers.

Completion of the nine-foot channel from Cairo to Pittsburgh was near. Plans were already then being laid for the dedication. Traffic on the rivers was growing as locks and dams were finished and turned mile after mile of the Ohio into a economical, slack-water system. Fifteen million tons in 1925 grew to nearly twenty-one million tons of commerce by 1929.[9] Steel shipped from Pittsburgh to the Lower Ohio and

[8] U.S. Army, Chief of Engineers, *Annual Report*, 1930, Pt. 1, p. 1311.
[9] *Ibid.*, 1930, Pt. 2, p. 25.

Mississippi nearly doubled in three years. Crude oil began to move in quantity to Louisville and Ashland. And coal, of course, showed a marked increase, constituting fully half the ton-mileage recorded.[10] In all these statistics could be found a Howard-built boat: the barges and work boats for the Engineers who built the dams and locks; the towboats—the *Patricia Barrett* for the common-carrier Barrett Line of Cincinnati, the *Donora* for the Carnegie-Illinois Steel Corporation, *Cop-R-Loy* for the Wheeling Steel Corporation, the *Catherine Davis* for the Island Creek Coal Company; ferry boats; packet boats; excursion boats; little boats; steamboats; diesel boats; diesel-electric boats. The Howard Ship Yards by 1929 had built them all.

[10] *Ibid.*, 1930, Pt. 2, pp. 25, 32.

CHAPTER IX

1929
and
After

THE *Loretta M. Howard*

S o WITH traffic on the rivers assured, with nine-feet of water from
Pittsburgh to New Orleans in sight, and with barges clearly destined
to predominate, the president of the Howard Ship Yards and Dock Company consulted with the secretary and treasurer of the corporation, Loretta M. Howard (his wife), and others and decided to design and build
the most efficient towboat then possible. It would be offered as a stock
design. He would construct it to operate on the Upper Ohio as well as
the Mississippi, for the waters now would be nearly the same. It would
not be a behemoth like the *Sprague* of 1,479 gross tons, for such specialization limited application. Thus, it came to be 145 by 30 by 4.9 feet,
with a gross tonnage of 336. It was a stern-wheeler with simple Frisbie
engines of eighteen-inch diameter and six-foot stroke which developed
600 horsepower. The engines were economical, trouble free, and easy to
operate. It was a good design. It offered adequate power for the day's
barge load. Six hundred horsepower was less than the *Cordova's* 800, of
course, but it was equal to or better than half the towboats on the Ohio.
Jim did not use the propeller-driven tunnel-type hull, for that was yet too
far advanced for use as a stock design. And, apparently, when steam
driven it offered too small an advantage over the more common stern-
wheeler. The new Howard boat was not intended to be radical; rather
Jim reasoned that standardization of the river and the almost universal
use of barges called for the economies of a standardized towboat as well.

Loretta (M.) Howard, steel-hulled, stern-wheel towboat launched in 1929. Built by James E. Howard to be the most efficient towboat possible and of stock design, she was launched by President Herbert Hoover on October 23, 1929.

So he sought to build the best one he could that would appeal to the widest market. If it found acceptance, of course, it would offer certain economies in construction which would give added appeal for prospective buyers.

Jim was as well qualified for drawing up the designs as his grandfather had been. He had attended the Boston Technical Institute (MIT), had worked with several consulting engineers whom the Yards had employed over years, and, furthermore, he had worked in every department of the Yards. He was a captain and an engineer. In fact, his bent for boat building had just won for him a patent for a rudder arrangement that greatly facilitated and overcame much objection to a propeller-driven towboat. The *J. J. Hennen* had been built by the Yards in 1928 for the Hennen Brothers of Louisville, Kentucky. A small boat but 76 by 18 by 6 feet, she was diesel and propeller driven. In their release for the local newspaper at the boat's departure April 2, 1928, the Yards had written (in pencil):

> For work on Western Rivers, particularly in pushing tows, the handling or flanking of a boat is very essential. The old time stern wheelers with their multiple rudders can flank a tow neatly around a bend in the river but some of the later screw-propelled boats have not been able to handle tows with equal facility. Like her predecessor (the *H. S. Hennen*) this boat is of the concave stern type and is a single screw with two rudders forward and one aft of the wheel, which arrangement places all three rudders directly in the wheel current either backing or going ahead. This rudder arrangement for single screw boats is a new design and is patented by Howard Ship Yards. Any one of the three rudders can be replaced without docking the boat, which is a great advantage and timesaver over the older arrangements.

One may wonder why Jim Howard did not choose to build a diesel, propeller-driven towboat. Perhaps if he had the story would have ended differently, but in 1929 of the fleet of about 150 towboats of five gross tons or more then at work on the Ohio and Upper Mississippi, only six were large diesel propeller-driven craft. There were, perhaps, some forty-five smaller craft, smaller even than the *J. J. Hennen*. Many of the smallest boats were gas driven by very low horsepower engines—perhaps only

20 or so. In fact, the only dieselized, propeller-driven craft then extant were those for the old Kelly Barge Line, just incorporated into the American Barge Line of Louisville. The Keystone Sand and Supply Company had two diesel towboats of around 500 to 600 horsepower, but all the rest that were intended to take a tow down the river were still steam and stern-wheel driven.[1]

The plans for the Howards' stock towboat were drawn up. The lines were laid out on the loft-room floor, and the keel was laid on the 20th of August, 1929. The hull was to be completed for launching by October 23, 1929, for on that date the great nine-foot channel project on the Ohio was finished and dedicated at Louisville. President Herbert Hoover addressing the crowd talked of the Old Ohio all had known, and their grandparents, too, and he spoke of the New Ohio and the New Mississippi and the new waterways his government was pledged to complete in order to provide a public way for private enterprises to serve the nation's interests. He even called for the St. Lawrence waterway's completion and flood control for the Mississippi as well; each was but a capital investment in the nation's interest and prosperity. The total cost of these projects each year was small compared with the price of a battleship. He concluded by asserting it a duty to make the nation's great resources available to the people.[2] Then President Hoover went by auto caravan across the new highway bridge to Jeffersonville, east out Market Street to the Howard Ship Yards where he launched the new towboat— the *Loretta M. Howard*.[3] The hopes of many more than just the Howards rode with her down the ways and out onto the Ohio.

The next day the treasurer for the Howard Ship Yards and Dock Company paid the round-trip toll fares for the President's auto caravan across the river. Business is not only great plans and grand events, but petty cash, too. So October 1929 drew to a close.

Slowdown in the Yards

The Yards that year of 1929 launched twenty-one boats. They ranged

[1] Compiled from data in Leahy, *Who's Who on the Ohio River*, pp. 585–98.
[2] Address quoted in *ibid.*, pp. 698–702.
[3] While the boat itself carried the name *Loretta Howard*, it was registered with the Bureau of Customs, U.S. Treasury Department, as the *Loretta M. Howard*.

from the *Loretta M. Howard* and the big tank barges for the American Barge Line 150 feet long to the 30-foot-long wooden motor boats for the Corps of Engineers in Vicksburg. There was even a railroad transfer barge. Late in the year they launched a towboat, the *Wm. Larimer Jones*, for the Vesta Coal Company of Pittsburgh, nearly the same size as the *Loretta M. Howard*. The differences were only a few feet, but it had compound engines of 1,000 horsepower. In 1930 they launched and completed a sister ship, the *Titan*. Still there were no buyers for the *Loretta M. Howard*. Activity in the Yards slowed in 1930.

The year 1931 commenced. A wharf barge for the city of Peoria was begun early in February. The Yard's bid for another towboat for the Inland Waterways Corporation in St. Louis was accepted and that keel laid the last of April. It was only a few feet larger than the *Loretta M. Howard*, but, again, it had engines of 1,000 horsepower.

Another contract from the Corps of Engineers in Cincinnati started work on a maneuver boat. But there was no demand that year for a large, economical towboat. The American Bridge Company, U.S. Steel subsidiary, had 17,700 tons of boats under way, and then the Dravo Contracting Company was building 16,600 tons. The McClintic-Marshall Company in Pittsburgh, a subsidiary of Bethlehem Steel, had twenty-one steel boats under construction, for a total of 22,290 tons. But the smaller yards and the independent ones had a lean year. Total output was half that of the year before.[4] It was cut in half again the following year. The Great Depression in the land left all in shoaler waters, and in Jeffersonville events in the office overshadowed the waning din in the Yards.

From its keel laying in July of 1929 through 1931, the *Loretta M. Howard* had absorbed some $60,000 of the Yards' working capital. It needed, perhaps, another $25,000 to complete it, but in the climate of the growing shortage of credit and equity investment then, a buyer had to be found before Jim Howard could find the means to finish his stock boat. Buyers were hard to find. Those companies able to build were doing so advantageously, but they were the larger corporations with planning and investment horizons of a decade or more. The *Loretta M. Howard*

---

[4] Leahy, *Who's Who on the Ohio River*, p. 565; U.S. Bureau of the Census, *Historical Statistics of the United States Colonial Times to 1957*, p. 448.

had not been designed for them. They could afford to build specialized craft for specific traffic and expect to complete their plans. But smaller towboat owners, common carriers, had to allow for more variation in trades and traffic and could not run the risk of putting all their capital in one hull. For them the standardized towboat would have made sense on the new Ohio. But they were either not encouraged by business events to buy the *Howard*, or else they were unable to do so. The Yards began to feel the pinch of the working capital shortage. Payment on bills was being delayed and operations required an even smoother and quicker flow of funds than before. The treasurer became busier than ever with many trips to secure payments, persuade angry creditors to wait, to compromise. This job she did very well.

DISASTER

THEN disaster. First, the Hennens who so proudly ordered the *J. J. Hennen* were unable to complete payment for her, or even her bills and wages. So Jim Howard had to take her back and seek ways to settle the claims against her so he could get the Yards' money back. It was not a large sum, but it was vitally needed. Then the Inland Waterways Corporation denied payment owing on their towboat, the *Mark Twain*, delivered in February 1932. Apparently the Inland Waterways Corporation feared the threat of suits against the Howard Ship Yards and the *Mark Twain* by her unsatisfied creditors. That sum, too, was not excessively large, but the Yards suddenly found they could not operate. The *Howard*, the *Hennen*, the *Mark Twain*, some of the finest boats, were dragging the company under.

Early in February 1932, though, Jim succeeded in selling the *Loretta M. Howard* to a company newly formed to tow coal for a Cincinnati electric-generating utility. Roy McBride, a river pilot, secured the contract and launched the McBride Lines, Incorporated, in Louisville on the strength of that contract and his experience as a river pilot. Since, of course, he did not have the cash for the towboat and could not get it at a bank, he contracted to buy the *Howard* on time, paying a monthly installment of $2,000 until the agreed-upon price of $100,000 was met. The low price was a concession made in the face of the hard times, and the monthly payment arrangement only meant that the Howards would have to persuade some of their own creditors to accept a partial payment each month, too. But it was a sale, it was income, and the Yards were sorely pressed. By then they could not even find the cash to pay for their customary ad in the *Waterways Journal*.

February 1932 held promise of a better day ahead. The *Mark Twain* was completed and delivered, even if not paid for. The plant could be shut down and overhead reduced. The *Loretta M. Howard* was sold, even if not paid for. A contract for a boat for the Corps of Engineers at Kansas City was awarded to the Howards and the keel for the *Sergeant Floyd* was laid at noon on March 17, 1932.

But it was only the calm in the passage of the eye of a hurricane. The depression deepened in the nation and in the Valley. Gracious Howard creditors found they could no longer be lenient and a few strident ones pressed so seriously for payment that the larger creditors were forced to intercede in order to save their own accounts. Then, late in 1932, a creditors' committee was formed, as in countless other cities and situations in the nation. It was composed of a representative of the Clark County State Bank which had a $15,000 mortgage claim, and other area businessmen with large accounts against the Yards. Members were John B. Funk, vice-president of the Howard Ship Yards and vice-president of the Clark County State Bank, chairman; Oscar J. Braun, manager, General Asbestos and Supply Company, Louisville; Charles T. Hertzsch, district superintendent, American Car and Foundry Company, Jeffersonville; John L. Pratt, treasurer, Neill-LaVielle Supply Company, Louisville; Herman W. Marcus, vice-president, Marcus Paint Company, Louisville; and Herbert F. Boehl, attorney, Jeffersonville. The committee was not punitive in its attitude and it earnestly sought ways to help keep the Howards in operation. Obviously there were few buyers for the Yards in 1932, and the only way any creditor could be paid was by the Yards continuing in operation and making profits.

The only boat built in 1932, the *Sergeant Floyd*, was completed, paid for, and contributed about $21,000 to the company's overhead. The Yards were forced to pass up bidding on a dozen government projects by reason of delinquent accounts, and the Inland Waterways Corporation continued to withhold $20,664 payment on the *Mark Twain* as long as there were liens or threat of liens against her. The *Hennen* lay idle at the bank, too. The creditors' committee sought to secure bids and performance bonds that would allow the Yards to continue in business. Early in 1933 it was planned to pay all creditors one fifth of their accounts on the condition that all creditors relinquished their claims and notes in return for bonds secured by the *Loretta M. Howard*, now the *Dorothy McBride*, and the property of the Yards. The bonds would have been retired in four years.

At this juncture, the Howard Ship Yards and Dock Company was still a viable organization. Current liabilities mounted to over $150,000, but the current assets of the company, represented by the *Loretta M. Howard*, the *J. J. Hennen*, the *Mark Twain*, and the company's own operating towboat, the *Ed. J. Howard*, were at least $125,000. The only loss the company had thus far actually sustained was in the disposal of the *Loretta M. Howard*. Her price of $100,000 was easily $25,000 to $35,-000 less than she might have been expected to bring. But she was sold under duress, in difficult times when many more companies with far greater losses were merely being reshuffled and emerging to produce again. The Howard Ship Yards and Dock Company was attempting to pay all of its liabilities in full.

The balance sheet was that for a sizable firm, even after agreement was reached with the creditors in February 1933. Yet the real asset was not stated—the one hundred-year-old prestige, good will, and experience of the Howards.

The ways lay idle throughout 1933, save for the building of a wood boat but eighteen feet in length for use in towing a ferryboat hull across a small river. It was ordered by the Kentucky Highway Commission, and the Yards had trouble in securing payment. The McBride Lines defaulted on their purchase agreement and, furthermore, allowed $4,000 in liens to be filed against the *Loretta M. Howard*. These the creditors' committee had to pay in order to save her. The National Surety Company, which had issued a bond for the *Mark Twain*, went into receivership and defaulted, of course. The proposed settlement for the creditors had to be revised with the two largest creditors, the Clark County State Bank and Clyde Howard with claims of $31,000, foregoing a cash settlement and accepting bonds instead. The Yards, thus, had fixed interest and prin-

TABLE 12. *Howard Ship Yards and Dock Company Statement of Financial Condition at December 31, 1932*

Giving Effect to Proposed Agreement with Creditors

ASSETS

Current Assets		
Accounts Receivable		
Inland Waterways	$ 20,664.56	
McBride Lines	10,000.00	
Escrow Payment	6,000.00	
Tug *J. J. Hennen*	3,500.00	
Less Cash Settlement		
to creditors	30,446.90	
to Bond Sinking Fund	352.47	
Other Accounts		
Receivable	4,845.11	
Inventories	23,455.19	$ 37,863.81
Fixed Assets		
Land and Equipment		154,028.91
Other Assets		
Steamer *Ed. J. Howard*	3,500.00	
Prepaid Expenses	959.86	4,459.86
Sinking Fund for Bonds		
Bailment Lease on *Loretta M. Howard*		82,400.00
		$278,752.58

LIABILITIES

Current Liabilities		
Due Officers and Employees	$ 1,678.61	
Accrued Expenses		
Interest	2,045.31	
Labor	1,666.83	
Taxes	6,978.06	
Less claim against		
U.S. for damages to		
be applied against		
taxes due	5,203.50	7,165.31
Fixed Liability		
Bonds Payable	78,556.34	78,556.34
Net Worth		
Capital Stock	171,375.00	
Surplus	21,655.93	193,030.93
		$278,752.58

SOURCE: Howard MSS.

cipal payments of $19,639.09 to make in each of the next four years. Once they were retired, the Yards would be free and clear again.

Early in 1934, Jim had noted in a letter to a friend that it took about $60,000 a year to keep the Yards running. Whether he meant it as gross revenues or as a contribution to overhead is not clear, but the Yards had not seen either gross revenues or overhead revenues of $60,000 since 1931. Three years is a long time for either a farm or a shipyard to lie idle. By 1934, with contractual commitments of at least $19,000 a year, the dissolution of the Yards had begun.

Paint began to peel. Unpainted wood began to rot. Steel began to rust, and rusting failed to carry its burden. The ribs began to show, and time took the planking away. There were no funds for maintenance.

Early in 1934, the Howards' towboat, the *Ed. J. Howard*, was lost by fire. But that loss was offset by the Inland Waterways Corporation's settlement for the *Mark Twain* of $20,460.69. The *J. J. Hennen* was sold for $16,500, only about 65 cents on the dollar. The *Loretta M. Howard/ Dorothy McBride* was sold to the Wisherd Line Steamers. They renamed her the *D. W. Wisherd*. The Yards won an Army Engineers' contract for a small gas boat forty feet long. Their bid of $5,237 was well below the $7,450 bid by the McClintic-Marshall Corporation. But no boats were built in 1935. The *Paul F. Thomas* ferryboat for Cincinnati was built on the Madison ways in 1934, however, but that did not arrest the ravages of time in Jeffersonville.

In February 1936 the creditors' committee was satisfied and dissolved. Though there was still a mortgage on the Yards of $15,000 held by the Clark County Bank, Clyde Howard's mortgage of $15,800 was canceled by conveying the Madison Marine Ways to him. Jim was free at last to do business the way he thought best. He set out to rebuild the Howard Ship Yards.

He bid, and won, a contract for two gasoline launches for the Tennessee Valley Authority. Each was 60 by 10 by 4 and powered with a 100 horsepower gasoline engine. Correspondence brimmed with the pride Jim felt in building these boats to his own, Howard, standards. But that was all for 1936. Then came January of 1937.

A heavy rain late in January fell on frozen ground all along the Upper Ohio Valley and the creeks and streams began to swell. From

Olean, New York, to Parsons, West Virginia, water ran off to Pittsburgh, Cincinnati, then Louisville. The wickets on the Ohio dams were laid flat, and the water rose in a wave that did not crest until January 26. At the crest, water stood six-feet high in the gilt-and-ivory drawing room of the Howard mansion in Jeffersonville. Jim and his family retreated to the second and third floors, but they had had to leave much behind—such as the sandalwood Steinway. Water, sand, mud flowed through the rooms, files, boxes, electric motors. Then an oil barge overturned upstream and coated all with lines of fetid scum. There were no boats launched in all of 1937 or 1938. When the Howards approached the Red Cross and other relief agencies, they were informed that such relief or low-interest loans were intended only for those who could not borrow elsewhere. So they retired and cleaned and painted as best they could. When some of their land was bought for the new flood-protection levee in 1938, the check went straight to the bank. The Yards and the home lie outside the levee.

In 1939 Jim built a little diesel towboat for the Two Rivers Barge Line in Cincinnati. The *Wm. S. Brokamp* was but 44 by 14 by 3.8. Two small ferryboats followed. In 1940 the *Frank Costanzo* slid down the ways. It was the last boat the Howard Ship Yards and Dock Company ever was to build.

A decade consumed what a family had been building for a century. As late as August 1941 Jim was still seeking capital. He needed money to repair, to rebuild. At one point, attempting to prepare the Yards for inspection by the Navy so as to be able to bid on new construction, Jim estimated that even $10,000 would turn the tide. A telegram, copy in the files, instructed an agent either to seek a loan from the Defense Loan Corporation or else find a buyer for the plant. But neither had materialized when the war came.

In the emergency following December 7, 1941, an inspection team from Washington looked at the site of the Yards, viewed the empty loft, the unused offices, and the ways. They easily recognized the potential and recommended the Navy acquire it. The Howard Ship Yards went to war.

Epilogue: The Fate of the Yards Since 1942

CHAPTER X

T HE LOUISVILLE *Times* reported on February 10, 1942, that the Navy had assumed control of the Howard Ship Yards and Dock Company and planned construction of a new-type vessel. The *Courier-Journal* added that the Navy job would send two thousand men to Jeffersonville. It was also reported that the War Department had commenced condemnation proceedings on twenty-seven acres in Jeffersonville which would permit the Navy to start clearing ground for additions to the Yards upstream. The project was to be under the direction of Lt. F. G. Healey, then naval supervisor of sub-chaser construction at the Jeffersonville Boat and Machine Company yards. Little more was ever reported about the reasons for, or the manner in which, the Navy acquired the historic Howard Ship Yards. To meet the war emergency, control and ownership was by process of eminent domain through the Federal District Court of Southern Indiana in New Albany.

Under the war-induced demand for boats, barges, and ships, the Yards demonstrated phenomenal capabilities. The record since the end of World War II has likewise been no less outstanding, but it is another chapter, if not another story, that had its beginning in 1938. In that year, the expanding American Commercial Barge Lines Company bought the moribund Sweeney shipyard just downstream from the Howards. The facility was made a wholly-owned subsidiary for boat and barge construction and marine repair as well. By the next year, 1939, the United

States Coast Guard and the Bureau of Marine Inspection and Navigation were listing the Jeffersonville Boat and Machine Company as builder of several barges, with the towboat, *National*, following in 1940.[1]

Given the growth of inland waterways commerce and the profitability of the parent company, the shipyard prospered and won a subchaser contract when the Navy began its expansion program. Thus, by 1942 it was eminently rational for the Navy to award its contracts to an operating concern with an assured labor force and demonstrated financial capability.

For the Navy, then, the management of Jeffersonville Boat and Machine Company, or Jeffboat as it came to be called, rebuilt and expanded the Howard Ship Yards. By adding Jeffboat's original yard and twenty more acres upstream, the Yards eventually encompassed sixty-four acres strung out for a mile and a quarter along the river front. Improvements included not only giant cranes capable of turning a fifty-ton boat upside down, but also new machine and assembly shops, seventeen miles of railroad siding, and, finally, a rail connection with the main rail lines in Jeffersonville. Production facilities were improved and rearranged to form an assembly line that greatly speeded boat construction. As a result, Jeffboat was able to deliver 123 LSTs (Landing Ship, Tank) and 26 subchasers by 1946.[2]

Shortly after the war's end, the Navy offered the improved Howard Yards to the highest bidder, and thus title passed to Jeffboat, Incorporated. Towboats, barges, and oceangoing ships have continued to flow from Jeffersonville.

It has been well over a century now since young Jim Howard drew the outlines of the *Hyperion* in the mud of the river bank. The changes in boatbuilding at that site would doubtlessly seem incredible to the men who sawed the planks for the *Hyperion*. Yet the changes and the history of the Howard Ship Yards in Jeffersonville, Indiana, are but a microcosm of the nation. From 1834 to 1929, the Howard Ship Yards were but one firm of the multitude that told the story of American free

---

[1] American Commercial Lines, Incorporated, *This Is American Commercial Lines* (Jeffersonville, Indiana: American Commercial Lines, Inc., 1966), and *The Courier-Journal Magazine* (Louisville), December 5, 1965, p. 14.
[2] *Ibid.*

enterprise—indeed free-for-all enterprise in 1834. Jim Howard and his shipyard were an example of the unleashing of unique abilities which were matched and channeled to their most appropriate use. It was testimony indeed as to the real wealth of a nation.

The story told after 1929 is an equally valid testimony of the economy's great folly of the thirties which neither the wit nor strength of good men could overcome by their own unaided efforts. Then challenged by the war, with families, farms, and factories disrupted, the Yards and the nation, recovered their industrial vigor. Since 1946, new ships and barges have gone down the ways to establish an incredible record.

From the third-floor billiard room of Ed. J. Howard's mansion, across East Market Street, one can see and appreciate the activity and production in the Yards. The home now houses the Clark County Historical Society Howard Steamboat Museum, and in its quiet rooms and halls is preserved the story of the generations of Howards, and many others, who built the steamboats that helped to build America.

Tarascon, side-wheel packet launched in 1863. Built for the Louisville & Henderson Mail Line, she was used to transport troops during the Civil War and ran for awhile on the Alabama River. She was retired in 1877.

DeKoven, *railroad transfer barge launched in 1894.*

Arthur Hider, steel-hulled, stern-wheel towboat launched in 1898. She is shown here new at the Howard Ship Yards.

City of Memphis, wooden-hulled, stern-wheel packet launched in 1898. Built for the St. Louis & Tennessee River Packet Company for the St. Louis–Memphis trade, she was sold about 1910 and renamed the S. B. Duncan. She burned at Vicksburg in 1912.

Morning Star, side-wheel packet launched in 1901. She was built for the Louisville & Evansville Packet Company, and after long service in various trades and as a cruise ship, she was bought by the Coney Island Company of Cincinnati and converted into an excursion boat. She burned at Cincinnati in 1922.

America, stern-wheel packet launched in 1918. She was built on the hull of the burned-out Indiana *in 1917 and ran in the Cincinnati–Louisville trade to replace the* City of Louisville *and the* City of Cincinnati. *She later became an excursion boat.*

FROM PADDLE WHEELS TO PROPELLERS   187

HOWARD STEAMBOAT MUSEUM

LaBelle, steel-hulled, stern-wheel towboat launched in 1921. She is shown here on grade at the Howard Ship Yards.

View from wharf barge of the grade at Howard Ship Yards about 1930.

APPENDIXES

APPENDIX A

Output by Years[1]

TABLE 1. *The Howard Ship Yards in Jeffersonville*

Year Built	Rig	Hull	Name of Vessel	Service	Home Port	Dimensions	Price
1834	stp	w	*Hyperion*	pkt	Apa	107.0 x 18.0 x 8.0	
	srw	w	*Black Locust*	fer	Lou	110.0 x 25.0 x 4.5	
1835	stp	w	*Tecumseh*	pkt	—	115.0 x 16.0 x 5.0	
1836 to 1847			James Howard moved his yards to Madison and Louisville			See Table 2 in Appendix A.	
1848	bge	w	Dredgeboat	mis			
	stp	w	*Emperor*	pkt	Mob	240.0 x 32.0 x 8.0	
	stp	w	*Louisiana*	pkt	Nol	240.0 x 31.0 x 7.0	
	stp	w	*Mary Foley*	pkt	Nol	200.0 x 31.0 x 7.0	
	stp	w	*Prairie Bird*	fer	Lou	100.0 x 30.0 x 4.5	
1849	stp	w	*Falcon*	pkt	Nol	220.0 x 32.0 x 6.5	
	stp	w	*Fanny Smith*	pkt	Lou	220.0 x 32.0 x 6.5	
	stp	w	*Isabella*	pkt	Mob	175.0 x 30.0 x 7.0	
	stp	w	*Lexington*	pkt	Lou	220.0 x 32.0 x 6.5	
	stp	w	*St. Charles*	pkt	Mob	230.0 x 31.0 x 7.0	
1850	stp	w	*Blue Wing* No. 2	pkt	Lou	150.0 x 30.0 x 6.5	
	stp	w	*John Simpson*	pkt	Lou	180.0 x 30.0 x 6.5	
	stp	w	*Swan*	pkt	Nol	108.0 x 22.3 x 5.0	
	bge	w	*U.S. Survey* No. 1	mis	—		
	bge	w	*U.S. Survey* No. 2	mis	—		

[1]For sources and explanation of column headings and abbreviations, see the notes at the end of Appendix A, p. 227 below.

Table 1—(*Continued*)

Year Built	Rig	Hull	Name of Vessel	Service	Home Port	Dimensions			Price
1851	stp	w	Dr. Smith	pkt	Gal	120.0 x 30.0 x	5.0		
	stp	w	Frank Lyon	pkt	Mob	210.0 x 31.0 x	8.0		
	stp	w	Glendy Burke	pkt	Nol	245.0 x 33.0 x	8.0	$	4,778
	stp	w	Kate Swinney	pkt	StL	180.0 x 30.0 x	6.5		
	stp	w	Lucy McConnell	fer	Lou	100.0 x 28.0 x	4.5		
	stp	w	Peter Dalman	pkt	Nol	200.0 x 30.0 x	7.5		
	stp	w	Southern Belle	pkt	Mob	240.0 x 31.0 x	8.0		
	stp	w	Trinity	pkt	Gal	175.0 x 28.0 x	6.5		
	stp	w	W. B. Clifton	pkt	Lou	225.0 x 33.0 x	6.5		
1852	srw	w	Athey Watchen	fer	Lou	150.0 x 40.0 x	5.5		
	stp	w	Brunette	pkt	StL	180.0 x 29.0 x	6.0		
	stp	w	Empress	pkt	Lou	285.0 x 34.0 x	7.5		
	stp	w	H. M. Wright	pkt	Nol	210.0 x 32.0 x	8.0		
	stp	w	Jennie Bealle	pkt	Mob	185.0 x 31.0 x	6.0		
	stp	w	Magnolia	pkt	Mob	180.0 x 31.0 x	7.5		
	stp	w	Messenger	pkt	Mob	185.0 x 32.0 x	7.5		
	stp	w	Octavia	pkt	Mob	180.0 x 30.0 x	6.0		
	stp	w	St. Francis	pkt	Lou	150.0 x 28.0 x	5.5		
	stp	w	Sam Dale	pkt	Mob	210.0 x 30.0 x	7.5		
	stp	w	W. P. Swinney	pkt	Vic	170.0 x 39.0 x	6.0		
	stp	w	Sallie Spann	pkt	Mob	180.0 x 30.0 x	6.0		
1853	srw	w	Alice W. Glaze	pkt	Nol	140.0 x 32.0 x	7.0		
	stp	w	Atakapas	pkt	—	180.0 x 32.0 x	7.0		
	stp	w	C. D. Jr.	pkt	Nol	200.0 x 30.0 x	7.5		
	stp	w	Ceres	pkt	Nol	185.0 x 32.0 x	7.0		
	stp	w	Geo. W. Jones	pkt	—	110.0 x 29.0 x	6.5		
	stp	w	Gopher	pkt	—	110.0 x 29.0 x	6.5		
	stp	w	Jas. H. Lucas	pkt	StL	230.0 x 35.0 x	7.0		
	stp	w	Josiah A. Bell	pkt	Gal	180.0 x 36.0 x	7.5		
	stp	w	Lucy Bell	pkt	Mob	180.0 x 32.0 x	6.0		
	stw	w	Runaway	pkt	Nol	125.0 x 26.0 x	5.0		
	stp	w	S. S. Prentice	pkt	Vic	180.0 x 29.0 x	7.0		
	stp	w	Southerner	pkt	Cin	240.0 x 34.0 x	6.0		
1854	stp	w	Ben Franklin	pkt	Lou	300.0 x 40.0 x	7.5		
	stp	w	Capitol	pkt	Nol	235.0 x 35.0 x	8.0		
	stp	w	David Tatum	pkt	StL	220.0 x 32.0 x	6.0		
	stp	w	Fanny Bullitt	pkt	Lou	245.0 x 35.0 x	7.0		
	stp	w	Marion	pkt	Lou	130.0 x 30.0 x	5.0		3,500
	stp	w	National	pkt	Mem	170.0 x 30.0 x	6.0		
	stp	w	Rainbow	pkt	Lou	235.0 x 35.0 x	7.0		
1855	stp	w	Carrier	pkt	Lou	200.0 x 33.0 x	6.0		

TABLE 1—(*Continued*)

Year Built	Rig	Hull	Name of Vessel	Service	Home Port	Dimensions			Price
	stw	w	*Diamond*	pkt	Lou	155.0 x 40.0 x	5.5		
	stw	w	*John Tompkins*	pkt	Lou	160.0 x 36.0 x	5.0	$	4,800
	stp	w	*P. C. Wallis*	pkt	Vic	160.0 x 32.0 x	5.5		
	stp	w	*R. L. Cobb*	pkt	Lou	160.0 x 30.0 x	4.5		3,200
	stw	w	*R. M. Patton*	pkt	Lou	160.0 x 33.0 x	5.5		
	bge	w	*Parker*	bge	Rer	130.0 x 26.0 x	5.0		2,200
	stp	w	*Scotland*	pkt	Lou	225.0 x 38.0 x	7.5		
	stp	w	*Victoria*	pkt	Gal	140.0 x 30.0 x	5.5		
1856	stp	w	*Col. Edwards*	pkt	Nol	155.0 x 31.0 x	6.5		5,000
	stp	w	*Dove*	pkt	Lou	150.0 x 30.0 x	5.5		
	stp	w	*Governor Pease*	pkt	Gal	160.0 x 32.0 x	6.0		
	stp	w	*John Warner*	pkt	StL	220.0 x 36.0 x	6.5		
	stp	w	*Kate Howard*	pkt	StL	235.0 x 36.0 x	6.5		
	stp	w	*N. J. Eaton*	pkt	—	220.0 x 35.0 x	6.5		
	stp	w	*Pete Whetstone*	pkt	Lou	225.0 x 38.0 x	7.5		
	stw	w	*Princess*	pkt	Nas	155.0 x 30.0 x	3.5		
	stp	w	*Silver Heels*	pkt	Lou	180.0 x 29.0 x	5.5		
	stp	w	*Tom Peacock*	pkt	—	120.0 x 30.0 x	6.0		
	stp	w	*W. R. Douglas*	pkt	Lou	145.0 x 30.0 x	6.0		4,250
	stp	w	*Woodford*	pkt	Lou	250.0 x 35.0 x	6.5		
1857	stp	w	*Alonzo Child*	pkt	StL	236.0 x 38.0 x	7.0		11,000
	stp	w	*Diana*	pkt	Lou	275.0 x 37.0 x	7.0		15,000
	srw	w	*Jefferson*	fer	Nol	120.0 x 30.0 x	4.5		
	stp	w	*John D. Perry*	pkt	Lou	220.0 x 33.0 x	6.0		
	stp	w	*Jas. G. Smith*	fer	StL	90.0 x 28.0 x	4.5		
	stp	w	*Music*	pkt	Nol	190.0 x 35.0 x	7.0		
	srw	w	*New Orleans*	fer	Nol	120.0 x 30.0 x	4.5		
	stp	w	*Platte Valley*	pkt	Lou	226.0 x 33.0 x	6.0		
	stp	w	*South Western*	pkt	StL	220.0 x 36.0 x	6.5		
	stp	w	*Twilight*	pkt	StL	215.0 x 33.0 x	6.0		
	bge	w	*Wiggins* No. 1	bge	StL	150.0 x 26.0 x	5.0		2,250
	bge	w	*Wiggins* No. 2	bge	StL	150.0 x 26.0 x	5.0		2,250
1858	srw	w	*Aline*	fer	Fra	125.0 x 30.0 x	6.0		3,350
	stp	w	*Grand Duke*	pkt	Nol	205.0 x 38.0 x	8.0		9,500
	stp	w	*Judge Porter*	pkt	Fra	140.0 x 30.0 x	6.0		
	stw	w	*Rescue*	pkt	Nol	100.0 x 24.0 x	4.0		
	stp	w	*St. Francis* No. 3	pkt	Mem	160.0 x 29.0 x	6.0		5,500
1859	stp	w	*Bayou City*	pkt	—	165.0 x 28.0 x	5.0		
	stp	w	*D. F. Kenner*	pkt	Nol	215.0 x 37.0 x	8.0		12,200
	stp	w	*J. D. Swain*	pkt	Fra	150.0 x 30.0 x	6.0		6,000
	stp	w	*James Woods*	pkt	Nas	257.0 x 37.0 x	7.0		

TABLE 1—(*Continued*)

Year Built	Rig	Hull	Name of Vessel	Service	Home Port	Dimensions		Price
	stp	w	*Jno. M. Sharp*	pkt	Vic	155.0 x 30.0 x	5.0	
	stp	w	*Lafourche*	pkt	Nol	185.0 x 34.0 x	7.5	$ 10,400
	stp	w	*Laurel Hill*	pkt	Nol	200.0 x 38.0 x	8.5	14,000
1860	stp	w	*Acadia*	pkt	Nol	188.0 x 35.0 x	7.0	9,800
	srw	w	*Isaac Bowman*	fer	Lou	160.0 x 39.0 x	5.5	14,600
	stp	w	*J. F. Pargoud*	pkt	Nol	234.0 x 38.0 x	8.0	14,000
	stp	w	*Jno. A. Cotton*	pkt	Nol	248.0 x 38.0 x	8.0	14,600
	stw	w	*Little Sallie*	pkt	Nol	100.0 x 23.0 x	3.5	1,600
	stp	w	*Mary T.*	pkt	Nol	185.0 x 34.0 x	8.0	10,000
	stp	w	*Memphis*	pkt	StL	263.0 x 38.0 x	7.0	14,000
	stp	w	*Robert Campbell, Jr.*	pkt	Lou	226.0 x 41.0 x	6.0	12,200
1861	stp	w	*Major Anderson*	pkt	Lou	245.0 x 36.0 x	5.5	28,755
1862	stp	w	*General Buell*	pkt	Lou	248.0 x 36.0 x	5.5	27,425
	stp	w	*Ruth*	pkt	StL	273.0 x 46.0 x	8.0	
	stp	w	*Wren*	pkt	Lou	150.0 x 30.0 x	5.5	13,770
	stp	w	*James Thompson*	fer	Lou	155.0 x 37.0 x	5.0	4,800
1863	stp	w	*Blue Wing* No. 3	pkt	Lou	150.0 x 30.0 x	5.5	
	stp	w	*Bostona* No. 3	pkt	Cin	240.0 x 36.0 x	5.5	
	stp	w	*Julia*	pkt	StL	241.0 x 41.0 x	7.0	
	stp	w	*Olive Branch*	pkt	StL	283.0 x 42.0 x	8.0	
	stp	w	*Tarascon*	pkt	Lou	249.0 x 36.0 x	6.0	40,900
1864	stp	w	*Ida Handy*	pkt	StL	258.0 x 45.0 x	8.0	
	stp	w	*Morning Star*	pkt	Lou	250.0 x 36.0 x	6.0	
	stp	w	*Ruth* No. 2	pkt	StL	300.0 x 49.0 x	9.5	
	flt	w	L and C Mail Line Wharfboat	wfb	Lou	200.0 x 50.0 x	5.0	
1865	stp	w	*North Missouri*	rrt	StL	160.0 x 30.0 x	5.3	
	stp	w	*Virginia*	pkt	StL	226.0 x 42.0 x	6.8	
1866	bge	w	*Galveston*	bge	Gal	120.0 x 25.0 x	6.0	
	bge	w	*Wm. Dwyer*	bge	Gal	126.0 x 25.0 x	6.0	
	bge	w	*Wm. R. Jarmon*	bge	Gal	126.0 x 25.0 x	6.0	
	stp	w	*Belle Memphis*	pkt	StL	260.0 x 40.0 x	7.0	
	srw	w	*Birdie Brent*	fer	StL	112.0 x 35.0 x	4.5	
	stp	w	*H. M. Shreve*	pkt	StL	198.0 x 35.0 x	5.5	
	srw	w	*Jessie*	fer	Nol	132.0 x 35.0 x	5.0	
	stp	w	*Stonewall*	pkt	StL	224.0 x 42.0 x	6.8	
1867	stw	w	*Dove* No. 2	pkt	Cin	116.0 x 26.0 x	4.5	

TABLE 1—(*Continued*)

Year Built	Rig	Hull	Name of Vessel	Service	Home Port	Dimensions	Price
	stp	w	Early Bird	pkt	Nol	125.0 x 25.5 x 4.5	
	stp	w	Frank Pargoud	pkt	Nol	255.0 x 41.0 x 9.3	
	stp	w	Governor Allen	pkt	Nol	217.0 x 40.0 x 8.0	
1868	stp	w	Belle of Alton	pkt	StL	227.0 x 35.0 x 6.0	
	srw	w	East St. Louis	fer	StL	175.0 x 53.0 x 6.0	
	stp	w	St. Francis	pkt	Mem	172.0 x 32.0 x 6.0	
	stp	w	Thos. M. Bagley	pkt	Gal	166.0 x 30.0 x 6.5	
	sts	w	Trade Palace	pkt	Nol	160.0 x 30.0 x 5.5	
1869	stw	w	Big Sunflower	pkt	Nol	125.0 x 28.0 x 4.0	
	stw	w	Gladiola	pkt	Nol	136.0 x 34.0 x 4.5	
	stp	w	La Belle	pkt	Nol	176.0 x 35.0 x 6.5	
	stw	w	Texarkana	pkt	—	135.0 x 35.0 x 5.5	
	stw	w	Texas	pkt	Nol	135.0 x 35.0 x 6.0	
	stw	w	Trenton	pkt	Nol	130.0 x 32.0 x 4.0	
	stp	w	Ben Franklin	pkt	Cin	255.0 x 37.0 x 6.0	
1870	bge	w	Bayou City	bge	Hou	125.0 x 25.0 x 6.0	$ 5,000
	stw	w	Cherokee	pkt	Lou	131.0 x 32.0 x 4.0	
	stp	w	City of Chester	pkt	StL	241.0 x 38.0 x 7.0	
	stp	w	City of Vicksburg	pkt	StL	265.0 x 42.0 x 8.0	
	bge	w	Dixie	bge	Hou	125.0 x 25.0 x 6.0	5,000
	stp	w	Grand Tower	pkt	StL	265.0 x 42.0 x 8.0	
	bge	w	Howard	bge	Hou	125.0 x 25.0 x 6.0	
	stp	w	Idlewild	pkt	Evs	214.0 x 35.0 x 5.5	
	srw	w	James Wathen	fer	Lou	150.0 x 37.0 x 6.0	22,000
	stw	w	John Howard	pkt	Gal	170.0 x 40.0 x 6.5	29,800
	stp	w	James Howard	pkt	Nol	328.0 x 54.0 x 10.0	
	stw	w	Jessie Taylor	pkt	Nol	156.0 x 37.0 x 7.0	
	bge	w	Paul	bge	Gal	90.0 x 24.0 x 6.0	3,100
	stp	w	Diana	pkt	—	165.0 x 32.0 x 6.0	
1871	bge	w	Beaver	bge	Hou	125.0 x 25.0 x 6.0	5,000
	flt	w	Hornell Millspaw	wfb	Lou	225.0 x 45.0 x 5.0	12,750
	bge	w	Grey Eagle	bge	Evs	85.0 x 18.0 x 4.0	700
	stp	w	Grey Eagle	pkt	Lou	238.0 x 36.0 x 6.0	42,000
	bge	w	Houston	bge	Hou	125.0 x 25.0 x 6.0	5,000
	stw	w	John Howard	pkt	Nol	181.0 x 36.0 x 6.5	27,850
	bge	w	L & N and M & L RR	bge	Nas	100.0 x 20.0 x 4.5	1,065
	bge	w	Lee	bge	Hou	125.0 x 25.0 x 6.0	5,000
	stp	w	Lizzie	pkt	Gal	165.0 x 35.0 x 5.0	37,000
	bge	w	Otter	bge	Hou	125.0 x 25.0 x 6.0	5,000
	bge	w	Rusk	bge	Hou	125.0 x 25.0 x 6.0	5,000
	stw	w	St. Mary	pkt	Nol	146.0 x 34.0 x 6.0	9,000

TABLE I—(*Continued*)

Year Built	Rig	Hull	Name of Vessel	Service	Home Port	Dimensions		Price
	bge	w	*Tarascon*	bge	Evs	85.0 x 18.0 x	4.0	$ 700
	bge	w	*Terry*	bge	Hou	125.0 x 25.0 x	6.0	5,000
	stp	w	*City of Helena*	pkt	StL	266.0 x 42.0 x	7.8	74,100
	bge	w	Barge	bge	Evs	85.0 x 18.0 x	4.0	
1872	stp	w	*Concordia*	fer	Nat	86.0 x 25.0 x	4.0	10,000
	stw	w	*John S. Bransford*	pkt	Lou	150.0 x 30.0 x	4.0	17,650
	bge	w	*L & N and M & L RR*	bge	Nas	120.0 x 20.0 x	4.5	1,064
	bge	w	*Little Fayette*	bge	Evs	130.0 x 24.0 x	4.5	3,000
	stw	w	*Longfellow*	pkt	Evs	112.0 x 20.0 x	4.0	3,000
	bge	w	M. V. T. No. 47	bge	StL	210.0 x 40.0 x	8.0	12,350
	bge	w	M. V. T. No. 48	bge	StL	210.0 x 40.0 x	8.0	12,350
	stw	w	*R. T. Bryarly*	pkt	Nol	150.0 x 33.0 x	4.5	18,350
	flt	w	L & N and M & L RR	wfb	Nas	150.0 x 36.0 x	4.0	6,150
	flt	w	L & N and M & L RR	wfb	Nas	150.0 x 36.0 x	4.0	6,150
	mis	w	Portland Canal Lock Gates	mis	Lou			12,000
	flt	w	Wharfboat	wfb	Nas	150.0 x 36.0 x	4.0	6,400
1873	stw	w	*Arch P. Green*	pkt	Cin	110.0 x 22.0 x	3.0	5,000
	bge	w	*Arnold Nugent* No. 1	bge	Lou	90.0 x 18.0 x	4.0	734
	bge	w	*Arnold Nugent* No. 2	bge	Lou	90.0 x 18.0 x	4.0	734
	bge	w	*Arnold Nugent* No. 3	bge	Lou	90.0 x 18.0 x	4.0	732
	bge	w	*Atlantic*	bge	Evs	160.0 x 35.0 x	5.0	6,000
	stw	w	*B. H. Cook*	pkt	Evs	151.0 x 30.0 x	4.5	5,800
	stw	w	*Dolphin*	pkt	StL	135.0 x 23.0 x	4.0	14,000
	sts	w	*Ida*	pkt	Pad	71.0 x 14.0 x	7.5	
	stp	w	*H. S. McComb*	rrt	Cai	195.0 x 45.0 x	7.0	41,600
	bge	w	*John Howard* No. 3	bge	Ark	137.0 x 27.0 x	4.5	3,000
	bge	w	*Little Nell*	bge	Lou	135.0 x 28.0 x	5.5	2,800
	bge	w	M. V. T. No. 49	bge	StL	213.0 x 40.0 x	8.0	13,000
	bge	w	M. V. T. No. 50	bge	StL	213.0 x 40.0 x	8.0	13,000
	stw	w	*Red Cloud*	pkt	Evs	176.0 x 34.0 x	5.0	26,375
	srw	w	*Three States*	fer	Cai	150.0 x 35.0 x	4.5	20,000
	stp	w	*Z. M. Sherley*	fer	Lou	153.0 x 36.0 x	6.0	15,000
	flt	w	Pump Boat	mis	Lou	45.0 x 12.0 x	3.0	400
	mis	w	Kentucky River Lock Gates	mis	Lou			665
	mis	w	Portland Canal Gates	mis	Lou			8,700
	mis	w	Portland Canal Gates	mis	Lou			9,250
1874	bge	w	*Emerke*	bge	Jef	73.0 x 14.0 x	4.0	600
	stw	w	*Fawn*	pkt	Lou	180.0 x 34.0 x	5.0	14,700
	bge	w	*Relief*	bge	Gal	95.0 x 25.0 x	7.0	3,800
	bge	w	*Utica*	bge	Jef	75.0 x 16.0 x	4.0	775

TABLE 1—(*Continued*)

Year Built	Rig	Hull	Name of Vessel	Service	Home Port	Dimensions		Price
	mis	w	Kentucky River Lock Gates	mis	Lou			$ 2,147
1875	stw	w	*Assumption*	pkt	Nol	150.0 X 36.0 X	3.5	
	stw	w	*Bonnie Lee*	pkt	Nol	165.0 X 30.0 X	4.0	
	bge	w	*Chicago ICRR*	rrt	Cai	175.0 X 37.0 X	6.0	
	bge	w	*Jim Black*	bge	StL	135.0 X 27.0 X	6.0	
	stp	w	*Junius S. Morgan*	pkt	Cai	195.0 X 45.0 X	7.0	
	bge	w	*Pin Hook*	bge	Nol	80.0 x. 18.0 X	3.0	
	bge	w	*Porter White*	bge	StL	135.0 X 27.0 X	6.0	
	stp	w	*Rene Macready*	pkt	Mem	140.0 X 29.0 X	4.5	
	srw	w	*Kate Fisher*	fer	StL	117.0 X 28.0 X	4.0	
	stw	w	*Timmie Baker*	pkt	Vic	100.0 X 21.0 X	3.0	
	bge	w	U.S. No. 17	bge	StL	135.0 X 28.0 X	5.0	
	bge	w	U.S. No. 18	bge	StL	135.0 X 28.0 X	5.0	
	bge	w	U.S. No. 19	bge	StL	135.0 X 28.0 X	5.0	
	bge	w	U.S. No. 20	bge	StL	135.0 X 28.0 X	5.0	
1876	stw	w	*Alberta*	pkt	Mem	116.0 X 25.0 X	3.5	
	stw	w	*C. W. Anderson*	pkt	Whe	160.0 X 31.0 X	4.5	
	stw	w	*Celina*	pkt	Lou	140.0 X 25.0 X	3.0	
	stw	w	*E. B. Stahlman*	pkt	Evs	145.0 X 27.0 X	3.0	
	stp	w	*Rob't. E. Lee*	pkt	Lou	306.0 X 48.0 X	10.0	
	stw	w	*Walker Morris*	pkt	Cai	996.0 X 19.0 X	4.0	
	stw	w	*Yazoo Valley*	pkt	Nol	180.0 X 36.0 X	6.5	
1877	stw	w	*Headlight*	pkt	StL	141.0 X 24.5 X	3.5	8,350
	stw	w	*Delner*	twb	Umr	136.0 X 26.5 X	4.0	5,200
	stw	w	*John G. Fletcher*	frt	Lou	120.0 X 24.7 X	3.5	3,500
	bge	w	*Lewis Hite*	bge	Lou	199.5 X 20.0 X	4.5	850
	bge	w	*Allen Hite*	bge	Lou	199.5 X 20.0 X	4.5	850
	stw	w	*Mattie Hays*	frt	Lou	100.5 X 20.5 X	3.5	3,000
	stw	w	*G. Gunby Jordan*	frt	Cha	126.0 X 25.3 X	3.5	10,000
	stw	w	*Dora Cabler*	frt	Cum	155.0 X 30.0 X	4.5	8,050
	stw	w	*Fashion*	pkt	Lou	219.5 X 35.8 X	5.0	20,714
	bge	w	*James Howard*	bge	Gal	110.5 X 26.6 X	9.0	5,000
	bge	w	Barge No. 1	bge	Nol	100.0 X 18.0 X	3.5	1,075
	bge	w	Barge No. 2	bge	Nol	100.0 X 18.0 X	3.5	1,075
	bge	w	Barge No. 3	bge	Nol	100.0 X 18.0 X	3.5	1,075
	bge	w	Barge No. 4	bge	Nol	100.0 X 18.0 X	3.5	1,075
	flt	w	Landing Dock	wfb	Roc	100.0 X 20.0 X	5.0	1,500
	bge	w	*Stella Clifton*	bge	Lou	199.5 X 20.0 X	4.5	850
	stw	w	*Winnie*	frt	—	110.5 X 24.2 X	3.6	6,650
	stp	w	*James Guthrie*	pkt	Lou	240.0 X 36.7 X	5.7	28,250

TABLE 1—(*Continued*)

Year Built	Rig	Hull	Name of Vessel	Service	Home Port	Dimensions	Price
1878	stp	w	John W. Cannon	pkt	Nol	252.5 X 43.0 X 9.4	$ 68,480
	stp	w	J. M. White	pkt	Nol	310.0 X 49.0 X 11.1	103,500
	stp	w	New Shallcross	fer	Lou	158.0 X 36.6 X 6.0	13,000
	stw	w	Laura Lee	pkt	Nol	206.2 X 37.2 X 6.5	16,000
	stw	w	Jewel	pkt	Cin	174.5 X 32.9 X 5.0	15,300
	stw	w	B. S. Rhea	pkt	Nas	162.0 X 32.0 X 4.5	15,800
	bge	w	Barge No. 5	bge	Nol	120.0 X 20.0 X 4.0	15,500
	bge	w	Barge No. 6	bge	Nol	120.0 X 20.0 X 4.0	15,500
	stw	w	Herbert	twb	—	85.0 X 19.4 X 3.7	1,350
	stp	w	Ed Richardson	pkt	Nol	300.0 X 48.6 X 10.7	51,700
1879	stp	w	City of Greenville	pkt	Mem	281.0 X 44.4 X 9.2	67,750
	bge	w	Victor	bge	Gal	115.0 X 26.5 X 7.5	5,750
	stw	w	C. N. Davis	pkt	Cum	140.0 X 27.0 X 3.0	4,725
	stw	w	City of Yazoo	pkt	Nol	200.0 X 38.0 X 6.8	25,000
	stp	w	Rainbow	pkt	Lou	263.0 X 40.0 X 6.0	21,000
	stw	w	Wm. Fagan	pkt	Oua	165.0 X 35.0 X 5.0	18,000
	stw	w	Charmer	pkt	Rer	185.0 X 34.0 X 5.8	18,300
	stp	w	Jesse K. Bell	pkt	Rer	217.6 X 40.0 X 7.5	25,000
	2ss	w	Wash Gray	twb	Jef	87.0 X 18.0 X 6.5	7,500
	flt	w	Wharf Boat	wfb	Hen	150.0 X 36.0 X 4.8	6,500
1880	arw	w	Horse-powered Ferry Boat	fer	Nas	70.0 X 53.0 X 2.5	2,250
	stw	w	Milwaukee	rrt	Umr	136.0 X 30.4 X 5.3	12,000
	stw	w	Gus Fowler	pkt	Cai	160.0 X 29.6 X 5.0	12,200
	stp	w	City of Providence	pkt	StL	270.5 X 44.4 X 8.3	71,850
	stp	w	Concordia	fer	Nas	90.3 X 24.5 X 4.5	4,000
	stp	w	Joseph Henry	mis	Lou	180.0 X 32.0 X 5.9	18,394
	bge	w	Anchor Line Barge No. 1	bge	StL	166.5 X 32.8 X 7.0	8,000
	stw	w	Alberta	pkt	Ark	150.0 X 28.5 X 3.5	4,825
	bge	w	Anchor Line Barge No. 2	bge	StL	166.5 X 32.8 X 7.0	8,000
	stw	w	Clyde	pkt	Evs	180.0 X 32.0 X 5.0	23,000
	stw	w	Thomas D. Fite	pkt	Cum	149.0 X 29.0 X 4.0	6,500
	stp	w	Belle Memphis	pkt	StL	265.0 X 42.0 X 8.3	63,450
	bge	w	Durland and Perkins Barge	rrt	Evs	195.0 X 35.0 X 5.5	6,750
1881	stp	w	W. Butler Duncan	rrt	Pad	200.0 X 45.0 X 7.0	43,350
	flt	w	Landing Dock	wfb	Jef	112.0 X 22.0 X 4.3	2,174
	stw	w	Ella	frt	Cum	149.0 X 28.0 X 3.0	4,063
	stw	w	S. P. Ewald	frt	Cum	149.0 X 30.0 X 4.3	7,100
	stp	w	City of Vicksburg	pkt	StL	270.0 X 44.3 X 8.3	73,350

TABLE 1—(*Continued*)

Year Built	Rig	Hull	Name of Vessel	Service	Home Port	Dimensions			Price
	stw	w	*J. P. Drouillard*	frt	Cum	165.0 x 31.3 x	4.9	$	7,000
	stp	w	*City of New Orleans*	pkt	Nol	285.0 x 48.3 x	9.1		87,000
	stp	w	*City of Baton Rouge*	pkt	Nol	285.0 x 48.3 x	9.3		84,300
	bge	w	*Hermit*	bge	Lou	99.5 x 20.0 x	4.7		950
	bge	w	*Guy Clark*	bge	Lou	99.5 x 20.0 x	4.7		950
	bge	w	Crane Boat	bge	—	60.0 x 28.0 x	3.5		850
	bge	w	Crane Boat	bge	—	60.0 x 28.0 x	3.5		850
	bge	w	Crane Boat	bge	—	60.0 x 28.0 x	3.5		850
	stw	w	*City of Nashville*	pkt	Cum	149.0 x 31.3 x	4.5		7,600
	stw	w	Durland and Perkins Barge	rrt	Evs	203.0 x 35.5 x	5.6		7,989
1882	stp	w	*City of Cairo*	pkt	StL	271.0 x 44.5 x	8.4		75,350
	bge	w	Barge No. 1	bge	StL	136.0 x 27.0 x	5.9		3,350
	bge	w	Barge No. 2	bge	StL	136.0 x 27.0 x	5.9		3,350
	bge	w	Barge No. 3	bge	StL	136.0 x 27.0 x	5.8		4,000
	bge	w	Barge No. 4	bge	StL	136.0 x 27.0 x	5.8		4,000
	stp	w	*J. W. Spencer*	fer	StL	132.5 x 35.0 x	5.0		15,450
	bge	w	U.S. Barge No. 60	bge	StL	136.0 x 26.5 x	5.9		3,550
	stw	w	*Charley DePauw*	twb	Jef	127.0 x 23.0 x	4.5		11,350
	flt	w	Landing Dock	wfb	Rii	95.0 x 18.0 x	4.5		1,500
	stw	w	*J. H. Hillman*	pkt	Cum	149.5 x 28.8 x	3.5		9,925
	stp	w	*Arkansas City*	pkt	StL	271.0 x 44.5 x	8.3		75,350
	stw	w	*J.G. Parke*	twb	Rii	140.0 x 28.0 x	3.8		18,750
	bge	w	U.S. No. 61	bge	Rii	136.0 x 26.5 x	5.9		3,550
	bge	w	U.S. No. 62	bge	Rii	136.0 x 26.5 x	5.9		3,550
	bge	w	Durland and Perkins Barge	rrt	Evs	208.0 x 35.5 x	5.6		8,052
	stw	w	*S. I. Parisot*	pkt	Nol	225.0 x 40.5 x	7.7		41,000
	stp	w	*W. C. Hite*	fer	Lou	156.0 x 36.4 x	6.3		22,200
	stw	w	*W. H. Cherry*	frt	Cum	168.5 x 32.0 x	5.0		18,650
	bge	w	*Waldo*	bge	Gal	140.0 x 26.0 x	6.0		4,500
	stw	w	*Sam J. Keith*	pkt	Cum	160.4 x 32.0 x	5.0		11,000
	stp	w	*City of St. Louis*	pkt	StL	300.0 x 49.0 x	8.8		86,850
	bge	w	U.S. No. 82	bge	StL	100.0 x 25.0 x	5.0		2,000
	bge	w	U.S. No. 83	bge	StL	100.0 x 25.0 x	5.0		2,000
	bge	w	U.S. No. 84	bge	StL	100.0 x 25.0 x	5.0		2,000
	bge	w	U.S. No. 85	bge	StL	100.0 x 25.0 x	5.0		2,000
1883	bge	w	U.S. Barge No. 100	bge	StL	100.0 x 25.0 x	5.0		2,000
	stw	w	*Alto*	frt	Mob	166.0 x 34.5 x	4.8		8,473
	bge	w	U.S. Pile Driver No. 39	mis	StL	80.0 x 20.0 x	3.8		1,950
	bge	w	U.S. Pile Driver No. 40	mis	StL	80.0 x 20.0 x	3.8		1,950

TABLE 1—(*Continued*)

Year Built	Rig	Hull	Name of Vessel	Service	Home Port	Dimensions		Price
	bge	w	U.S. Pile Driver No. 41	mis	StL	80.0 x 20.0 x	3.8	$ 1,950
	bge	w	U.S. Pile Driver No. 42	mis	StL	80.0 x 20.0 x	3.8	1,950
	bge	w	U.S. Pile Driver No. 43	mis	StL	80.0 x 20.0 x	3.8	1,950
	bge	w	U.S. Pile Driver No. 44	mis	StL	80.0 x 20.0 x	3.8	1,950
	bge	w	U.S. Pile Driver No. 45	mis	StL	80.0 x 20.0 x	3.8	1,950
	bge	w	U.S. Pile Driver No. 46	mis	StL	80.0 x 20.0 x	3.8	1,950
	stw	w	*General Gilmore*	twb	StL	140.0 x 28.0 x	4.0	16,675
	bge	w	U.S. No. 166	bge	StL	120.0 x 30.0 x	6.0	2,650
	bge	w	U.S. No. 167	bge	StL	120.0 x 30.0 x	6.0	2,650
	bge	w	U.S. No. 168	bge	StL	120.0 x 30.0 x	6.0	2,650
	bge	w	No. 4	bge	StL	135.0 x 27.0 x	6.0	3,800
	bge	w	No. 5	bge	StL	135.0 x 27.0 x	6.0	3,800
	stp	w	*Henry Sackman*	rrt	StL	220.0 x 46.0 x	6.0	40,000
	srw	w	*Carlos S. Greeley*	fer	StL	160.0 x 48.5 x	6.2	14,340
	bge	w	No. 6	bge	StL	135.0 x 27.0 x	6.0	3,800
	stw	w	*Osceola*	twb	Jef	133.0 x 24.0 x	4.5	15,300
	bge	w	No. 7	bge	StL	135.0 x 27.0 x	6.0	3,800
	stp	w	*W. F. Nesbit*	pkt	Nas	200.0 x 35.0 x	6.0	27,400
	stw	w	*Benton McMillan*	pkt	Cum	155.0 x 33.0 x	5.0	16,750
	stp	w	*W. F. Osborn*	rrt	Cai	285.0 x 45.0 x	7.0	57,500
	bge	w	Lime Boat	bge	Lou	80.0 x 16.5 x	5.0	700
1884	flt	w	Landing Barge	wfb	Cai	200.0 x 24.0 x	5.0	6,000
	stp	w	*City of Bayou Sara*	pkt	StL	296.0 x 48.3 x	9.8	78,750
	bge	w	No. 8	bge	StL	135.0 x 27.0 x	6.0	3,650
	bge	w	No. 9	bge	StL	135.0 x 27.0 x	6.0	3,650
	flt	w	Landing Dock	wfb	Cai	200.0 x 30.0 x	5.0	7,500
	stp	w	*Pargoud*	pkt	Nol	242.5 x 42.8 x	8.0	45,500
	bge	w	*Comanchee*	bge	Mem	140.0 x 27.0 x	6.0	3,800
	bge	w	*Apache*	bge	Mem	140.0 x 27.0 x	6.0	3,800
	stw	w	*Alberta*	frt	—	145.0 x 28.0 x	3.6	9,750
	bge	w	*Mohave*	bge	Mem	140.0 x 27.0 x	6.0	3,800
	bge	w	*Shoshone*	bge	Mem	140.0 x 27.0 x	6.0	3,800
	flt	w	Wharf Boat	wfb	Mem			2,299
1885	stp	w	*City of Natchez*	pkt	StL	296.0 x 48.7 x	9.8	75,000
	stp	w	*John Smith*	pkt	Nas	70.0 x 14.0 x	2.7	1,175
	srw	w	*Samuel B. Wiggins*	fer	StL	170.0 x 48.5 x	6.5	15,067
	stw	w	*H. K. Bedford*	pkt	Whe	148.0 x 27.0 x	3.3	5,600

TABLE I—(*Continued*)

Year Built	Rig	Hull	Name of Vessel	Service	Home Port	Dimensions			Price
	flt	w	Louisville Pump Boat	mis	Lou	50.0 x 14.0 x	3.0	$	600
	stw	w	*Alert*	twb	Nas	133.0 x 24.0 x	4.0		14,561
	stp	w	*City of Owensboro*	pkt	Lou	240.0 x 38.0 x	6.0		19,500
	stw	w	*Grace Velie*	twb	Hel	80.0 x 18.0 x	3.5		1,450
	stw	w	*Milton H. Smith*	pkt	Cha	110.0 x 24.0 x	4.0		7,561
	stw	w	Honduran Steamer	twb	For	53.0 x 22.0 x	2.5		1,650
	stp	w	Steamboat Hull	twb	Cht	155.0 x 28.0 x	4.5		3,500
1886	stp	w	Steamboat Hull	twb	Rer	130.0 x 26.0 x	5.0		3,641
	bge	w	MVT Fuel Barge	bge	StL	165.0 x 32.0 x	8.0		3,725
	bge	w	MVT Fuel Barge	bge	StL	165.0 x 32.0 x	8.0		3,725
	stp	w	*Chattahoochee*	mis	Cha	125.0 x 25.0 x	5.0		4,000
	stw	w	*William Porter*	pkt	Pad	150.0 x 30.0 x	4.0		6,250
	stw	w	*Pactolus*	pkt	Apa	135.0 x 28.0 x	4.5		13,500
	stw	w	*B. S. Rhea*	pkt	Nas	162.0 x 30.0 x	4.5		6,650
	srw	w	*John J. Brown*	fer	Nol	110.0 x 25.0 x	5.0		5,702
	stw	w	*Fannie Fearn*	pkt	Apa	135.0 x 31.7 x	5.0		6,000
	flt	w	Wharf Boat	wfb	Cai	150.0 x 32.0 x	5.0		7,500
	stw	w	*John Fowler*	pkt	Nas	149.0 x 27.0 x	3.8		8,700
	stp	w	*Oliver Bierne*	pkt	Nol	260.0 x 44.0 x	8.0		39,000
	stw	w	*Teche*	pkt	Nol	190.0 x 38.0 x	5.5		20,000
	stw	w	*Blanks Cornwell*	pkt	Vic	140.0 x 28.0 x	4.0		8,650
1887	flt	w	Coal Float	mis	Lou	140.0 x 28.0 x	2.3		1,775
	stw	w	*Matt F. Allen*	pkt	Cum	159.5 x 28.0 x	4.0		5,800
	stp	w	*New South*	pkt	Cin	254.0 x 42.0 x	7.0		32,500
	stw	w	*Joseph L. Stephens*	fer	Bon	102.0 x 28.0 x	4.0		7,000
	stw	w	*Roy Lynds*	fer	StL	85.0 x 24.0 x	3.5		4,850
	stp	w	*Crystal City*	pkt	StL	230.0 x 40.0 x	7.0		45,000
	stw	w	*Pearl*	frt	Cum	140.0 x 22.0 x	2.7		2,220
	stw	w	*E. G. Ragon*	pkt	Lou	165.0 x 31.0 x	4.5		10,500
	bge	w	Fuel Barge	bge	StL	170.0 x 32.0 x	8.0		5,500
	stp	w	*City of Monroe*	pkt	StL	270.0 x 44.0 x	8.0		66,147
	stw	w	*Hallette*	pkt	Nol	160.0 x 30.0 x	4.5		11,500
1888	flt	w	Landing Dock	wfb	Mem	119.0 x 24.0 x	5.3		3,250
	bge	w	*Swab*	bge	StL	155.0 x 30.0 x	6.0		4,000
	bge	w	*Ostrich*	bge	StL	155.0 x 30.0 x	6.0		4,000
	bge	w	Crane Boat	mis	StL	75.0 x 26.0 x	3.5		1,200
	stp	w	*Sunshine*	pas	Lou	175.0 x 37.0 x	5.8		21,750
	bge	w	Museum Boat	mis	Lou				6,000
	bge	w	Theater Boat	mis	Lou				6,000
	bge	w	Sand Barge No. 1	bge	StL	120.0 x 28.0 x	7.0		3,000
	bge	w	Sand Barge No. 2	bge	StL	120.0 x 28.0 x	7.0		3,000
	bge	w	Sand Barge No. 3	bge	StL	120.0 x 28.0 x	7.0		3,000

TABLE 1—(*Continued*)

Year Built	Rig	Hull	Name of Vessel	Service	Home Port	Dimensions		Price
	flt	w	Wharf Boat	wfb	StL	150.0 x 28.0 x	4.3	$ 2,850
	stw	w	I. T. Rhea	pkt	Nas	150.0 x 30.0 x	4.0	4,500
	stw	w	L. T. Armstrong	pkt	—	154.0x 29.0 x	4.3	6,700
	stw	w	Joe Fowler	pkt	Pad	180.0 x 32.0 x	5.0	20,800
	stw	w	Lafourche	pkt	Nol	165.0 x 38.0 x	7.0	22,700
	stw	w	Garland	pkt	Nol	160.0 x 30.0 x	4.5	13,250
	bge	w	Charlie	bge	Nol	125.0 x 20.0 x	4.0	1,600
	bge	w	Bob	bge	Nol	125.0 x 20.0 x	4.0	1,600
	stw	w	Paul Tulane	pkt	Nol	210.0 x 40.0 x	7.0	34,500
	stw	w	The New Idea	pkt	Nol	125.0 x 26.0 x	4.0	4,500
	stw	w	Matt F. Dortch	pkt	Nas	160.0 x 29.7 x	3.0	4,000
1889	bge	w	Adelaide	bge	StL	170.0 x 35.0 x	8.0	5,000
	flt	w	Boat House	mis	Lou	100.0 x 30.0 x	4.0	4,285
	stp	w	Florence	fer	StL	130.0 x 34.0 x	5.2	9,000
	sts	w	Aid	twb	Pit	51.0 x 12.0 x	6.0	875
	stw	w	Tell City	pkt	Lou	190.0 x 35.0 x	5.0	21,350
	stp	w	Kate Adams	pkt	Mem	240.0 x 34.0 x	7.0	48,000
	bge	w	No. 16	bge	StL	135.0 x 27.0 x	5.7	4,000
	bge	w	No. 17	bge	StL	135.0 x 27.0 x	5.7	4,000
	bge	w	Rock Barge	bge	StL	152.0 x 27.0 x	5.0	3,700
	bge	w	Hull for Cook Boat	mis	—	120.0 x 21.0 x	3.0	700
	flt	w	Float No. 1	wfb	Lou	55.0 x 20.0 x	3.5	675
	stp	w	Rush	fer	Lou	115.0 x 36.0 x	4.5	6,000
	stw	w	Lady Lee	pkt	Mem	165.0 x 35.0 x	4.5	10,000
	stp	w	E. B. Wheelock	twb	Nol	160.0 x 30.0 x	4.5	14,245
	bge	w	T. & P. R. R. Barge 1	bge	Nol	120.0 x 20.0 x	4.0	2,000
	bge	w	T. & P. R. R. Barge 2	bge	Nol	120.0 x 20.0 x	4.0	2,000
	stp	w	C. E. Satterlee	twb	Nol	160.0 x 30.0 x	4.5	14,245
	stw	w	City of Savannah	pkt	StL	190.0 x 32.0 x	5.5	13,000
	flt	w	Float No. 2	wfb	Lou	55.0 x 20.0 x	3.5	675
	bge	w	Cinderella	bge	Nol	120.0 x 20.0 x	4.0	2,000
	bge	w	Wm. Shakespeare	bge	Nol	120.0 x 20.0 x	4.0	2,000
	stp	w	Valley Queen	pkt	Nol	190.0 x 35.0 x	4.5	19,000
	stw	w	J. E. Trudeau	pkt	Nol	160.0 x 30.0 x	4.5	16,000
1890	stw	w	Janie Rae	pkt	Evs	110.0 x 20.0 x	3.0	3,000
	stp	w	City of Hickman	pkt	StL	285.0 x 44.5 x	9.5	66,000
	bge	w	MVT Co. No. 101	bge	StL	225.0 x 36.0 x	9.0	11,000
	bge	w	MVT Co. No. 102	bge	StL	225.0 x 36.0 x	9.0	11,000
	flt	w	Wharf Boat	wfb	StL	250.0 x 49.0 x	6.0	7,250
	bge	w	Chester	bge	StL	185.0 x 35.0 x	6.5	8,500
	bge	w	Helena	bge	StL	185.0 x 35.0 x	6.5	8,500
	stw	w	Rowena Lee	pkt	Mem	165.0 x 35.0 x	4.5	12,000
	stw	w	Ouachita	pkt	Nol	185.0 x 38.0 x	3.5	30,000

TABLE 1—(*Continued*)

Year Built	Rig	Hull	Name of Vessel	Service	Home Port	Dimensions		Price
	stw	w	*City of Sheffield*	pkt	StL	180.0 x 35.0 x	5.5	$ 14,000
	stw	w	*Jno. W. Hart*	pkt	Nas	165.0 x 28.0 x	3.0	8,250
1891	srw	w	*Henry L. Clarke*	fer	Nas	170.0 x 48.5 x	6.5	17,320
	stp	w	*Delta*	rrt	Vic	226.0 x 45.0 x	7.0	41,960
	stp	w	*City of Jeffersonville*	fer	Jef	150.0 x 34.5 x	6.3	14,500
	stw	w	*City of Paducah*	pkt	StL	190.0 x 33.0 x	5.5	13,500
	stp	w	*George A. Madill*	frt	StL	265.0 x 45.0 x	7.0	53,000
	stw	w	*Dolphin* No. 2	twb	StL	150.0 x 30.0 x	4.5	9,500
	bge	w	Sand Barge	bge	StL	120.0 x 28.0 x	6.0	3,000
	bge	w	*Commerce*	bge	StL	190.0 x 35.0 x	6.5	8,500
	bge	w	*Vidalia*	bge	StL	190.0 x 35.0 x	6.5	8,500
	2ss	s	*Josie*	fer	Nol	95.0 x 25.0 x	9.0	17,000
	stw	w	*Alex Perry*	pkt	Nas	149.9 x 28.5 x	3.5	7,150
	stw	w	*Emily*	fer	Phi	89.0 x 32.0 x	3.0	7,440
	bge	w	*Pelican*	bge	StL	135.0 x 27.0 x	5.7	4,100
	stw	w	*Ora Lee*	pkt	Mem	140.0 x 32.0 x	4.0	8,900
	stw	w	*Mabel Comeaux*	pkt	StL	178.0 x 36.0 x	6.5	21,000
	stw	w	*Natchez*	pkt	Nol	225.0 x 40.0 x	8.0	43,000
	stw	s	*Santa Fe*	twb	Nol	65.0 x 16.0 x	3.0	8,000
	stw	w	*T. P. Leathers*	pkt	Nol	220.0 x 40.0 x	6.5	42,500
	stw	w	*Colbert*	twb	Flo	125.0 x 24.0 x	3.0	9,500
	bge	w	U.S. Barge	bge	Flo	80.0 x 20.0 x	4.0	950
	bge	w	*Pelican*	bge	StL	165.0 x 30.0 x	6.0	4,250
	bge	s	*Santa Maria*	bge	For	40.0 x 12.0 x	2.5	2,000
	bge	s	*Providencia*	bge	For	40.0 x 12.0 x	2.5	2,000
	stw	w	*Hull*	pkt	Ark	100.0 x 24.0 x	3.5	2,193
1892	stp	w	*Grey Eagle*	pkt	StL	250.0 x 40.0 x	5.5	23,000
	stw	w	*Parlour City*	pkt	Nol	125.0 x 26.0 x	3.0	10,000
	stw	w	*City of Peoria*	pkt	StL	130.0 x 26.0 x	4.5	12,000
	stp	w	*Columbia*	fer	Lou	170.0 x 35.0 x	6.0	17,750
	srw	w	*Madison*	fer	StL	150.0 x 44.5 x	6.5	15,000
	flt	w	Landing Dock	wfb	Lou			2,150
	bge	w	Coal Flat No. 7	bge	StL	87.0 x 21.0 x	7.0	1,650
	bge	w	Coal Flat No. 8	bge	StL	87.0 x 21.0 x	7.0	1,650
	stw	w	*W. K. Phillips*	pkt	Nas	165.0 x 29.3 x	4.0	8,500
	bge	w	Coal Flat	bge	Lou	150.0 x 28.0 x	2.7	1,800
	srw	s	*Thomas Pickles*	fer	StL	130.0 x 54.0 x	7.0	29,000
	bge	w	Coal Flat	bge	Lou	150.0 x 26.0 x	2.7	1,800
	stp	w	*City of New Albany*	pkt	Lou	225.0 x 35.0 x	6.0	19,000
	stw	w	*Ashland City*	pkt	Nas	120.0 x 20.3 x	3.9	3,975
	bge	w	Coal Flat	bge	Lou	140.0 x 21.0 x	2.7	1,700
	flt	w	Landing Dock	wfb	Lou	55.0 x 20.0 x	3.0	650
	bge	w	Transfer Barge	rrt	Iro	240.0 x 22.0 x	5.0	8,000

TABLE 1—(*Continued*)

Year Built	Rig	Hull	Name of Vessel	Service	Home Port	Dimensions	Price
1893	stw	w	*Huntsville*	twb	Nas	125.0 x 24.0 x 4.0	$ 15,000
	bge	w	RR Barge No. 1	rrt	Nas	130.0 x 32.0 x 5.5	4,000
	bge	w	RR Barge No. 2	rrt	Nas	170.0 x 32.0 x 5.5	6,000
	srw	w	*Alonzo C. Church*	fer	StL	170.0 x 48.5 x 6.5	17,320
	bge	w	Derrick Boat	mis	Chi	90.0 x 36.0 x 3.0	2,000
	bge	w	Coal Float	bge	Lou	146.0 x 28.0 x 3.0	1,750
	2ss	w	*Help*	twb	Lou	55.0 x 14.0 x 3.5	1,500
	stw	w	*City of Camden*	pkt	Nol	175.0 x 35.0 x 5.0	19,000
	bge	w	C. E., U.S.A. Barge	bge	StL	100.6 x 25.0 x 5.4	2,550
	bge	w	C. E., U.S.A. Barge	bge	StL	100.6 x 25.0 x 5.4	2,550
	bge	w	C. E., U.S.A. Barge	bge	StL	100.6 x 25.0 x 5.4	2,550
	bge	w	C. E., U.S.A. Barge	bge	StL	100.6 x 25.0 x 5.4	2,550
	bge	w	*The Ram*	mis	StL	140.0 x 36.0 x 8.0	7,000
	stw	w	*City of Little Rock*	pkt	Mem	145.0 x 28.0 x 3.3	9,400
	stw	w	*John Howard*	pkt	Oua	180.0 x 37.0 x 6.0	17,540
	stw	w	*Shawnee*	pas	Lou	35.0 x 8.0 x 3.0	991
	stw	w	*P. D. Staggs*	pkt	Nas	160.0 x 29.0 x 3.0	5,900
	bge	w	C. E., U.S.A. Barge	bge	StL	135.0 x 28.0 x 5.0	3,650
	bge	w	C. E., U.S.A. Barge	bge	StL	135.0 x 28.0 x 5.0	3,650
	bge	w	C. E., U.S.A. Barge	bge	StL	135.0 x 28.0 x 5.0	3,650
1894	bge	w	C. E., U.S.A. Quarter Boat	bge	StL		5,390
	bge	w	C. E., U.S.A. Quarter Boat	bge	StL		5,390
	bge	w	C. E., U.S.A. Quarter Boat	bge	StL		5,390
	bge	w	C. E., U.S.A. Quarter Boat	bge	StL		5,390
	bge	w	Barge	bge	StL	135.0 x 28.0 x 5.0	3,650
	bge	w	Barge	bge	StL	135.0 x 28.0 x 5.0	3,650
	bge	w	Barge	bge	StL	135.0 x 28.0 x 5.0	3,650
	stp	w	*City of Louisville*	pkt	Lou	300.0 x 42.0 x 7.0	72,500
	bge	w	Snag Boat	mis	Vic	116.0 x 24.0 x 3.0	4,000
	stw	s	*General Reyna Barrios*	twb	For	90.0 x 20.0 x 4.0	9,250
	bge	s	Barge	bge	For	80.0 x 18.0 x 3.5	2,700
	bge	s	Barge	bge	For	80.0 x 18.0 x 3.5	2,700
	bge	s	Barge	bge	For	80.0 x 16.0 x 3.5	2,400
	bge	s	Barge	bge	For	80.0 x 16.0 x 3.5	2,400
	stw	s	*E. R. Andrews*	twb	Ppw	165.0 x 32.5 x 5.0	25,500
	bge	w	Barge	bge	StL	100.0 x 22.0 x 4.0	1,350
	stw	w	*Clyde*	pkt	StL	175.0 x 33.0 x 5.0	11,500
	stp	w	*Dekoven*	rrt	Pad	220.0 x 36.0 x 6.0	20,000
	bge	w	Barge	bge	StL	200.0 x 31.0 x 5.5	5,000

TABLE I—(*Continued*)

Year Built	Rig	Hull	Name of Vessel	Service	Home Port	Dimensions			Price
	bge	w	Barge	bge	StL	200.0 x 31.0 x	5.5	$	5,000
	bge	w	Barge	bge	StL	200.0 x 31.0 x	5.5		5,000
	bge	w	Barge	bge	StL	200.0 x 31.0 x	5.5		5,000
	stw	w	*Imperial*	pkt	Nol	210.0 x 40.0 x	7.0		24,500
	bge	w	C. E., U.S.A. Barge	bge	Mem	135.0 x 28.0 x	5.0		3,750
	bge	w	C. E., U.S.A. Barge	bge	Mem	135.0 x 28.0 x	5.0		3,750
	bge	w	C. E., U.S.A. Barge	bge	Mem	135.0 x 28.0 x	5.0		3,750
	bge	w	C. E., U.S.A. Barge	bge	Mem	135.0 x 28.0 x	5.0		3,750
	stw	w	*Fritz*	twb	Cai	120.0 x 26.0 x	4.0		5,000
1895	stw	w	*City of Warsaw*	fer	War	100.0 x 24.0 x	3.9		2,200
	bge	w	Barge	bge	StL	200.0 x 37.0 x	7.0		5,850
	bge	w	Barge	bge	StL	200.0 x 37.0 x	7.0		5,850
	bge	w	Barge	bge	StL	200.0 x 37.0 x	7.0		5,850
	bge	w	Fuel Flat	bge	StL	110.0 x 22.0 x	4.0		1,100
	stw	w	*W. T. Scovell*	twb	Nol	160.0 x 31.0 x	3.0		12,500
	bge	w	Dump Scow	bge	StL	110.0 x 22.0 x	4.0		1,350
	bge	w	Dump Scow	bge	StL	110.0 x 22.0 x	4.0		1,350
	stw	w	*Rose Hite*	pkt	Lou	150.0 x 28.0 x	3.5		6,500
	bge	w	Dump Scow	bge	Cin	75.0 x 20.0 x	5.0		2,750
	stw	w	*General H. L. Abbot*	twb	StL	170.0 x 32.0 x	5.0		27,375
	stw	w	*Will A. Cummins*	pkt	Nas	160.0 x 30.0 x	4.0		7,000
	bge	w	C. E., U.S.A. Barge	bge	Cht	135.0 x 28.0 x	5.0		3,385
	bge	w	C. E., U.S.A. Barge	bge	Cht	135.0 x 28.0 x	5.0		3,385
	bge	w	C. E., U.S.A. Barge	bge	Cht	135.0 x 28.0 x	5.0		3,385
	bge	w	C. E., U.S.A. Barge	bge	Cht	135.0 x 28.0 x	5.0		3,385
	bge	w	*Vidette*	bge	Nol	100.0 x 24.0 x	4.0		1,900
	bge	w	Barge	bge	Nol	100.0 x 24.0 x	4.0		1,900
	stw	w	*Reuben Dunbar*	pkt	Nas	160.0 x 28.5 x	4.0		7,000
	stw	w	*Patrol*	twb	—	130.0 x 28.0 x	4.9		9,980
	stw	w	*Charlie Curlin*	frt	Lou	87.0 x 18.0 x	3.5		4,000
	stp	w	*Anna Dale*	rrt	Cai	250.0 x 42.0 x	8.0		13,500
	stp	w	*Wash Gray*	twb	Lou	90.0 x 19.0 x	8.0		4,000
	bge	w	Barge	bge	Vic	110.0 x 24.0 x	3.5		1,650
	bge	w	Barge	bge	Vic	110.0 x 24.0 x	3.5		1,650
	stw	w	*Tarascon*	pkt	Lou	190.0 x 35.0 x	5.0		12,250
1896	stw	w	*Verapaz*	twb	For	90.0 x 18.0 x	3.0		5,000
	bge	s	Barge	bge	For	85.0 x 18.0 x	2.5		3,000
	bge	s	Barge	bge	For	85.0 x 18.0 x	2.5		3,000
	bge	w	Sand Barge	bge	Lou				600
	stw	w	*MacKenzie*	twb	Lou	125.0 x 25.0 x	4.5		4,560
	stw	s	*El Peten*	twb	Nol	90.0 x 20.0 x	4.0		6,000
	bge	s	Barge	bge	Nol	65.0 x 18.0 x	2.5		2,500
	bge	s	Barge	bge	Nol	65.0 x 18.0 x	2.5		2,500

TABLE I—(*Continued*)

Year Built	Rig	Hull	Name of Vessel	Service	Home Port	Dimensions			Price
	stw	s	Towboat	twb	For	100.0 x 20.0 x	4.0	$	6,000
	bge	s	Barge	bge	For	90.0 x 20.0 x	4.0		2,500
	bge	s	Barge	bge	For	90.0 x 20.0 x	4.0		2,500
	stw	w	*Lookout*	twb	Cht	110.0 x 25.0 x	3.0		9,000
	2ss	s	*Ollie*	fer	Nol	125.0 x 30.0 x	4.5		4,400
	stw	w	*Istrouma*	fer	Brl	150.0 x 30.0 x	5.0		6,800
	stw	w	*H. W. Buttorff*	pkt	Nas	160.0 x 30.0 x	4.0		7,000
	stw	w	*Bluff City*	pkt	StL	225.0 x 42.0 x	6.0		36,500
	stw	w	*Eliza*	twb	Pit	110.0 x 25.0 x	3.0		3,700
	stw	w	Hull for U.S. Dredge	mis	—	185.6 x 34.9 x	4.7		14,000
1897	stw	w	*Jim T. Duffy, Jr.*	twb	Mem	120.0 x 26.0 x	4.0		4,500
	stw	w	*Colonel G. L. Gillespie*	twb	Evs	110.0 x 25.0 x	3.0		3,700
	stw	s	*H. C. Haarstick*	twb	StL	115.0 x 22.0 x	10.0		15,500
	stw	w	*Dolphin* No. 3	twb	StL	155.0 x 32.0 x	5.0		19,000
	stw	w	*W. C. Hite*	fer	Lou	156.0 x 36.0 x	6.5		14,750
	bge	w	Transfer Barge	bge	StL	230.0 x 28.0 x	7.0		7,500
	stp	s	*Andrew Christy*	fer	StL	176.0 x 48.0 x	7.0		27,000
	stw	w	*Bob Dudley*	frt	Nas	157.0 x 28.5 x	3.5		6,000
	flt	w	Landing Dock	wfb	Mem	120.0 x 40.0 x	4.0		3,750
	stw	w	*Chiska*	twb	StL	160.0 x 30.0 x	6.0		25,900
	stp	w	*Rob't. E. Lee*	pkt	Mem	245.0 x 43.0 x	6.5		27,000
	stw	w	*Tennessee*	pkt	StL	170.0 x 32.0 x	4.5		8,500
	bge	w	Drilling Scow	mis	Lou	72.0 x 22.0 x	4.0		
	bge	w	Drilling Scow	mis	Lou	72.0 x 22.0 x	4.0		
	stw	s	Hull for U.S. Dredge	mis	StL	160.0 x 40.0 x	6.5		50,000
	stw	s	Hull for U.S. Dredge	mis	StL	160.0 x 40.0 x	6.5		50,000
	stw	w	*Electra*	pkt	Nol	175.0 x 35.0 x	4.5		17,000
	stw	w	*Sunrise*	pkt	Nol	180.0 x 36.0 x	5.0		19,750
	stw	w	*John W. Thomas*	pkt	Nas	160.0 x 26.5 x	3.5		4,600
	stp	w	*James Lee*	pkt	Mem	230.0 x 43.0 x	6.5		27,000
1898	stp	w	*Belle of the Bends*	pkt	Vic	210.0 x 32.0 x	7.0		33,500
	stw	w	*Cumberland*	twb	Nas	130.0 x 36.0 x	4.0		9,600
	bge	w	Coal Float	bge	Lou	160.0 x 28.0 x	2.5		1,150
	stw	w	Yukon River Packet	pkt	Ala	225.0 x 40.0 x	6.0		25,000
	stw	w	Yukon River Packet	pkt	Ala	225.0 x 40.0 x	6.0		25,000
	stw	w	Yukon River Packet	pkt	Ala	225.0 x 40.0 x	6.0		25,000
	stw	w	Yukon River Towboat	twb	Ala	160.0 x 32.0 x	5.0		12,000
	stw	w	*Georgia Lee*	pkt	Mem	210.0 x 43.0 x	6.0		18,000
	stw	w	*Julian Poydras*	pkt	Brl	160.0 x 30.0 x	5.0		12,000
	stw	w	*City of Memphis*	pkt	StL	200.0 x 36.0 x	6.0		12,000
	stw	w	*Henry Harley*	pkt	Nas	160.0 x 29.0 x	4.0		11,750

TABLE I—(*Continued*)

Year Built	Rig	Hull	Name of Vessel	Service	Home Port	Dimensions		Price
	stw	w	Gem	twb	Nol	135.0 x 28.0 x	4.2	$ 10,500
	bge	w	Ready	bge	Nol	100.0 x 20.0 x	3.0	1,800
	bge	w	Relief	bge	Nol	100.0 x 20.3 x	3.0	1,800
	stp	s	Kate Adams	pkt	Mem	240.0 x 40.0 x	7.0	43,750
	stw	s	Arthur Hider	twb	Mem	160.0 x 30.0 x	5.0	33,850
	stw	w	America	pkt	Nol	200.0 x 38.0 x	7.0	30,000
	stw	w	J. B. Richardson	pkt	Nas	165.0 x 30.0 x	4.2	18,000
	stw	w	Greenwood	frt	Gre	130.0 x 28.0 x	3.5	4,250
	stw	w	Mary	pkt	Mob	177.0 x 33.0 x	4.5	19,850
	bge	w	House Boat, CMN	hbt	Lou	70.0 x 24.0 x	4.0	850
	flt	w	Landing Dock	wfb	Lou	100.0 x 30.3 x	3.0	2,000
1899	stp	w	City of Cincinnati	pkt	Cin	307.0 x 41.0 x	6.5	40,000
	stw	w	Ouachita	frt	—	140.0 x 32.0 x	4.0	10,000
	stw	w	Red River	frt	Nol	155.0 x 28.0 x	4.0	12,000
	bge	w	Barge	bge	StL	200.0 x 33.0 x	5.5	5,000
	bge	w	Barge	bge	StL	200.0 x 33.0 x	5.5	5,000
	bge	w	Barge	bge	StL	200.0 x 33.0 x	5.5	5,000
	bge	w	Barge	bge	StL	200.0 x 33.0 x	5.5	5,000
	bge	w	Barge	bge	StL	200.0 x 33.0 x	5.5	5,000
	bge	w	Barge	bge	StL	200.0 x 33.0 x	5.5	5,000
	bge	w	Barge	bge	StL	200.0 x 33.0 x	5.5	5,000
	stw	w	Peters Lee	pkt	Mem	220.0 x 42.0 x	6.0	19,000
	stw	s	W. R. King	twb	—	190.0 x 40.0 x	5.5	67,750
	flt	w	Wharf Boat	wfb	Cla	165.0 x 35.0 x	4.0	3,460
	stw	w	Mary	fer	War	100.0 x 24.0 x	3.9	3,000
	stw	w	Rees Lee	pkt	Mem	220.0 x 42.0 x	6.0	19,000
	bge	w	Coal Barge	bge	Pad	100.0 x 24.0 x	7.0	2,000
	bge	w	Coal Barge	bge	Pad	100.0 x 24.0 x	7.0	2,000
	stw	s	U.S. Tender	mis	—	100.0 x 24.0 x	4.0	15,000
	stw	s	U.S. Tender	mis	—	100.0 x 24.0 x	4.0	15,000
	stw	s	U.S. Tender	mis	—	100.0 x 24.0 x	4.0	15,000
	bge	w	Mattress Barge	mis	—	160.0 x 32.0 x	5.0	3,500
	bge	w	Mattress Barge	mis	—	160.0 x 32.0 x	5.0	3,500
	stw	w	Bayless Lee	pkt	Mem	190.0 x 38.0 x	5.8	14,700
1900	stw	w	Rowena Lee	pkt	Mem	190.0 x 38.0 x	5.8	14,700
	bge	w	Coal Barge	bge	StL	130.0 x 25.0 x	7.0	1,600
	bge	w	Coal Barge	bge	StL	130.0 x 25.0 x	7.0	1,600
	bge	w	Sand Barge	bge	StL	130.0 x 30.0 x	7.0	3,450
	stp	w	Indiana	pkt	Lou	285.0 x 42.0 x	6.0	30,000
	stp	w	Col. A. McKenzie	twb	—	160.0 x 32.0 x	5.0	32,000
	bge	w	Barge	bge	Nol	108.0 x 18.0 x	3.3	1,650
	bge	w	Barge	bge	Nol	108.0 x 18.0 x	3.3	1,650
	stw	w	M. W. Kelley	pkt	Cog	150.0 x 32.0 x	4.0	13,000

TABLE 1—(*Continued*)

Year Built	Rig	Hull	Name of Vessel	Service	Home Port	Dimensions		Price
	stw	w	*Alma*	pkt	Nol	155.0 x 32.0 x	4.0	$ 12,500
	bge	w	Barge	bge	Nol	120.0 x 24.0 x	4.0	1,950
	bge	w	Barge	bge	Nol	120.0 x 24.0 x	4.0	1,950
	bge	w	C & O Railroad Transfer	rrt	Iro	240.0 x 22.0 x	5.0	6,000
	stw	w	*E. T. Slider*	twb	Nai	110.0 x 24.0 x	3.2	4,000
	bge	w	Barge	bge	Cin	200.0 x 33.0 x	6.0	6,000
	bge	w	Barge	bge	Cin	200.0 x 33.0 x	6.0	6,000
	bge	w	Coal Barge	bge	Cin	135.0 x 26.0 x	7.8	1,650
	bge	w	Barge	bge	Cin	135.0 x 26.0 x	7.8	1,650
	bge	w	Barge	bge	Cin	135.0 x 26.0 x	7.8	1,650
	bge	w	Barge	bge	Cin	135.0 x 26.0 x	7.8	1,650
	flt	w	Landing Dock	wfb	Lou	60.0 x 20.0 x	3.0	1,000
1901	stw	w	*Lida*	twb	Evs	121.0 x 26.0 x	3.4	6,500
	stp	w	*Morning Star*	pkt	Evs	225.0 x 38.0 x	5.8	22,500
	stw	w	*J. S.*	pas	Rii	175.0 x 36.8 x	5.0	13,450
	flt	w	Pumpboat Hull	mis	Pit	26.0 x 14.0 x	3.9	325
	stw	w	*Wm. McClelland*	twb	StL	150.0 x 28.0 x	4.5	11,000
	bge	w	Dredge Boat	mis	Pad	80.0 x 30.0 x	6.8	
	stw	w	*Gold Dust*	pkt	Mem	170.0 x 34.0 x	5.0	6,000
	stw	w	*Sadie Lee*	pkt	Mem	140.0 x 31.0 x	5.0	10,000
	bge	w	Barge	bge	StL	175.0 x 35.0 x	7.0	6,320
	stw	w	*Vega*	twb	Ppw	104.0 x 17.3 x	3.3	9,805
	stw	s	*Steel Queen*	fer	Pit	125.0 x 28.0 x	3.4	11,675
	stw	w	*A. D. Allen*	pkt	Lra	125.0 x 27.0 x	3.5	4,500
	stw	w	*H. M. Carter*	pkt	Shv	155.0 x 28.0 x	4.0	11,000
	stw	w	*G. W. Thomas*	twb	Pit	150.0 x 27.5 x	4.0	10,500
	stw	w	*Senator Cordill*	pkt	Nat	170.0 x 34.0 x	5.0	28,950
1902	flt	w	Boat House	mis	Cin	92.0 x 22.0 x	3.5	3,600
	flt	w	Landing Dock	wfb	Lou			2,350
	stw	w	*Stacker Lee*	pkt	Mem	225.0 x 45.0 x	6.0	21,600
	stw	w	*City of Savannah*	pkt	StL	200.0 x 38.0 x	6.0	17,000
	bge	w	Barge	bge	StL	120.0 x 28.0 x	6.0	3,438
	bge	w	Barge	bge	StL	120.0 x 28.0 x	6.0	3,438
	bge	w	Barge	bge	StL	120.0 x 28.0 x	6.0	3,438
	bge	w	Barge	bge	StL	120.0 x 28.0 x	6.0	3,438
	stw	w	*Shiloh*	pkt	StL	150.0 x 29.0 x	4.0	9,250
	flt	w	Life Saving Boat House	mis	Lou			6,880
	stw	w	*Beauregard*	mis	Mem	128.0 x 30.0 x	4.3	5,810
	bge	w	Sand Barge	bge	Brl	100.0 x 24.0 x	4.0	3,250
	flt	w	Sand Digger	mis	Nai			1,400
	flt	w	Sand Digger	mis	Nai			1,400

TABLE 1—(*Continued*)

Year Built	Rig	Hull	Name of Vessel	Service	Home Port	Dimensions			Price
	stp	w	*Ste Genevieve*	rrt	Cai	215.0 x 45.0 x	8.0	$	67,500
	srw	s	*A. M. Halliday*	fer	Nol	120.0 x 57.5 x	7.0		20,700
1903	bge	w	Derrick Boat	mis	Nai				1,400
	bge	w	Sand Digger	mis	Nai				1,465
	stw	w	*Guntersville*	pkt	Nas	150.0 x 30.0 x	4.0		18,500
	bge	w	Sand Barge No. 1	bge	StL	130.0 x 30.0 x	7.0		4,473
	bge	w	Sand Barge No. 2	bge	StL	130.0 x 30.0 x	7.0		4,473
	bge	w	Sand Barge No. 3	bge	StL	130.0 x 30.0 x	7.0		4,473
	bge	w	Sand Barge No. 4	bge	StL	130.0 x 30.0 x	7.0		4,473
	bge	w	Sand Barge No. 5	bge	StL	130.0 x 30.0 x	7.0		4,473
	stw	w	*Wymoka* (New Deck & Cabin)	mis	—				7,900
	bge	w	Coal Float	bge	Jef	145.0 x 26.0 x	3.0		1,660
	stw	w	Steamboat Hull	twb	Brl	120.0 x 27.0 x	4.0		3,752
	stw	w	*Lyda*	twb	Pad	122.0 x 24.0 x	3.3		3,000
	bge	w	Dredge	mis	Nas				5,000
	stw	w	*Henry*	mis	Nas	90.0 x 20.0 x	3.0		4,535
	stw	w	*John*	mis	Nas	90.0 x 20.0 x	3.0		4,535
	bge	w	Barge	bge	Nas				1,505
	bge	w	Barge	bge	Nas				1,505
	bge	w	Barge	bge	Nas				1,505
	bge	w	Barge	bge	Nas				1,505
	bge	w	Dump Scow	mis	Nas				3,650
	bge	w	Dump Scow	mis	Nas				3,650
	bge	w	Sand Barge	bge	—	110.0 x 26.0 x	6.0		2,300
	stw	w	*Columbia*	frt	Nol	170.0 x 30.0 x	4.4		8,998
	stw	w	*Roberts*	frt	Mrl	135.0 x 27.0 x	4.0		12,500
	stw	w	*Bob Blanks*	pkt	Mrl	175.0 x 35.0 x	5.0		25,000
	stw	w	*Handy*	pkt	Mrl	110.0 x 22.0 x	3.0		8,825
	stw	w	*Frank B. Hayne*	pkt	Mrl	130.0 x 26.0 x	4.0		9,000
	stw	w	*Charley Jutte*	twb	Pit	150.0 x 27.0 x	4.2		11,850
1904	flt	w	Landing Dock	wfb	Mci	150.0 x 30.0 x	5.0		5,110
	flt	w	Landing Dock	wfb	Mci	150.0 x 30.0 x	5.0		5,110
	bge	w	Barge	bge	Cai	100.0 x 20.0 x	4.0		2,090
	bge	w	Derrick Boat Hull	mis	Cai	100.0 x 40.0 x	5.0		3,450
	stw	s	*H. St. L. Coppee*	twb	Mem	140.0 x 30.0 x	6.0		53,900
	bge	w	Sand Barge	bge	StL	130.0 x 30.0 x	7.0		4,800
	bge	w	Sand Barge	bge	StL	130.0 x 30.0 x	7.0		4,800
	stw	w	*Golden Eagle*	pkt	Brl	175.0 x 35.0 x	5.0		15,035
	bge	w	Sand Barge	bge	StL	120.0 x 28.0 x	6.0		3,950
	bge	w	Sand Barge	bge	StL	120.0 x 28.0 x	6.0		3,950
	bge	w	Fuel Flat Boat	bge	StL	80.0 x 20.0 x	6.0		1,650
	bge	w	Barge	bge	Cin	100.0 x 25.0 x	6.0		2,500

TABLE 1—(*Continued*)

Year Built	Rig	Hull	Name of Vessel	Service	Home Port	Dimensions			Price
	stw	w	*Kentucky*	pkt	StL	175.0 x 33.0 x	4.5		$ 13,500
	stw	w	*City of Saltillo*	pkt	StL	200.0 x 36.0 x	6.0		17,350
	srw	w	*Perryville*	fer	Chi	100.0 x 27.0 x	4.0		3,300
	stw	w	*Margaret E. Ray*	fer	—	40.0 x 10.0 x	3.0		750
	bge	w	Barge	bge	Vic	110.0 x 24.0 x	3.0		2,100
	stw	w	*Bowling Green*	pkt	Evs	123.0 x 32.0 x	5.5		18,600
	stw	w	*Nugent*	twb	Lou	120.0 x 24.0 x	4.0		7,250
	stw	w	*Three States*	pas	Cai	150.0 x 32.0 x	4.5		12,525
	bge	w	Derrick Boat	mis	—	100.0 x 26.0 x	4.0		1,700
1905	srw	s	*A. Baldwin*	fer	Nol	125.0 x 44.0 x	7.0		19,500
	stw	w	*Scimitar*	mis	StL	135.0 x 26.0 x	4.0		16,650
	srw	s	*L. H. Morrero*	fer	Nol	113.0 x 42.0 x	7.0		15,550
	stw	w	*Jennie Barbour*	twb	Fra	110.0 x 28.0 x	4.0		8,076
	gas	w	*White Oak*	frt	Cum	90.0 x 18.0 x	3.0		3,350
	bge	w	Dredge	mis	StL	125.0 x 30.0 x	6.0		4,595
	bge	w	Dredge	mis	StL	130.0 x 30.0 x	7.0		6,700
	bge	w	Sand Barge	bge	StL	130.0 x 30.0 x	7.0		4,850
	bge	w	Sand Barge	bge	StL	130.0 x 30.0 x	7.0		4,850
	bge	w	Sand Barge	bge	StL	130.0 x 30.0 x	7.0		4,850
	bge	w	Flat Boat for Caulking	mis	StL	24.0 x 8.0 x	1.0		100
1906	stw	w	*H. M. Carter* (New Cabin)	pkt	Nol				4,756
	bge	w	Sand Barge	bge	Mci	100.0 x 30.0 x	6.0		3,583
	bge	w	Sand Barge	bge	Mci	100.0 x 30.0 x	6.0		3,583
	bge	w	Sand Barge	bge	Mci	100.0 x 30.0 x	6.0		3,583
	stw	w	*J. O. Cole*	twb	Cin	130.0 x 26.0 x	4.5		5,400
	stw	w	*Wm. Edenborn*	twb	Nol	145.0 x 31.0 x	5.0		12,835
	bge	w	Excursion Barge	pas	Nai	75.0 x 16.0 x	2.5		1,000
	gas	w	Excursion Boat	pas	Nai	52.0 x 12.0 x	2.5		1,300
	bge	w	Pile Driver	mis	StL	80.0 x 36.0 x	3.0		2,700
	stw	w	*Concordia*	pkt	Nat	150.0 x 30.0 x	5.0		11,700
	stw	w	*Mary A. Anderson*	twb	Gal	100.0 x 28.0 x	3.5		10,000
	stw	w	*Columbia* (New Cabin)	pkt	Nol				4,000
	stw	w	*John A. Patton*	pkt	Cht	165.0 x 32.0 x	4.5		19,500
	stp	w	*Alton*	pkt	StL	240.0 x 35.0 x	6.0		19,950
	bge	w	Barge	bge	Vic	70.0 x 16.0 x	4.0		1,100
1907	stw	s	*Jas. E. Ransdell*	mis	Vic	137.0 x 32.0 x	5.0		42,443
	stw	s	*Ben Humphrey*	mis	Vic	137.0 x 32.0 x	5.0		42,443
	bge	w	Sand Barge	bge	StL	130.0 x 30.0 x	7.0		5,000
	flt	w	Wharfboat	wfb	StL	150.0 x 40.0 x	6.0		9,000

TABLE 1—(*Continued*)

Year Built	Rig	Hull	Name of Vessel	Service	Home Port	Dimensions			Price
	bge	w	Coal Float	bge	Lou	150.0 x 26.0 x	2.4	$	2,500
	flt	w	Wharfboat With Cargo Box	wfb	Evs	150.0 x 40.0 x	5.0		7,750
	stw	w	*John Quill*	pkt	Mob	170.0 x 35.0 x	4.5		21,000
	bge	w	Mattress Barge	mis	Vic	135.0 x 34.0 x	5.0		
	bge	w	Mattress Barge	mis	Vic	135.0 x 34.0 x	5.0		
	stw	w	*Merrill*	twb	Mar	115.0 x 22.0 x	3.5		14,000
	bge	w	Railroad Transfer Barge	rrt	Cai	225.0 x 36.0 x	6.7		13,950
1908	bge	s	Dredge	mis	Cin	125.0 x 34.0 x	6.8		27,689
	stw	w	*City of Muskogee*	pkt	Muk	125.0 x 28.0 x	3.5		10,000
	bge	w	Derrick Hull	mis	StL	120.0 x 30.0 x	6.0		5,000
	stw	w	*Northern*	twb	Nai	125.0 x 25.5 x	4.0		9,250
	stw	s	*Mammoth Cave*	mis	Lou	140.0 x 34.0 x	5.0		30,830
	stw	w	*Hiwassee*	twb	Pad	100.0 x 20.0 x	3.0		10,000
	stw	w	*Chilhowee*	twb	Pad	100.0 x 20.0 x	3.0		10,000
	bge	w	Barge	bge	Lou	160.0 x 34.0 x	6.0		6,436
	bge	w	Barge	bge	Lou	160.0 x 34.0 x	6.0		6,436
	bge	w	Fuel Flat Boat	bge	Pad	100.0 x 20.0 x	6.0		2,200
	stw	w	*R. C. McCalla*	mis	Mob	100.0 x 28.0 x	5.0		19,000
	stw	w	*Tombigbee*	mis	Mob	100.0 x 28.0 x	5.0		19,000
	bge	w	Mattress Barge	mis	Vic	135.0 x 34.0 x	5.0		7,100
	bge	w	Mattress Barge	mis	Vic	135.0 x 34.0 x	5.0		7,100
1909	stw	w	*J. H. Menge*	pkt	Mrl	191.0 x 37.0 x	6.5		33,500
	stw	w	*Kentucky*	twb	Cin	127.0 x 30.0 x	5.5		24,600
	mis	s	Guards for the *Kate Adams*	mis					7,000
	stw	w	*James L. Hale*	twb	Mob	70.0 x 16.0 x	3.0		2,970
	flt	w	Wharfboat	wfb	Mem	300.0 x 50.0 x	6.5		2,250
	stw	w	*G. W. Hill*	pkt	StL	190.0 x 36.0 x	5.0		28,850
	stw	w	*City of Florence*	pkt	Nas	130.0 x 26.0 x	3.0		14,000
	stw	w	*Ed Myer*	pkt	Car	125.0 x 22.0 x	3.0		9,835
	bge	w	Barge	rrt	Cin	224.0 x 36.0 x	6.0		12,000
	bge	w	Barge	rrt	Cin	225.0 x 36.0 x	6.0		12,000
	mis	w	Texas Deck for *B. S. Rhea*	mis					320
	stw	w	*Nashville*	pkt	Nas	156.0 x 33.0 x	4.5		22,850
1910	stw	s	*Plaquemine*	twb	Nol	116.0 x 28.0 x	5.0		38,700
	bge	w	Barge	rrt	—	225.0 x 36.0 x	6.0		12,000
	bge	w	Barge	rrt	—	225.0 x 36.0 x	6.0		12,000
	stw	w	*Peerless*	fer	Lou	100.0 x 36.0 x	3.5		4,000
	stw	s	*Teche*	twb	Nol	86.0 x 19.0 x	4.5		16,850

TABLE I—(*Continued*)

Year Built	Rig	Hull	Name of Vessel	Service	Home Port	Dimensions			Price
	stw	w	*Gladys*	fer	StL	95.0 x 25.0 x	4.0	$	5,025
	3gs	s	*Polly*	pas	Lou	95.0 x 15.0 x	3.0		18,000
1911	stw	w	*H. S. Chamberlain*	twb	Nas	140.0 x 30.0 x	4.0		18,500
	stp	w	Excursion Boat	pas	StL	165.0 x 24.0 x	5.5		15,000
	stw	s	*General Craighill*	twb	Whe	116.0 x 27.0 x	4.2		27,550
	bge	w	Dump Scow	bge	Cin	75.0 x 17.0 x	6.3		3,220
	bge	w	Sand Barge	bge	Lou	110.0 x 26.0 x	6.0		3,650
	bge	w	Sand Barge	bge	Lou	110.0 x 26.0 x	6.0		3,650
	flt	w	Landing Dock	wfb	Ask	40.0 x 16.0 x	3.0		487
	bge	w	Dump Scow	bge	Cin	75.0 x 17.0 x	6.3		3,220
1912	stp	s	*Julius S. Walsh*	fer	StL	169.0 x 50.0 x	7.0		83,000
	stp	s	*W. S. McChesney, Jr.*	fer	StL	180.0 x 50.0 x	7.0		83,000
	stw	s	*Issaquena*	twb	Vic	145.5 x 30.0 x	6.0		55,640
	stw	s	*Jupiter*	twb	StL	99.0 x 20.0 x	4.5		17,175
	stw	s	*Saturn*	twb	StL	99.0 x 20.0 x	4.5		17,175
	stw	w	*Corker*	pkt	Cin	130.0 x 30.0 x	4.5		8,224
	bge	w	Sand Barge	bge	Evs	100.0 x 26.0 x	6.0		2,750
	bge	w	Sand Barge	bge	Evs	100.0 x 26.0 x	6.0		2,750
	bge	w	Derrick Boat	mis	Evs	66.0 x 34.0 x	4.0		2,295
	bge	w	Derrick Boat	mis	Evs	66.0 x 34.0 x	4.0		2,295
	bge	w	Sand Digger Hull	mis	Evs	100.0 x 22.0 x	4.0		1,950
	stw	w	*Saint Louis*	pkt	StL	210.0 x 38.0 x	6.0		21,950
	mis	w	New Cabin and Texas Deck on *Lucille Nowland*	mis	—				5,000
	stw	w	Cairo Ferry Boat	fer	Cai	120.0 x 28.0 x	4.0		5,700
	bge	w	Fuel Flat Boat	bge	Lou	60.0 x 16.0 x	4.5		800
1913	stw	s	*Cherokee*	twb	Lou	120.0 x 26.0 x	4.6		17,257
	stw	w	*Peoria*	pkt	StL	240.0 x 38.0 x	6.0		26,000
	stw	w	*C. C. K.*	fer	Chi	90.0 x 24.0 x	4.0		4,768
	stw	w	*Joe Horton Fell*	pkt	Nas	160.0 x 30.0 x	4.5		19,750
	bge	w	Barge	bge	Evs	100.0 x 26.0 x	6.0		2,750
	bge	w	Barge	bge	Evs	100.0 x 26.0 x	6.0		2,750
	bgt	s	Barge	bge	Lou	70.0 x 22.0 x	4.8		4,000
	bgt	s	Barge	bge	Lou	70.0 x 22.0 x	4.8		4,000
	bge	w	Barge	bge	Bir	60.0 x 15.0 x	3.0		675
	bge	w	Barge	bge	Bir	60.0 x 15.0 x	3.0		675
	stw	w	Steamboat Hull	frt	Lou	75.0 x 16.0 x	3.5		1,200
	bge	s	Derrick Boat Hull	mis	StL	80.0 x 36.0 x	5.0		7,775
	flt	w	Landing Dock	wfb	Lou				833
	flt	w	Landing Dock	wfb	Lou				833
	flt	w	Landing Dock	wfb	Lou				833

TABLE 1—(*Continued*)

Year Built	Rig	Hull	Name of Vessel	Service	Home Port	Dimensions			Price
	flt	w	Boat House	mis	Lou	60.0 x 24.0 x	4.0	$	1,925
1914	stw	w	*Homer Smith*	pas	Pit	240.0 x 40.0 x	7.0		29,619
	bge	s	Derrick Boat Hull	mis	Lou	70.0 x 32.0 x	5.0		5,600
	bge	s	Derrick Boat Hull	mis	Lou	70.0 x 32.0 x	5.0		5,600
	bge	s	*Shippingport*	mis	Lou	100.0 x 22.0 x	5.0		5,825
	bge	s	*Portland*	mis	Lou	100.0 x 22.0 x	5.0		5,825
	bge	s	Pumpboat Hull	mis	—	110.0 x 36.0 x	5.5		10,793
	bge	s	Derrick Boat	mis	Cin	70.0 x 32.0 x	5.0		5,500
	bge	s	Derrick Boat	mis	Cin	70.0 x 32.0 x	5.0		5,500
	bge	s	Derrick Boat	mis	Lou	80.0 x 26.0 x	5.0		5,225
	bge	s	Pumpboat Hull	mis	Lou	50.0 x 16.0 x	5.0		2,275
	stw	s	Towboat Hull	twb	Rii	125.0 x 31.0 x	4.0		13,836
	stw	s	Towboat Hull	twb	Rii	125.0 x 31.0 x	4.0		13,836
	stw	s	Towboat Hull	twb	Rii	125.0 x 31.0 x	4.0		13,836
	stw	s	Towboat Hull	twb	Rii	125.0 x 31.0 x	4.0		13,836
	stw	s	*Standard*	twb	Nol	130.0 x 30.0 x	6.0		32,000
	stw	w	*Three States*	fer	Cai	120.0 x 28.0 x	4.5		11,000
	stw	w	*Edna* (Hull Only)	fer	StL	65.0 x 20.0 x	3.5		1,600
	bge	w	Flat Boat	bge	StL	100.0 x 20.0 x	7.0		2,385
1915	stw	s	*Chalmette*	twb	Nol	89.0 x 21.0 x	4.5		19,425
	bge	s	Barge	bge	Nol	124.0 x 30.0 x	7.5		8,250
	bge	s	Barge	bge	Cin	60.0 x 26.0 x	3.5		3,750
	bge	s	Derrick Boat	mis	Cin	70.0 x 32.0 x	5.0		5,550
	bge	s	Derrick Boat	mis	Cin	70.0 x 32.0 x	5.0		5,550
	bge	w	*Hattie Brown*	pkt	Lou	125.0 x 25.5 x	4.5		4,355
	stw	w	*Kathryn E. Nugent*	twb	Lou	52.0 x 12.0 x	6.0		2,000
	gas	w	Gasoline Launch	pas	StL				610
	40s	s	Inco No. 1	frt	StL	240.0 x 42.0 x	6.5		
1916	stw	s	*Minnesota*	pas	Spm	115.0 x 30.0 x	5.0		30,000
	srw	s	*H. O. Penick*	fer	—	120.0 x 54.0 x	7.0		21,000
	srw	s	*S. Halliday*	fer	Nol	130.0 x 56.0 x	7.0		20,000
	srw	s	*Joseph Bisso*	fer	Nol	120.0 x 54.0 x	7.0		21,000
	srw	s	*City of Baton Rouge*	fer	—	120.0 x 54.0 x	7.0		22,000
	stw	s	*Pilgrim*	pas	Lou	200.0 x 36.0 x	6.0		17,554
	stw	w	*Paducah*	pkt	StL	170.0 x 33.0 x	5.0		15,000
1917	srw	s	*Martin Behrman*	fer	Nol	126.5 x 31.2 x	7.2		20,000
	mis	w	Cabin for the *Indiana*	mis	Lou				19,850
	gas	w	*B. M. White*	twb	Lou	60.0 x 12.0 x	6.0		6,800
1918	stp	w	*General Logan*	twb	Lou	90.0 x 18.0 x	3.0		16,600
	bge	w	Barge	bge	Lou	90.0 x 18.0 x	3.0		1,873

Table 1—(*Continued*)

Year Built	Rig	Hull	Name of Vessel	Service	Home Port	Dimensions		Price
	bge	w	Barge	bge	Lou	90.0 x 18.0 x 3.0	$	1,873
	bge	w	Barge	bge	Lou	90.0 x 18.0 x 3.0		1,873
	bge	w	Barge	bge	Lou	90.0 x 18.0 x 3.0		1,873
	bge	w	Barge	bge	Lou	90.0 x 18.0 x 3.0		1,873
	bge	w	Barge	bge	Lou	90.0 x 18.0 x 3.0		1,873
	bge	w	Barge	bge	Lou	90.0 x 18.0 x 3.0		1,873
	bge	w	Barge	bge	Lou	90.0 x 18.0 x 3.0		1,873
	bge	w	Barge	bge	Lou	90.0 x 18.0 x 3.0		1,873
	bge	w	Barge	bge	Lou	90.0 x 18.0 x 3.0		1,873
	bge	w	Barge	bge	Lou	90.0 x 18.0 x 3.0		1,873
	bge	w	Barge	bge	Lou	90.0 x 18.0 x 3.0		1,873
1919			Unknown					
1920	bge		Barge	bge	Ask			
	bge		Barge	bge	Ask			
	bge		Barge	bge	Ask			
	bge		Barge	bge	Ask			
	bge		Barge	bge	Ask			
	bge		Barge	bge	Ask			
	bge		Barge	bge	Ask			
	bge		Barge	bge	Ask			
	stw		*Vim*	twb				
	2ss	s	*Cordova*	twb	Mob	140.0 x 24.0 x 8.0		
	2ss	s	*Demopolis*	twb	Mob	140.0 x 24.0 x 8.0		
1921	stw	s	*Hoffman*, C. E., U.S.A.	twb				
	bge	s	Derrick Hull	mis	Nas			
	stw	s	*Labelle* Hull	twb	Pit	148.5 x 34.4 x 5.6		
	stw	s	*Duffy*	twb	Lou	125.0 x 25.0 x 4.6		
	stw	s	*Mamie S. Barrett*	twb	Lou	123.2 x 30.0 x 5.0		
	gaw	s	*D. A. B.*	twb	Pit	63.0 x 16.0 x 3.0		
		s	Hull					
		s	Hull					
	bge	s	Derrick Hull	mis	Nas			
	bge	s	Derrick Hull	mis	Nas			
	stw	s	*Penniman*	twb		148.0 x 30.0 x 5.0		
1922	stw	s	*Tullulah*	twb		127.5 x 23.0 x 4.5		
			Hyacinth		Nol			
	stw		*Atlantico*	twb	For			
	gas		*D and H*					
	bge		Barge		Mem			

Table 1—(*Continued*)

Year Built	Rig	Hull	Name of Vessel	Service	Home Port	Dimensions		Price
1923	2ss	s	*Montgomery*	twb	Mob	140.0 x 24.0 x	8.0	
	stw	s	*Cape Girardeau*	pkt	StL	210.0 x 38.0 x	6.5	
	bge		Barge	bge	Nai			
	bge		Barge	bge	Nai			
	bge		Barge	bge	Nai			
	bge		Barge	bge	Nai			
	bge		Barge	bge	Nai			
	bge		Barge	bge	Nai			
	?		*Griffy*	?	?	65.0 x 11.9 x	2.5	$ 1,625
	bge	s	*Ferry Park*	mis	Lou	60.0 x 14.0 x	2.4	
1924		s	Ferry boat hull	fer		85.0 x 110.0 x 2.7		1,800
		s	Ferry boat hull	fer				
		s	Ferry boat hull	fer				
		s	*Elinor*	twb				
	olw		*Kanawha*	twb		80.0 x 20.7 x	3.7	
	stw	s	*Donora*	twb	Pit	140.0 x 32.0 x	6.0	
			Am. Steel and Wire Boat					
	stw	s	*Sequoyah*	twb		138.0 x 29.0 x	6.3	
1925	bge	s	Barge	bge				
		s	Ferry boat hull	fer	Vic			
		s	Ferry boat hull	fer	Nol			
		s	Ferry boat hull	fer	Nol			
			Hull					
			Hull					
			Hull					
			Hull					
	sts	s	*Algiers*	fer	Nol	144.0 x 55.0 x	7.7	
	stp	s	*Charles J. Miller*	fer	Mem	130.0 x 32.0 x	5.0	
	stw	s	*Chicot*	twb	StL	107.2 x 23.5 x	4.8	
	stw	s	*Jerome D. Beeler*	twb	Evs	107.2 x 23.5 x	4.8	
	sts	s	*New Orleans*	fer	Nol	144.0 x 55.0 x	7.7	
	stw	s	*Samuel L. May*	twb	Pit	130.0 x 28.0 x	5.0	
	bge	s	*Burnside*	fer	Lou	70.0 x 12.0 x	2.0	
1926	elw	s	*Gouverneur*	twb	Chc	121.9 x 23.0 x	5.0	
			Hull for A. C. French	fer	Buk			
			Hull for A. C. French		Buk			
	sts	s	*Louisiana*	fer	Brl	144.5 x 55.0 x	9.3	
	bge	s	Maneuver Boat Hull USCE	mis	Vic	60.0 x 26.0 x	3.7	
	bge	s	Concrete-Mixer Hull USCE	mis	Vic	128.0 x 42.0 x	7.0	

TABLE 1—(*Continued*)

Year Built	Rig	Hull	Name of Vessel	Service	Home Port	Dimensions	Price
	ols	s	*Pilgrim*	fer	Cai	100.0 x 30.0 x 5.0	
	stw	s	Excursion Stock Boat	pas		240.0 x 40.0 x 7.0	
	stw	s	*George W. Miller*	frt	Apa	138.0 x 32.0 x 4.9	
	stw	s	*Patricia Barrett*	twb	Cin	75.0 x 40.0 x 6.4	
	stw	s	*Mississippi* (Hull only)	twb	StL	213.0 x 38.0 x 7.3	
	bge	s	Barge for South America	bge	For	85.0 x 17.0 x 4.0	
	bge	s	Barge for South America	bge	For	85.0 x 17.0 x 4.0	
	bge	s	Concrete-Mixer Hull	mis	Mem	120.0 x 45.0 x 7.0	
	bge	s	*Boonsborough* No. 11	bge	Lou	93.0 x 20.0 x 2.0	
1927	bge	s	Car Carrier	bge	Brl	285.0 x 60.0 x 9.5	
		s	Kentucky River Ferry	fer	Rik	93.0 x 20.0 x 2.5	
	gaw	s	*Dugan*	fer	Lou	40.0 x 14.5 x 2.5	
	bge	s	Ft. Gage Dredge for U.S.	mis	StL		
	bge	s	Barge for C.E., U.S.A.	bge	StL	55.0 x 16.0 x 3.0	
	bge	s	Barge for C.E., U.S.A.	bge	StL	55.0 x 16.0 x 3.0	
	bge	s	Barge for C.E., U.S.A.	bge	StL	55.0 x 16.0 x 3.0	
	bge	s	Barge for C.E., U.S.A.	bge	StL	55.0 x 16.0 x 3.0	
	bge	s	Barge for C.E., U.S.A.	bge	StL	55.0 x 16.0 x 3.0	
	bge	s	Barge for C.E., U.S.A.	bge	StL	55.0 x 16.0 x 3.0	
	bge	s	Barge for C.E., U.S.A.	bge	StL	55.0 x 16.0 x 3.0	
	bge	s	Barge for C.E., U.S.A.	bge	StL	55.0 x 16.0 x 3.0	
	bge	s	Barge for C.E., U.S.A.	bge	StL	55.0 x 16.0 x 3.0	
	bge	s	Barge for C.E., U.S.A.	bge	StL	55.0 x 16.0 x 3.0	
	bge	s	Barge for C.E., U.S.A.	bge	StL	55.0 x 16.0 x 3.0	
	bge	s	Barge for C.E., U.S.A.	bge	StL	55.0 x 16.0 x 3.0	
	bge	s	Barge for C.E., U.S.A.	bge	StL	55.0 x 16.0 x 3.0	
	bge	s	Barge for C.E., U.S.A.	bge	StL	55.0 x 16.0 x 3.0	
	bge	s	Barge for C.E., U.S.A.	bge	StL	55.0 x 16.0 x 3.0	
	bge	s	Barge for C.E., U.S.A.	bge	StL	55.0 x 16.0 x 3.0	
	bge	s	Barge for C.E., U.S.A.	bge	StL	100.0 x 25.0 x 5.0	
	bge	s	Barge for C.E., U.S.A.	bge	StL	55.0 x 16.0 x 3.0	
	bge	s	Derrick Boat	mis	Lou	80.0 x 30.0 x 4.5	
	mis	s	Landing Apron 1	mis	Jef		
	mis	s	Landing Apron 2	mis	Jef		
	mis	s	Landing Apron 3	mis	Jef		
	bge	s	Barge for C.E., U.S.A.	bge	StL	100.0 x 25.0 x 5.0	
	bge	s	Barge for C.E., U.S.A.	bge	StL	100.0 x 25.0 x 5.0	

TABLE 1—(*Continued*)

Year Built	Rig	Hull	Name of Vessel	Service	Home Port	Dimensions	Price
	bge	s	Barge for C.E., U.S.A.	bge	StL	100.0 x 25.0 x 5.0	
	bge	s	Barge for C.E., U.S.A.	bge	StL	100.0 x 25.0 x 5.0	
	bge	s	Barge	bge	Pba	100.0 x 25.0 x 5.0	
	bge	s	Barge	bge	Pba	100.0 x 25.0 x 5.0	
	bge	s	Barge	bge	Pba	100.0 x 25.0 x 5.0	
	stw	s	Hull	fer	Lou	40.0 x 14.0 x 3.0	
	bge	s	Barge	bge	StL	100.0 x 25.0 x 5.0	
	flt	s	Steel Guide Docks	wfb	Nai	120.0 x 24.0 x 4.0	
	flt	s	Steel Guide Docks	wfb	Nai	120.0 x 24.0 x 4.0	
	flt	s	Steel Guide Docks	wfb	Nai	120.0 x 24.0 x 4.0	
	flt	s	Steel Guide Docks	wfb	Nai	120.0 x 24.0 x 4.0	
	olw	s	*Traveler*	fer	Kwf	100.0 x 30.0 x 5.0	
1928	ols	s	*J. J. Hennen*	twb	Lou	76.0 x 18.0 x 6.0	
	bge	s	Barge	bge	Lou	110.9 x 28.0 x 7.3	
	bge	s	Barge	bge	Lou	110.9 x 28.0 x 7.3	
	flt	s	Wharfboat	wfb	Lou	132.0 x 30.0 x 4.3	
	stw	s	*Catherine Davis*	twb	Cin	135.5 x 26.5 x 5.0	
	gaw	s	*Sallie H.*	twb	Nas	64.7 x 18.0 x 3.5	
	bge	s	Barge for C.E., U.S.A.	bge	Huw	80.0 x 26.0 x 5.0	
	bge	s	Barge for C.E., U.S.A.	bge	Huw	80.0 x 26.0 x 5.0	
	bge	s	Barge for C.E., U.S.A.	bge	Huw	80.0 x 26.0 x 5.0	
	bge	s	Needle Flat Boats	mis	Lou	40.0 x 14.0 x 3.5	
	bge	s	Needle Flat Boats	mis	Lou	40.0 x 14.0 x 3.5	
	bge	s	Needle Flat Boats	mis	Lou	40.0 x 14.0 x 3.5	
	bge	s	Needle Flat Boats	mis	Lou	40.0 x 14.0 x 3.5	
	bge	s	Needle Flat Boats	mis	Lou	40.0 x 14.0 x 3.5	
	bge	s	Needle Flat Boats	mis	Lou	40.0 x 14.0 x 3.5	
	bge	s	Needle Flat Boats	mis	Lou	40.0 x 14.0 x 3.5	
	bge	s	Needle Flat Boats	mis	Lou	40.0 x 14.0 x 3.5	
	bge	s	Needle Flat Boats	mis	Lou	40.0 x 14.0 x 3.5	
	bge	s	Rock Barge	bge	Nol	120.0 x 30.0 x 7.0	
	bge	s	Rock Barge	bge	Nol	120.0 x 30.0 x 7.0	
	olw	s	*Porterfield*	twb	Vic	79.0 x 18.5 x 4.0	
1929	stw	s	*Cop-R-Loy*	twb	Whe	73.0 x 20.0 x 3.7	
	bge	s	Supply Barge	bge		100.0 x 30.0 x 5.0	
	stw	s	*Loretta M. Howard*	twb	Jef	145.0 x 30.0 x 4.9	$ 60,000
	bge	s	A. B. L. 201	tnk	Lou	150.0 x 35.0 x 9.8	
	bge	s	A. B. L. 202	tnk	Lou	150.0 x 35.0 x 9.8	
	bge	s	A. B. L. 203	tnk	Lou	150.0 x 35.0 x 9.8	
	bge	s	A. B. L. 204	tnk	Lou	150.0 x 35.0 x 9.8	
	bge	s	Houseboat Hull	hbt	Lou	50.0 x 14.0 x 3.5	
	gas	w	Motor Boat, C. E., U.S.A.	mis	Vic	30.0 x 7.5 x 2.6	

TABLE I—(*Continued*)

Year Built	Rig	Hull	Name of Vessel	Service	Home Port	Dimensions	Price
	gas	w	Motor Boat, C. E., U.S.A.	mis	Vic	30.0 x 7.5 x 2.6	
	gas	w	Motor Boat, C. E., U.S.A.	mis	Vic	30.0 x 7.5 x 2.6	
	gas	w	Motor Boat, C. E., U.S.A.	mis	Vic	30.0 x 7.5 x 2.6	
	gas	w	Motor Boat, C. E., U.S.A.	mis	Vic	30.0 x 7.5 x 2.6	
	bge	s	A. B. L.	tnk	Lou	130.0 x 30.0 x 11.0	
	bge	s	A. B. L.	tnk	Lou	130.0 x 30.0 x 11.0	
	bge	s	A. B. L.	tnk	Lou	130.0 x 30.0 x 11.0	
	bge	s	A. B. L.	tnk	Lou	130.0 x 30.0 x 11.0	
	bge	s	Track Barge	rrt	—	195.0 x 30.0 x 6.5	
	stw	s	*Wm. Larimer Jones*	twb	Pit	139.5 x 34.0 x 7.5	
	sts	s	*Wm. H. Klein*	twb	Cht	121.0 x 28.5 x 4.7	
	gaw	s	*Carmen*	twb	Evs	40.5 x 14.3 x 2.8	
1930	bge	s	Sand Barge	bge	Lou	110.9 x 28.0 x 7.7	
	bge	s	Sand Barge	bge	Lou	110.9 x 28.0 x 7.7	
	gas	s	Motor Boat, C. E., U.S.A.	mis	Vic	31.0 x 7.5 x 2.5	
	gas	s	Motor Boat, C. E., U.S.A.	mis	Vic	31.0 x 7.5 x 2.5	
	gas	s	Motor Boat, C. E., U.S.A.	mis	Vic	31.0 x 7.5 x 2.5	
	gas	s	Motor Boat, C. E., U.S.A.	mis	Vic	31.0 x 7.5 x 2.5	
	flt	s	Wharf Boat	wfb	Rii	230.0 x 45.0 x 8.0	
		s	Ferry	fer	Wak	68.0 x 20.0 x 3.3	
	stw	s	*Titan*	twb	Pit	136.0 x 34.0 x 7.3	
	olw	s	*Helen H.*	twb	Lou	85.0 x 22.0 x 4.3	
1931	flt	s	Wharf Boat	wfb	Pei	230.0 x 45.0 x 8.0	
	stw	s	*Mark Twain*	twb	StL	157.0 x 42.0 x 6.0	$ 20,664
		s	Maneuver Boat Hull, C.E.	mis	Cin	75.0 x 24.0 x 4.5	
		s	Ferry	fer	Evs	59.0 x 17.0 x 2.5	
	gas	s	Work Boat, C. E., U.S.A.	mis	Lou	31.0 x x	
	gas	s	Work Boat, C. E., U.S.A.	mis	Lou	31.0 x x	
	gap	s	Motor Boat, C. E., U.S.A.	mis	Sci	22.0 x x	
	flt	s	Float	wfb	—	40.0 x 10.0 x 3.0	
	flt	s	Float	wfb	Ask	40.0 x 10.0 x 3.0	

TABLE I—(*Continued*)

Year Built	Rig	Hull	Name of Vessel	Service	Home Port	Dimensions	Price
	flt	s	Float	wfb	Ask	40.0 x 10.0 x 3.0	
	flt	s	Float	wfb	Ask	40.0 x 10.0 x 3.0	
	gap	s	*Everett Lee*	fer	Lou	60.0 x 30.0 x 3.0	
1932	ols	s	*Sergeant Floyd*, C.E.	mis	Kem	138.0 x 30.0 x 5.0	$ 21,000
1933	gas	w	Motor Boat	twb	Lou	18.0 x x	
1934	gas	s	*Turley*, C.E.,U.S.A.	mis	Lou	40.0 x 8.0 x 2.8	
	bge	w	Sand Barge	bge	StL	130.0 x 30.0 x 7.0	480
1935			Unknown				
1936	gas	s	T. V. A. No. 1	pas	Cht	60.0 x 10.1 x 4.0	
	gas	s	T. V. A. No. 2	pas	Cht	60.0 x 10.1 x 4.0	
1937			Unknown				
1938			Unknown				
1939	ols	s	*Wm. B. Brokamp*	twb	Cin	44.0 x 14.0 x 3.8	
	ols	s	*Shepard*	fer	Mem	62.7 x 28.0 x 4.2	18,000
	ols	s	*Taylor*	fer	Mem	62.7 x 28.0 x 4.2	18,000
	gas	s	Motor Boat, C. E., U.S.A.	mis	—		
	gas	s	Motor Boat, C. E., U.S.A.	mis	—		
	gas	s	Motor Boat, C. E., U.S.A.	mis	—		
	gas	s	Motor Boat, C. E., U.S.A.	mis	—		
	gas	s	Motor Boat, C. E., U.S.A.	mis	—		
1940	ols	s	*Frank Costanzo*	twb	Lou	71.4 x 20.0 x 5.4	

TABLE 2. *A Partial Listing of Output at Howard Ship Yards at Other Locations*

Year Built	Rig	Hull	Name of Vessel	Service	Home Port	Dimensions	Price
			YARDS AT MADISON, INDIANA				
1836	stp	w	*Irwinton*	pkt	Ap	121.0 X 21.5 X 4.5	
	stp	w	*Livingston*	pkt	Nol	150.0 X 18.0 X 6.5	
1837	bge	w	*Hard Times*	bge	—	110.0 X 19.0 X 6.0	
	bge	w	*Natches*	bge	—	110.0 X 19.0 X 6.0	
1839	stp	w	*John Armstrong*	pkt	Lou	136.0 X 22.0 X 5.0	
	stp	w	*New Argo*	pkt	Cin	135.0 X 22.0 X 5.0	
	stp	w	*Robert Fulton*	pkt	Lou	157.0 X 22.0 X 5.0	
1840	stp	w	*Governor Morehead*	pkt	Cin	122.0 X 20.0 X 4.2	
1843	stp	w	*Montezuma*	pkt	Mob	150.0 X 28.0 X 6.5	
1907	stw	w	*Levi Workum*	pkt	—	185.0 X 34.0 X 5.0	$ 14,250
1908	bge	w	Barge	bge	Lou	160.0 X 34.0 X 6.0	6,436
	bge	w	Barge	bge	Lou	160.0 X 34.0 X 6.0	6,436
1910	bge	w	Barge	rrt	—	225.0 X 36.0 X 6.0	12,000
1926	stw	w	*Interstate*	twb	Chi	112.3 X 24.5 X 3.6	
1934	stw	w	*Paul F. Thomas*	fer	Cin	107.0 X 30.0 X 4.0	
			YARDS AT LOUISVILLE AND SHIPPINGPORT				
1846	stp	w	*Courier*	pkt	Lou	141.5 X 20.5 X 5.0	
	stp	w	*General Jessop*	pkt	—	150.0 X X	
	stp	w	*James Hewitt*	pkt	Lou	195.0 X 27.5 X 6.5	
	stp	w	*Lavaca*	pkt	Gal	130.0 X X	
	stp	w	*Major Barbour*	pkt	Lou	141.0 X 21.0 X 4.6	
	stp	w	*Mobile*	pkt	Mob	167.0 X 23.0 X 7.0	
1850	stp	w	*Cuba*	pkt	Mob	180.0 X 29.0 X 7.0	
	stp	w	*Empress*	pkt	Mob	190.0 X 29.0 X 6.5	
	stp	w	*Helen*	pkt	Mob	180.0 X 26.0 X 6.5	
	stp	w	*Music*	pkt	Nol	175.0 X 29.0 X 7.0	
	stp	w	*S. W. Downs*	pkt	Lou	175.0 X 28.5 X 6.5	17,500
	stw	w	*Terrebonne*	pkt	Nol	120.0 X 24.0 X 4.5	
	stp	w	*Wade Allen*	pkt	—	175.0 X 24.0 X 6.0	

TABLE 2—(*Continued*)

Year Built	Rig	Hull	Name of Vessel	Service	Home Port	Dimensions	Price
			YARDS AT CINCINNATI				
1910	bge	w	Barge	rrt	—	225.0 x 36.0 x 6.0	$ 12,000
			YARDS AT MOUND CITY, ILLINOIS				
1923	stp	w	*Dan O'Sullivan*	twb	StL	125.0 x 28.0 x 5.0	
1925	stw	w	*Jim O'Sullivan*	twb	StL	130.0 x 30.0 x 5.5	

TABLE 3. *Tonnage Index of Output*[1] *at the Howard Ship Yards*

Year Built	Annual Total	5-Year Moving Average	Average Hull Tonnage	Year Built	Annual Total	5-Year Moving Average	Average Hull Tonnage
1834	154		154	1865	900	2518	450
1835	0		0	1866	3477	2325	386
1836	244		122	1867	1946	2056	486
1837	251		125	1868	1935	2914	387
1838	0			1869	2024	3078	289
1839	471		157	1870	5187	3384	399
1840	102		102	1871	4298	3833	269
1841	0			1872	3474	3542	316
1842	0			1873	4183	3105	246
1843	273		273	1874	568	2748	142
1844	0			1875	3003	2603	215
1845	0			1876	2510	2955	359
1846	908		227	1877	2749	3699	153
1847	0			1878	5944	3835	594
1848	1704	1541	426	1879	4305	4489	431
1849	2239	2093	448	1880	3657	4303	281
1850	2853	3066	285	1881	5788	5526	386
1851	3671	3526	408	1882	7820	5491	340
1852	4863	3923	405	1883	6061	5393	216
1853	4005	3923	364	1884	4130	5027	375
1854	4224	4103	528	1885	3167	4215	288
1855	2854	4022	317	1886	3659	3882	283
1856	4569	3516	381	1887	3760	4064	342
1857	4457	3378	371	1888	4396	4468	231
1858	1475	3628	295	1889	5037	5168	219
1859	3533	2812	442	1890	5189	5116	472
1860	4108	2326	517	1891	7460	5040	311
1861	485	2612	485	1892	3501	5183	219
1862	2030	2578	508	1893	4013	5275	201
1863	2903	1937	581	1894	5754	4281	240
1864	3365	2535	841	1895	5647	4787	217

[1]For official registration purposes, the measured gross ton is a unit of 100 cubic feet applied to the internal freight- or passenger-carrying capacity of a vessel. For Western Rivers steamboats, however, it often appears to be a capricious standard. See Hunter, *Steamboats on the Western Rivers*, p. 643.

The Tonnage Index of Output was devised in order to have a consistent standard for measuring the output of the Howard Ship Yards. It, too, is a unit of volume. It employs the builder's recorded dimensions for each hull. For example, the *Hyperion* measured 107 feet in length, 18 feet in width, and 8 feet in depth. Length times width times depth divided by 100 cubic feet yields the tonnage index of 154. Actual gross tonnage of the vessel was 125 because of some unknown exception. In the aggregate, the Tonnage Index of Output is a valid measure of the Yards' production. It also serves for cautious comparisons with industry gross tonnage.

TABLE 3—(*Continued*)

Year Built	Annual Total	5-Year Moving Average	Average Hull Tonnage	Year Built	Annual Total	5-Year Moving Average	Average Hull Tonnage
1896	2490	5291	147	1919	0	212	0
1897	6031	5467	302	1920	538	431	269
1898	6534	5382	297	1921	867	511	145
1899	6632	5513	301	1922	1664	633	83
1900	5224	5033	249	1923	984	942	246
1901	3143	4279	210	1924	611	1522	204
1902	3633	3766	303	1925	2083	1974	231
1903	2762	3209	184	1926	3764	2177	269
1904	4068	3004	194	1927	3950	3570	103
1905	2442	2893	222	1928	1977	3328	94
1906	2114	3008	176	1929	5576	2848	242
1907	3078	2875	257	1930	1374	2194	172
1908	3338	2867	209	1931	1366	1799	195
1909	3407	2662	341	1932	675	765	338
1910	2401	2661	300	1933	2	490	2
1911	1087	2292	121	1934	410	314	137
1912	3073	2189	220	1935	0	179	0
1913	1493	2010	115	1936	485	179	243
1914	2893	2397	161	1937	0	131	0
1915	1503	1896	188	1938	0	146	0
1916	3022	1715	378	1939	170	49	57
1917	572	1136	286	1940	77	49	77
1918	583	643	49	1941	0	49	0

TABLE 4. *Gross Revenues*

Year	Amount	Year	Amount
1858	$ 61,012	1893	$128,551
1859	86,393	1894	251,310
		1895	151,045
1860	89,528	1896	119,560
1861	28,755	1897	333,450
		1898	351,650
1871	235,865	1899	279,910
1872	108,464		
1873	186,790	1900	145,650
1874	22,022	1901	152,525
1877	107,064	1902	174,492
1878	326,130	1903	165,905
1879	199,525	1904	183,420
		1905	89,071
1880	238,969	1906	104,990
1881	328,376	1907	158,486
1882	433,277	1908	170,041
1883	237,888	1909	170,175
1884	172,299		
1885	145,664	1910	106,575
1886	137,043	1911	75,277
1887	192,792	1912	309,704
1888	172,200	1913	96,024
1889	202,750	1914	184,091
		1915	49,490
1890	179,500	1916	146,554
1891	349,763	1917	46,650
1892	157,625	1918	39,076

SOURCES: Cash Book, 1858–1863 and Daybooks Six, Seven, and Eight, Howard MSS. Prior to 1877 and subsequent to 1918, records of the vessels built, their dimensions, and the prices are only occasionally recorded or referred to in correspondence.

Explanation of Columns and Abbreviations

Year Built. When the source is Key Book or other data in the Howard MSS, the year built refers to the year of launching; otherwise the year built refers to the year in which the vessel was completed, as shown by the builder's certificate in the records of the U.S. Treasury Department, Bureau of Customs.

Rig. The rig of the vessel, or the means of propulsion. The rig abbreviations are identical to those used by the U.S. Treasury Department, Bureau of Customs, in the annual list, *Merchant Vessels of the United States.*

arw — animal powered, recessed wheel
bge — barge, unrigged, no means of self-propulsion
elw — electric, stern-wheel
flt — float, intended to be more or less permanently moored
gap — gas engine, side-wheel
gas — gas engine, screw-propeller
2gs — gas engine, two screw-propellers
gaw — gas engine, stern-wheel
grw — gas engine, center or recessed wheel
hbt — houseboat
olp — oil engine, side-wheel
ols — oil engine, screw-propeller
2os — oil engine, two screw-propellers
olw — oil engine, stern-wheel
orw — oil engine, center or recessed wheel
srw — steam engine, center or recessed wheel
stp — steam engine, side-wheel
sts — steam engine, screw propellers
2ss — steam engine, two screw-propellers
stw — steam engine, stern-wheel

Hull. The material used in constructing the hull. Abbreviations used are:

i — iron
s — steel
w — wood
o — other, including composite materials

Name of Vessel. The name given to a vessel at the time of launching or registration with the U.S. Treasury Department, Bureau of Customs.

Service. The type of service for which the vessel was primarily intended at the time of launching. Abbreviations used are:

bge — barge or other towed vessel
fer — ferry boat, either passenger and/or freight
frt — freight
mis — miscellaneous
pas — passenger
pkt — packet, combined freight and passenger
rrt — railroad transfer ferry
twb — towboat
wfb — wharfboat, an unrigged and stationary hull

Home Port. The port designated by the owner and approved by the Commissioner of Customs at the time the vessel was assigned its permanent document. Where the home port of registration was not available, the city of residence of the owner was used. Abbreviations used are:

Ale — Alexandria, La.
Als — Alaska, Yukon River primarily
Apa — Apalachicola, Fla.
Ark — Arkansas River
Ask — Ashland, Ky.

Bgk — Bowling Green, Ky.
Bir — Birmingham, Ala.
Bon — Boonville, Mo.
Brl — Baton Rouge, La.
Buk — Burnside, Ky.

Cai — Cairo, Ill.
Car — Carthage, Tenn.
Cha — Chatahoochee, Ala.
Chc — Chicago, Ill.
Chi — Chester, Ill.
Cht — Chattanooga, Tenn.
Cin — Cincinnati, Ohio
Cla — Clarksville, Tenn.
Cog — Columbus, Ga.
Cum — Cumberland River

Evs — Evansville, Ind.

Flo — Florence, Ala.
For — Foreign ports,
          principally Central America
Fra — Franklin, La.

Gal — Galveston, Tex.
Gre — Greenwood, Miss.

Hel — Helena, Ark.
Hen — Henderson, Ky.
Hou — Houston, Tex.
Hun — Huntington, W. Va.

Iro — Ironton, Ohio

Jef — Jeffersonville, Ind.

Kcm — Kansas City, Mo.
Kwf — Key West, Fla.

Lon — London, Ky.
Lou — Louisville, Ky.
Lra — Little Rock, Ark.

Mar — Marietta, Ohio
Mem — Memphis, Tenn.
Mob — Mobile, Ala.
Mci — Mound City, Ill.
Mrl — Monroe, La.
Muk — Muskogee, Okla.

Nai — New Albany, Ind.
Nas — Nashville, Tenn.
Nat — Natchez, Miss.
Nol — New Orleans, La.

Oua — Ouachita River, Ark.

Pad — Paducah, Ky.
Pba — Pine Bluff, Ark.
Pei — Peoria, Ill.
Phi — Philadelphia, Pa.
Pit — Pittsburgh, Pa.
Ppw — Point Pleasant, W. Va.

Rer — Red River, Ark.
Rii — Rock Island, Ill.
Rik — Richmond, Ky.
Roc — Rockport, Ind.

Sci — Sioux City, Iowa
Shv — Shreveport, La.
Spm — St. Paul, Minn.
StJ — St. Joseph, Mo.
StL — St. Louis, Mo.

Umr — Upper Missouri River

Vic — Vicksburg, Miss.

Wak — Warsaw, Ky.
War — Warsaw, Mo.
Whe — Wheeling, W. Va.

Dimensions.

Length. Builder's recorded length of the keel between perpendiculars, where available. Otherwise, length refers to the measured length recorded for purposes of registration with the U.S. Treasury Department, Bureau of Customs.

Width. Builder's recorded width of the hull at the main deck, where available. Otherwise, width refers to the measured width recorded for purposes of registration.

Depth. Builder's recorded depth of the hold, where available. Otherwise, depth refers to the measured depth of the hold used for purposes of registration. Depth of the hold is not the draft of the vessel.

Price. Builder's recorded contract price or the quoted price to the owner for a vessel.

Sources: Howard Ship Yards & Dock Co., MSS, Lilly Library, Indiana University, Bloomington, particularly "A Record of the Boats Built by the Howards," compiled through 1884, by John C. Howard and in later years, through 1932, by others, referred to as the Key Book; U.S. Treasury Department, Bureau of Customs, *Merchant Vessels of the United States;* Stephen G. Savage, James Howard of Jeffersonville, Master Builder of Steamboats (Unpublished Master's Thesis, Indiana University); and Lewis C. Baird, *Baird's History of Clark County Indiana* (Indianapolis, B. F. Bowen & Co., 1909), pp. 330–52.

APPENDIX B

Steamboats Constructed on the Western Rivers

Year	Number of Hulls	Gross Tons	Index of Tonnage 1850–60=100	Year	Number of Hulls	Gross Tons	Index of Tonnage 1850–60=100
1811	1	100.00	0.3	1841	90	15,870.52	53.1
1812				1842	102	16,794.88	56.2
1813	1	25.00	0.8	1843	55	9,385.82	31.4
1814	2	385.67	1.3	1844	129	25,395.24	85.0
1815	5	1,077.85	3.6	1845	119	20,104.70	67.3
1816	4	880.23	2.8	1846	150	25,560.32	85.6
1817	5	702.52	2.4	1847	120	22,438.82	75.1
1818	15	3,090.08	10.3	1848	120	27,271.03	91.3
1819	23	5,315.66	17.8	1849	139	28,353.24	94.9
1820	15	2,642.52	8.8	1850	109	20,910.87	70.0
1821	3	545.72	1.8	1851	132	26,711.10	89.4
1822	11	1,013.42	3.4	1852	155	35,259.24	118.1
1823	17	2,278.28	7.6	1853	126	33,452.44	112.0
1824	20	3,171.81	10.6	1854	142	33,805.39	113.2
1825	18	3,065.79	10.3	1855	116	30,926.03	103.5
1826	35	6,563.76	22.0	1856	138	32,632.65	109.3
1827	33	5,244.61	17.6	1857	163	37,080.30	124.2
1828	19	3,043.05	10.2	1858	127	31,481.40	105.4
1829	36	7,561.53	25.3	1859	85	13,838.52	46.3
1830	33	4,811.15	16.1	1860	162	32,432.03	108.6
1831	27	4,003.75	13.4	1861	146	30,459.57	102.0
1832	86	12,187.43	40.8	1862	49	6,653.34	22.3
1833	44	5,548.32	18.6	1863	118	21,721.76	72.7
1834	62	8,263.31	27.7	1864	206	44,656.06	149.5
1835	51	5,718.35	19.1	1865	187	50,081.84	167.7
1836	107	14,478.85	48.5	1866	153	46,755.49	156.5
1837	115	21,500.09	72.0	1867	63	18,551.74	62.1
1838	66	12,626.27	42.3	1868	93	20,742.46	69.5
1839	108	14,454.61	48.4	1869	79	21,022.75	70.4
1840	63	9,223.86	30.9	1870	116	35,506.15	118.9

Year	Number of Hulls	Gross Tons	Index of Tonnage 1850-60=100	Year	Number of Hulls	Gross Tons	Index of Tonnage 1850-60=100
1871	155	50,083.72	167.7	1901	111	22,888.00	73.4
1872	108	25,497.63	85.4	1902	161	9,836.00	31.5
1873	109	19,474.48	65.2	1903	150	8,597.00	35.6
1874	125	19,672.17	65.9	1904	187	10,821.00	34.7
1875	91	13,315.80	44.6	1905	173	6,477.00	20.8
1876	109	19,025.67	63.7	1906	167	6,591.00	21.1
1877	113	21,653.54	72.5	1907	165	7,288.00	23.4
1878	133	28,124.44	94.2	1908	207	6,114.00	19.6
1879	124	31,539.71	105.6	1909	207	5,940.00	19.1
1880	117	23,930.92	80.1	1910	193	5,488.00	17.6
1881	129	24,587.00	82.3	1911	202	6,393.00	20.5
1882	134	24,672.00	82.6	1912	205	5,286.00	17.0
1883	116	20,879.00	69.9	1913	234	7,930.00	25.4
1884	91	16,219.00	54.3	1914	132	8,009.00	25.7
1885	81	11,220.00	37.6	1915	144	5,499.00	17.6
1886	70	9,700.00	32.5	1916	140	4,973.00	16.0
1887	69	10,108.00	33.8	1917	157	6,185.00	19.8
1888	74	11,372.00	38.1	1918	135	5,409.00	17.3
1889	74	11,557.00	38.7	1919	107	3,716.00	11.9
1890	82	11,886.00	39.8	1920	185	10,300.00	33.0
1891	95	15,473.00	51.8	1921	131	10,829.00	34.7
1892	89	12,482.00	41.8	1922	125	15,422.00	49.5
1893	87	9,364.00	31.4	1923	128	12,581.00	40.4
1894	61	7,304.00	24.5	1924	264	27,908.00	89.5
1895	60	7,240.00	24.2	1925	209	9,826.00	31.5
1896	82	13,134.00	44.0	1926	159	9,846.00	31.6
1897	91	10,974.00	36.7	1927	140	16,191.00	51.9
1898	106	12,211.00	40.9	1928	167	25,021.00	80.3
1899	92	14,042.00	47.0	1929	129	10,506.00	33.7
1900	109	8,823.00	29.5	1930	117	6,815.00	21.9
1901	115	8,927.00	29.9	1931	97	11,600.00	37.2
1902	139	8,888.00	29.8	1932	85	5,550.00	17.8
1903	137	9,597.00	32.1	1933	65	7,166.00	23.0
1904	176	9,439.00	31.6	1934	96	12,299.00	39.4
1905	161	5,741.00	19.2	1935	112	9,928.00	31.8
1906	144	4,586.00	15.4	1936	164	44,256.00	142.0
	New Series			1937	118	20,645.00	66.2
1900	115	14,173.00	45.5				

SOURCES: U.S. Bureau of the Census, *Tenth Census* (1880), IV, *Transportation,* pp. 671–72; U.S. Bureau of the Census, *Special Reports: Transportation by Water,* 1906, p. 167; and U.S. Department of Commerce, Bureau of Marine Inspection and Navigation, *Merchant Marine Statistics,* 1936, pp. 46-48, 49, and 1937, p. 36. Subsequent issues of the *Merchant Marine Statistics* do not list the number or gross tonnage of vessels built by geographic division.

INDEX

Howard, Edmonds J., son of James Howard, 11n, 75, 139, 144; birth, 15; in partnership with his father, 56, 74, 81; mansion, 109, 110, 111, 112; production of Yards under, 116; builder of stern-wheelers, 116, 121; craftsmanship, 121; director, American Rivers Shipbuilding Co., 146; stockholder, Howard Ship Yards Co, 147; death, 153, 155

Howard, Edmonds John, 11n

Howard, James, 2, 11n, 132; sketch, 13–14; apprenticeship, 3, 14; builds first boat, 3, 4, 9–10, 180; location of shipyards, 10, 15, 23; steamboat clerk, 14; partners, 14–15, 23, 56, 74, 144; craftsmanship, 27, 34, 114, 121; home, 50; death and funeral, 73–74; estimate of, 74, 75, 140; preference for side-wheeler over stern-wheeler, 116, 117; on disadvantages of the propeller, 134

Howard, James, and Co. (James, John, and Edmonds J. Howard), 56, 144

Howard, James E., son of Edmonds J. Howard, 11n, 145, 146, 147, 154, 155, 157, 176, 177; president, Howard Ship Yards and Dock Co., 163; designs and builds the *Loretta M. Howard*, 167–70

Howard, John, father of James Howard, 13–14

Howard, John C., brother of James Howard, 14, 15, 56, 74, 81, 139, 144

Howard, Loretta M., 163, 167

Howard, Martha, mother of James Howard, 13

Howard, Thomas, brother of James Howard, 14

Howard Ship Yards, beginning, 14; locations, Port Fulton, 10; Madison, 15, 144, 146, 163, 176; Shippingport, 22; Louisville, 23; Jeffersonville, 23, 189; Mounds City, Ill., 146, 156; Cincinnati, 146, 156; production, 28, 44–45, 46, 62, 67–68, 92, 112, 116–21, 125, 133, 145, 166, 170–71, 193–223; advantages of Jeffersonville location, 28–30, 34; reasons for success, 34, 68, 114, 157, 164–65; innovations in construction, 35, 56, 150; and Panic of 1857, 36; effects of Civil War on, 46 ff.; in post-Civil War years, 67–68; gross revenues, 68, 92, 155, 176, 226; data on boats constructed, 68; change over from packet to towboat and barge, 92, 93, 105; from wood to steel, 124, 127–31; zenith, 112; effect of development of Great Lakes shipbuilding industry, 124–25; last packet, 131–32, 163; first towboats, 132; increase in barges built, 133; propeller-driven craft, 134, 135–36; tunnel-type hull, 135–36, 158–59; gas and diesel boats, 136; incorporations, 145–47, 163; decline in revenues, 155; sale considered, 156; production increased with river improvement, 166; in Great Depression, 171–76; and 1937 flood, 176–77; last boat built, 177; taken over by U.S. Navy, 177; example of American free enterprise, 80–81; tonnage index of output, 224–25

Howard Ship Yards and Dock Co., 157, 163; creditors committee, 173–74, 176; financial condition, 1932, 174–76; taken over by U.S. Navy, 177–80

Howard Ship Yards Co., 147–48, 156–57, 163

Hulls, wooden, 37, 121; strengthening of, 33, 115–16; iron, 122–23, 124; steel, 122–23; wood clad with iron plates, 123; tunnel-type, 135–36, 158–59; dimensions, 193–223; decline in size, 121

Hyperion, 3, 4, 10, 11, 14, 73, 136, 139, 180

Ice, transported by river, 104, 106

Ida Handy, 54

Inco No. 1, 135, 136, 148–51, 155, 156

Inland Navigation Co., Wilmington, Del., 148, 151

Inland Waterways Corp., Mobile, Ala., 157, 171, 172

Internal combustion engine, 136

Ione, 16

Iron, for steamboat equipment, availability of, 29–30; in steamboat construction, 121–24. *See also* Steel

Iron ore, transported by river, 104, 105

Ironton, Ohio, 28

Irwinton, 15

Isaac Bowman, 45

Island Creek Coal Co., 166

Paul F. Thomas, 176
Pegram, George, 51, 54–56, 70–73, 116
Peoria, 150
Pharr and Williams, 132
Pittsburgh, Pa., steamboat construction, 8, 28, 29–30, 62; shops for manufacturing steamboat equipment, 29–30
Polly, 8
Population, growth, in Ohio and Mississippi valleys, 4
Port Fulton (Jeffersonville), Ind., 10
Porter, John, Boonville, Mo., 70
Portsmouth, Ohio, 28
Pratt, John L., 173
Prices, Howard Ship Yards, 31, 44, 45, 49, 51, 52, 78, 86, 104, 176, 194–223; estimates, 38, 39–43; metal hulls and wooden hull, 122–23, 125–26, 127, 131; in Louisville area, 31. *See also* Fares, Freight rates
Profits, in steamboating, 16, 51, 56, 78, 142
Propeller, 91, 92, 124, 169–70; disadvantages of, 134–35; replaces the paddle wheel, 133–36, 159; in tunnel-type towboat, 158–59

Queen City Marine Railway and Dock Co., Cincinnati, 146, 156
Queen of the West, 53

Races, steamboat, 73; hazzards of, 25
Railroads, 9; first transfer barge, 56; in competition with steamboats, 60, 64–67, 101, 105, 106; built as feeders to water routes, 65; construction in North before the Civil War, 65; little effect on production of Howard Ship Yards after Civil War, 70; construction in South before the Civil War, 97–98; after the Civil War, 98–99; variation of gauges, 99–100; adoption of standard gauge, 100–101; freight handled, as compared with steamboats, 102–103
Red River Line, 145
Red River Transportation Co., 90
Rees, James, and Sons, Pittsburgh, 124, 127, 130
Regulations, of steamboats, 25, 26

Revenues, gross, of Howard Ship Yards, 68, 92, 155, 176, 226
Richmond, 83, 116
Ripley, Ohio, 28
Rivers, *see* Western Rivers
Rivers and Harbors Act, 162
Rivers and Harbors Congress, 161–62
Roach and Long, 38
Rob't. E. Lee, the racer, 73, 80, 86, 136
Rob't. E. Lee, the second, 62, 73, 74, 101, 105; speed of, and freight carried, 77–78; earnings, 78
Robinson and Minis, of Pittsburgh, 122
Ruth, first, 51; earnings, 56, 142
Ruth, second, 54–56

S. W. Downs, 23, 35
Safety devices, 26
Sailing ships, constructed in Ohio Valley, 8; on Western Rivers, 17
St. Louis, shipyards, 28; shops for manufacturing steamboat equipment, 30; home port of Howard-built boats, 34, 68, 70, 93, 95
Santa Fe, 124, 132
Saunders, E. E., 44
Sergeant Floyd, 173
Shallcross, 90
Shippingport (Louisville), Ky., Howard Ship Yards, 22, 222
Shreve, Henry M., 7, 161
Side-wheelers, decline, 62; replaced by stern-wheelers, 74–75, 90, 92, 115–16; description, 114
Sinnot, John C., 31, 33
South America, home ports of Howard-built boats, 124, 125
Southerner, 35
Speed, of Western Rivers steamboats, 13, 80, 85, 86, 136, 151
Steamboats, development, for use on Western Rivers, 7–9, 113–14; in development of the West, 9; demand for, 15 ff.; ostentation, 59–60, 62, 78, 86–90, 133. *See also* Construction, Design, Operation, Tonnage.
Steamboat Inspection Act, 25, 26
Steel, in steamboat construction, 122–27; first employed by Howards, 124–25; high cost, 125–26, 127, 131; replaces

Steel—*Continued*
    wood, 127–31; source of fabricated,
    130; shipped by river, 165–66
Stern-wheelers, replace side-wheelers,
    74–75, 90, 92, 115–16
Steubenville, Ohio, 28
Stuckey, Twomey Co., 38
Sweeney, J. M., 130, 156

T. P. Leathers, 94
Tabasco, Mexico, 132
Tarascon, 54, 182
Tecumseh, 15, 144
Tennessee Valley Authority, 176
Terrebonne, 115
Thompson, Cave, 145
Timber, sources of, 10, 29, 130–31; de-
    cline in tons transported by steam
    navigation, 104, 106. *See also* Wood
Titan, 171
Tobin, John W., 70, 81, 85, 90, 101–102
Tonnage, of Western River steamboats,
    4, 16–17, 19, 21, 27, 44–45, 46, 49, 60–
    62, 107, 108, 121, 123, 231; constructed
    at Howard Ship Yards, 44–45, 46, 49,
    67–68, 92, 116–21; decrease in, per
    hull, 92; constructed by Great Lakes
    shipbuilding industry, 125; percentage
    owned by individuals, partnerships,
    and corporations, 142–43; of barges,
    increase of, 162; measurement, 77–78,
    49–51, 224n; index of output, Howard
    Ship Yards, 224–25
Towboats, 91, 104, 130, 132–33; tunnel-
    type, screw-propelled, 157–60, 160–61;
    stock design stern-wheeler, 167–70
Trade Palace, 134, 135
Travel, by land and river, compared,
    5–6, 6–7
Trenton, 70, 81
Turnpikes, 6
Two Rivers Barge Line, 177
Typewriter, introduction of, 139

United States, 122
U.S. Government, customer of Howard
    Ship Yards, 125, 141, 166, 171, 173,
    176
U.S. Navy, takes over Howard Ship
    Yards, 177–80

Upper Mississippi River, decline in traf-
    fic, 106; passenger traffic, 103, 107–108

Valley Forge, 122
Vicksburg, Miss., home port of Howard-
    built boats, 49, 70, 93
Virginia, 56

W. T. Scovell, 127
W. W. Fry, 122
Wages, paid by Howard Ship Yards,
    31–32, 46, 52–53, 163; effect of Civil
    War on, 51–52
Walker, J. B., 35
Warrior River, 135, 157
Washington, 7
Watson, John, Co., 56
Western Iron Boat Building Co., St.
    Louis, 124
Western Rivers, shallow depths and ob-
    structions, 8, 17–20, 160–61; improve-
    ment, 29, 159–60, 161–62, 165–66, 167,
    170. *See also* under names of rivers
Western Trader, 8
Westmoreland, 47
Wheeling, W. Va., 8, 28
Wheeling Steel Corp., 166
Wheelock, Edwin D., New York City,
    146
White, J. M., of Cloverport, Ky., 85
White, J. M., of New Orleans, 35
White Collar Line, 144
White Oak, 136
White River, 20
Whistles, locomotive, 60, 64; steamboat,
    58–59, 64
Wiggins Ferry Co., St. Louis, 130
Wilderness Road, 5
Wm. Larimer Jones, 171
Wm. S. Brokamp, 177
Wood, in steamboat construction, 37,
    121–22; cheaper than steel, 122–23,
    125–26, 127; shift from, to steel, 127–
    31
World War I, 131, 153
World War II, 177–78, 181
Wren, 51, 56

Yazoo Valley, 73

Zularef, John, 36n, 144

THE TEXT OF THIS BOOK was set on the Linotype in JANSON, a robust "Old Face" of the Dutch school. Having in mind the proclivity of the early punch-cutters to wander, it is interesting to note that this type was cut in Amsterdam by Nicholas Kis, a Hungarian, *circa* 1690. It was erroneously named for Anton Janson, a Dutchman, who had been employed in Leipzig where the original matrices were discovered years later. These same mats are currently in the possession of the Stempel Foundry, Frankfurt, and the version you are reading was modeled directly on type produced from the original strikes.

This book is printed on BECKETT TEXT, a 70 pound laid finish book paper with matching end papers. The cloth cover is BANCROFT ARRESTOX imprinted with foil.

The typography and binding designs for this book were by JAMES H. OLIN with art work by RUSSELL HOLLENBECK.

This book was composed by TYPOSERVICE CORPORATION, printed by WM. B. BURFORD PRINTING COMPANY, and bound by H & H BOOKBINDING CO., INC., all of Indianapolis, Indiana.